Appetite For Freedom™

Video driven Bible study for women with food struggles

Taking back your health, God's way!

Heleen Woest

www.SurrenderedHearts.com

Appetite for Freedom: Taking back your health God's way

This book is not a medical model and none of the information in this book is meant to be a prescription for any kind of treatment, medical or other wise. References to other organizations and materials are for convenience only and are not intended as endorsements. The author has made every effort to present the current research accurately and assumes no responsibility for inaccuracies, omissions, or errors contained in the source materials. The author and publisher are not liable for misuse of information provided. The author and publisher are neither liable nor responsible to any person or entity for any loss, damage, or injury caused or alleged to be cause by the information in this book. The information in this book is for guidance only and is not to be treated as a substitute for professional eating disorder treatment by a physician or counselor.

All Scripture quotations, unless otherwise indicated are from the following versions with corresponding abbreviations:

AMP=*THE AMPLIFIED BIBLE, EXPANDED EDITION. Old Testament* copyright © 1965, 1987 by the Zondervan Corporation. *The Amplified New Testament* copyright © 1958, 1987 by the Lockman Foundation. Used by permission. Words in brackets [ ] and parentheses ( ) are those of The Amplified Bible translators, not the author.

NIV= *Holy Bible, NEW INTERNATIONAL VERSION.* Copyright © 1973, 1978 International Bible Society. Used by permission of Zondervan Bible Publishers.

Dedication

To the greatest grandma that a girl could ever wish for, my Oumatjie, Helena Hendriena Roode. Thank you for listening intently to my many essays and stories through the years, and encouraging me to never stop writing. When you moved on to heaven I lost my biggest fan, but I know exactly where to find you, in the arms of Jesus, where we'll meet again for sure.

Acknowledgments

To Tony: Thank you for loving me through all my ups and downs on this journey of finding answers for me and others. I'm not ashamed to admit that none of this would have been possible if God hadn't take pity on me and given me you. You are God's greatest gift to me, and you still make my heart skip a beat after twenty years.

To Jean, Terrance, Jason, and Christie: You are the reason I keep fighting for freedom and reaching for more of Jesus every day. To be your mom has been the joy of my life. I love you four sweeties so very much.

To my Mom and Dad: Thank you from the bottom of my heart for showing me throughout your lives that NOTHING compares to loving God. It is that love that carried me through and brought me to this place, and I know that it will guide me on. Thank you for being my greatest cheerleaders; I'm a lucky girl indeed.

To Paula Holt: What a great friend and encourager God gave me in you. Thank you for instilling courage in me and helping me brainstorm through countless issues. You were so instrumental in making all of this happen, and for that I will forever be grateful to you.

To Angie Riesterer, Angela Bayford, and Sarah Gallagher: Thank you so much for offering up hours of your time to edit this book. I am so grateful for the valuable contributions and suggestions you brought to this project. Your love, friendship, and encouragement inspired me more than you would ever know.

To our business small group at City Bible Church: Thank you Steve and Becky Scheidler, Wes and Paula Holt, and the other members of our small group who contributed financially and in many other ways to bring this dream into fruition and as a result touch the lives of those who desperately need this message of hope and healing.

To the leaders of All Things New at City Bible Church: Thank you Tim Nashif, Mark Jones, Lori Simpson, and Kari Rambukkange for allowing me to film the DVDs at All Things New and especially for assisting me and being patient with me as we worked out all the details.

To Mark Nashif: Thank you for doing such an excellent recording job and also for you grace, encouragement, and kindness throughout. It was a joy working with you.

To my friends and family: Thank you so much to each of you who prayed for me, came out to the recording nights, or helped lead the tables; thank you Sue Ober for praying with me weekly; thank you Sharon Riesterer, Linda Bryan, Rosie Thomas, and Linda Hulse for your counsel and encouragement; thank you Becky Scheidler, Paula Holt, Claire Seidler, and Lili Brown for making me look pretty; thank you Juliet Dwyer for feeding my family, and thank you Terrance Woest and Maile Dwyer for babysitting. I am so blessed by your love!

Contents

About the Author

Heleen Woest is a Christian author and speaker on the topic of food related struggles. She is married to Tony and mom to Jean, Terrance, Jason and Christie. She lives with her family in Beaverton Oregon where they are active members of City Bible Church.

Heleen was born and grew up in South Africa as a pastor's kid. She gave her heart to God when she was only a small child and loved Him ever since. Through the years she felt a deep compassion for the brokenhearted and people in bondage, as well as a yearning to teach about the love and mercy of God.

When she experienced first hand the healing power of God in her life after struggling with eating disorders, she reached out to women at her local church with similar struggles. She facilitated small groups for women with food related issues for the past ten years, first in California, and now at *All Things New*, a ministry of City Bible Church in Portland Oregon. In order to better help the ladies who joined her small groups, she delved into the Word of God for answers and studied the field of eating disorders and food addiction extensively.

In 2007, while taking a break from the small groups to tend to a precious new baby girl, Heleen wrote an eBook: *God will I ever be free?* She also developed a 12 week online program, *Women Struggling with Food*, based on the Bible and material by well-known Christian authors, counselors, and doctors. *Appetite for Freedom* is an updated version of her 12 week online program, which has been successfully used by women around the globe for a number of years now.

Heleen received a Bachelors degree from the University of South Africa and she continues to work on a Masters in Biblical Counseling. She has done a great deal of lay counseling under the supervision of experienced and godly counselors for more than a decade. She trusts God to use her humble offering of transparency to guide women to freedom in Christ. She is very aware of the fact that without God she can do nothing, but with God all things are possible!

Introduction

Thank you for allowing me into this very vulnerable area of your life. I pray that I will be worthy of your trust and that our 12 weeks together will be a blessed encounter with the King of all kings.

There is truly only one thing harder than having a struggle with food, and that is to ask for help. You took that scary step forward to show up for this study, and I know God is going to honor this leap of faith that you're taking. If you have been looking for a solution to your problem for a while, I anticipate that you may be skeptical and fearful that this program is just another hoax. I don't blame you because there sure are a lot of false promises out there. I can so relate to the devastating feeling of having your hopes shattered time and time again, and therefore I want to be honest with you from the start about what you can expect.

That said, I also want to emphasise from the start that our God is faithful and able to save and heal His people. If you received Jesus as your Lord and Savior then the saving, healing power of the Holy Spirit is available to you.

Will you be free after 12 weeks?
I believe that God can instantly set people free in such a way that they never look back. However, for the most part I saw women, like myself, having to walk out their journey to freedom, learning to trust God every step of the way. I didn't like it at the time, but today I can see a great deal more of God's purpose in making me walk the journey. I am happy to report that many ladies came back to testify that they fell less and less, until falling was no longer an issue in their lives. I don't have contact with everybody that went through my support groups or online program, but I often receive testimonies from ladies who developed a deep love-relationship with Jesus along this journey. They all agree that it is worth every drop of sweat and tears. This is why I want to help ladies who struggle with this painful issue get a great start, as well as prepare them for the rest of the journey.

I have seen ladies break free from their food struggles and eating disorders during the 12 weeks and I rejoiced with them! Here is one lady's testimony I received only a few weeks ago via email:
I have just finished the 12 week program. I cannot thank you enough for putting all this together, God has used you in a mighty way (and still is!!!)
God has done amazing things in my life over these 12 weeks, I haven't binged/purged once and God has dealt with some issues in my life that I didn't even know were affecting me! I have lived with bulimia for 14 years or so and although I have had episodes of not throwing up (sometimes for as long as 9 months) I have never been free. I truly believe that Jesus has now set me free once and for all, but I am also very aware that Satan is ready to dive in and knock me off track, so I need to keep walking closely with my Saviour.

After this initial victory most of these ladies had to walk the journey of consistently surrendering their lives to God. This means that some of them encountered times of falling and getting back up before they settled into a place of peace and freedom. I wrote this 12-week program with all of that in mind, and therefore included "tools" for ladies to use when the enemy trips them up or when they hit a crisis. My online program includes a members' forum where ladies encourage each other to stay the course and not give up as well as other tools they can come back to.

Face it - life happens, and we tend to fall back on the things that once brought us comfort if we don't keep our guard up. This is part of what I want to teach you in the coming weeks: How to keep your guard up and implement biblical principles into your busy life so that you can experience true freedom.

How long will it take to be totally free?

I can't say for sure why we all have different times of arriving at a place of freedom from this struggle. I suspect that it has to do with our individual relationships with God, our unique past experiences, and how soon we are ready to open our hearts for God to remove the layers of pain and brokenness. However, I do believe that we can ALL find God's freedom from bondage because Jesus came to set the captives free (Isaiah 61 and 11).

Even though the time frame differs for all of us, and freedom for me might look different than it does for you, our place of freedom will have a few things in common:

- It's a place where we know "life in abundance" as the Bible speaks of (John 10:10)
- It's a place where we love Jesus more than anything or anyone
- It's a place where we've learned to talk openly with Him about our journey, whether we're up or down, running free or barely making it
- It's a place where we have love, joy, peace, patience, kindness, goodness, faithfulness, gentleness, and self control in the midst of a broken world with problems and difficult people

You may be experiencing fear of failure

Fear of failure in this struggle is connected with chasing the illusion of a perfect track record where we never fall again. The enemy uses fear of failure in the lives of many people to keep them from reaching out for help and trying again. In our 12 weeks together, I would like to teach you how to keep going forward on this journey, further away from the struggle with food, by consistently focusing on the true desires in your heart and the victories along the way (not the failures). The fear will go away when you realize that falling is not your enemy; staying down and beating yourself up is. Also, your journey doesn't end after the 12 weeks so there is no pressure to hurry-up-and-get-it-together within a set time frame, but rather to grow wiser about God's power, Satan's schemes, and your own vulnerabilities in order to complete your journey.

Program Structure:

This program runs for 12 weeks (including the introduction week) and deals with eleven important topics surrounding food struggles. Every week has 5 days of interactive material based on Biblical principals, research, testimonies, and practical guidelines. You will have 7 days to complete 5 days worth of material. You will get the most out of this study if you also attend the weekly meetings where you will watch a 30 minute DVD and join other ladies in discussing the week's material. Throughout this study a little Bible icon will indicate that it's time for you to participate. You may be asked to look up a Scripture verse, ponder on a specific topic, or find a quiet place to pray.

It is God who will heal you and bring freedom to your life as you meet with Him in the weeks to come. I trust that the material will be a great blessing to you, but remember that it is not so much the material, but rather the "stirring" that it causes inside of you, as you open your heart to the Holy Spirit, that will bring lasting freedom.

In His Love
Heleen

WEEK 1
Taking the First Steps

Day 1
Finding New Hope

If you have been wrestling with food-related issues for as long as I did, you are probably pretty educated on the topic of eating disorders and food addiction. But just in case you're not sure, I will give you a quick overview.

What is an eating disorder?

An eating disorder is a compulsive behavior surrounding food that controls your life and also limits your freedom to eat in a healthy and normal way.

There are many different types of eating disorders. In this program we will mainly focus on the following types:

ANOREXIA:
An addiction to dieting or self starvation. This usually causes a total deterioration of a person's physical and mental health.

BINGE EATING DISORDER:
A pattern of powerful, and often secret, binge eating (quickly eating large amounts of high-calorie, sugary, fatty foods). This is often used as a drug to either numb unwelcome feelings or make life "better." As with compulsive overeating it usually causes serious weight gain.

BULIMIA:
A pattern of powerful, and often secret, binge eating (quickly eating large amounts of high calorie, sugary, fatty foods).The binge is usually followed by purging (removing the food eaten during the binge by using laxatives, diuretics, self-induced vomiting, compulsive exercise, or starvation). Because of the purge there isn't necessarily weight gain, but it is very harmful to one's health.

COMPULSIVE OVEREATING:
This resembles the binge in bulimia (which may or may not be done secretly) or "grazing" (constant eating) over a few hours. This usually is done to escape or drown out unwelcome emotions such as anger, inadequacy, embarrassment, fear, loneliness, pain, insecurity, or boredom. This usually causes serious weight gain.

People who struggle with food find themselves in a vicious cycle. This cycle will probably be all too familiar if you are in the grip of an eating disorder.

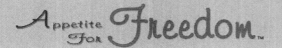

The Eating Disorder Cycle
1. Uncomfortable feelings of dissatisfaction, anxiety, and depression
2. A pressing desire to get rid of these feelings
3. Use of food to numb the feelings (binge, purge or starvation)
4. Feelings of guilt, shame, self-hate, and hopelessness after the food abuse
5. Resolution to never binge, purge or starve again
6. Lack of ability to honor these personal boundaries
7. Right back to number one to keep on repeating the cycle day after day…

Why do eating disorders occur?

Many professionals and experts in the field of eating disorders believe that our society and the media's obsession with weight plays a huge role to reinforce the practice of eating disorders. Others believe that certain issues such as dysfunctional families, controlling relationships, illness, death of a loved one, divorce, or sexual and physical abuse may trigger eating disordered behaviors. Some claim that hereditary factors play a part in eating disorders and that certain people might have inherited a predisposition to having an eating disorder.
However, everyone seems to agree that food struggles are complex. It's not an isolated incident that causes an eating disorder or food addiction, but rather a combination of factors. From my own experience I have to agree with this.

More importantly: What can be done?

This is probably not the first time you went looking for a solution to your problem. Just like me, you probably know all about the fad diets out there and have probably tried a few yourself.

In all seriousness, lots of plans make sense for people who want to shed a few pounds, but those "plans," even the Christian-based ones, fly out the window the minute life gets rough for someone with an eating disorder.

Would you picture the following scenario with me:
You get out of bed with the best intentions in the world. You have your "plan" ready: Today is going to be awesome! You're going to exercise, eat healthy, read your Bible, and be the best woman of God you can be. **Then life happens.** *You have a fight with your husband, your child gets sick, your car breaks, your boss overwhelms you with responsibilities and tasks, your past failures come out of the closet to haunt you, and you hear the familiar messages in your head that you will never "get it together." Without even realizing what you're doing, you walk over to the cupboard and "inhale" hand-fulls of sugary cereal. Guilt and shame flood over you. You did it again! What's the use, you might as well give up on this diet as well.*

People with food struggles are trapped in a never-ending conflict that cannot be cured by a diet. The only way we feel good about ourselves or accepted by others is when we look good, are skinny, and perform perfectly all the time. However, this is an unattainable goal, so we keep failing at these high expectations we set for ourselves, and keep "needing" food (or food abstinence) to cope with these emotions. We are trapped in a vicious cycle.

Some of us feel that food (or food abstinence) is the best thing we have going in our lives. Even though we know about the dangers involved, we feel that abstinence or purging gives us control while the large amounts of food make us happy (even if only for a moment). We're caught in this cycle and we really don't *want to* let it go. We will talk more about asking God to change our "want to" in the weeks to come.

There is LIFE after eating disorders and food addiction. There's peace, joy, healthy relationships, and a healthy body, but it's not found in fad diets or dangerous methods. These things just keep us spinning around in circles year after year, trapped in the never-ending conflict that I described above.

After many years, and countless diets, I finally found healing in letting God deal with all those places in me that fueled my food struggles. Even when I still find myself turning to food during high-stress periods in my life, I now recognize the horrible feeling when peace and joy are replaced by fear and I run from it as fast as I possibly can.

If you've once tasted the freedom in living a life surrendered to God you start to recognize the old signs of bondage quickly, and you cannot stand to live like that anymore.
Don't get me wrong, I am in no way condemning every food plan on the market. On the contrary, there are sound and helpful programs and books out there. What I'm saying is the best food plan in the world will not work if we don't first find healing for spirit, mind, and body.

Identifying the Problem

Carefully read through the list of questions below, and circle the numbers that apply to you. The answers stay between you and God, but be sure to use this tool to bring some truth to your heart and shake off denial for good.

1. Do you think about food or food abstinence all the time?
2. Are you preoccupied with a desire to be thinner and do you fear weight gain?
3. Do you starve to make up for binges?
4. Are you overweight despite concern by others for you to lose weight?
5. Do you binge and then vomit afterward?
6. Do you exercise excessively to burn off calories, rather than to stay fit?
7. Do you overeat by binging or by 'grazing' continuously?
8. Do you eat the same thing everyday and feel annoyed when you eat something else?
9. Do you use laxatives, diet pills, or diuretics as a method of weight control?
10. Do you hide stashes of food for future eating or binges?
11. Do you avoid all food with sugar and feel waves of shame and condemnation wash over you when you do eat sweets?
12. Is food your friend and do you often turn to food for comfort?
13. Would you rather eat alone and do you feel uncomfortable when you must eat with others?
14. Do you have specific ways you eat (or foods you eat) when you're emotionally upset, sad, angry, afraid, anxious or ashamed?
15. Do you become depressed or feel guilty after an eating binge?
16. Do you 'feel' fat even when people tell you otherwise?
17. Are you ever afraid that you won't be able to stop eating?
18. Have you tried to diet repeatedly only to sabotage your weight loss?

19. **Do you feel powerful when you are able to abstain from eating?**
20. **Do you have weight changes of more than 10 pounds after binges or fasts?**
21. **Do you feel your eating behavior is abnormal? Do you try to hide it from others?**
22. **Does feeling ashamed of your body weight result in more binging?**
23. **Do you make insulting jokes about your body weight or your eating?**
24. **Do you feel guilty after eating anything not allowed on your diet?**
25. **Do you follow unusual rituals while eating such as counting bites?**
26. **Do you feel out of control when you eat?**
27. **Do you feel that you do not deserve to eat?**
28. **Do you know the calorie content in all or almost all the food that you eat?**
29. **Do you feel the only control you have in your life is in the areas of food and weight?**
30. **Do you feel anger towards anyone who questions your eating habits?**
31. **Do you believe that everything in your life would be better if you lose weight?**
32. **Do you feel that you have to be perfect in everything that you do?**
33. **Do you view food as a substance that could be spiritually enhancing or hindering?**

If you answered yes to three or more of the above questions, you may be dealing with a disordered way of relating to food.

Please note that this is only an exercise in self discovery, designed to help you realize the seriousness of any compulsive eating habit, it's not a diagnostic tool. Please see your physician for further evaluation and a diagnostic test if you feel you have identified an eating disorder in yourself for the first time and are concerned about your health.

You may feel discouraged after doing this self evaluation test, but please remember that gaining knowledge about this area of your life is a step in the right direction. Once we recognize and admit to the brokenness in our lives, we can start moving forward out of the lies we believed for years, and start applying the truth of God's Word so we can be free.

The Bible clearly states in John 8:32 (NIV):
Then you will know the truth, and the truth will set you free.

Restoring your faith

The core foundation of this program is about restoring your faith in God and teaching you how to daily SURRENDER to Him. Not only will a full surrender to God cause you to stop looking for a way to "fix this thing" by yourself, but it will also help you start thinking about turning to others and especially to God for help. As long as we misplace our faith by trusting in our own best efforts, we won't be fully placing our faith in an almighty, all-powerful God.

This might be the first time that you are admitting to yourself that all of your best efforts to change yourself and "pick yourself up by the bootstraps" are not working. This might be the first time that you realize that God is the only one who can save you. In fact, you might not even believe it yet.

The way we build faith in God is by getting to know Him and His Word
Romans 10:17 (Amplified Bible)
So faith comes by hearing [what is told], and what is heard comes by the preaching [of the message that came from the lips] of Christ (the Messiah Himself)..

It's all about relationship. Think about the people on this earth that you trust and have faith in. They are usually people you know well. You know their character and they have proven themselves worthy of your trust. God has already proven that He can be trusted and that He loves us by giving us His Son (John 3:16). He calls us His children throughout the Bible and makes it clear that He wants to have a relationship with each one of us

GOD CAN DO ANYTHING. So if He didn't set you free from this food struggle, even after you've begged Him countless times to do so, then there is a reason, and He holds the answer. If you start to build a deep and intimate relationship with God, He will show you what is lacking in your relationship with Him and why you still find yourself in bondage. He speaks through His Word, His people, and the Holy Spirit. Don't stress if you're not familiar with what I'm talking about yet; I will explain this in the weeks to come. All you need to know right now is that in order for you to be set free from eating disorders, food addiction, or any other food struggle, you need a type of relationship with God that can go the distance.

Do you trust that God can and wants to help you?
- Maybe, like me, you didn't even realize that you stopped trusting God.
- You might even be blaming Him for the situation you find yourself in right now.
- Maybe, like me, you have been putting your trust in yourself, diets, different programs and people for a long time.
- Maybe, like me, you have to stop and remind yourself that you are turning your back on your ONLY HOPE - the only One who can save you!

Did you know that we need faith to please God, to keep hope alive, and to step into the purpose He has for our lives?

Please look up these scriptures about FAITH and write them in the spaces below:

Hebrews 11:6

_____
_____
_____

2 Corinthians 5:7

_____
_____
_____

Are you ready for your faith to be restored? Do you want to believe again? It's as easy as asking God. Take a look at this guy in the Bible who asked: Mark 9:24 (NIV)
Immediately the boy's father exclaimed, "I do believe; help me overcome my unbelief!"

I believe the boy's father really wanted to believe, but he didn't know how to do it, so he asked Jesus to get him there. Do you need help getting to a place of trusting God and giving your eating disorder over to Him? Starting asking Him today. God wants to increase your faith. He knows you, He knows how you work, and He is the only ONE who can heal you.

I invite you to join me in this prayer if you are ready to lay down unbelief

Lord, please forgive me for not trusting you to help me with my eating disorder. Forgive me for trying all this time to do it on my own and shutting you out of this part of my life.
I repent today from unbelief; please help me to believe that you can heal me.
I stand on Your Word today that says "...with God all things are possible" (Matthew 19:26). I will no longer believe the lies of the enemy. This food struggle is not too big for You, God, and it's not just some little thing that I have to take care of either.
I believe today that this is not something I will have to carry for the rest of my life.
Your Word says that You have come to set the captives free (Isaiah 61:1) and You don't want me to be in bondage. You want me to live a life of abundance (John 10:10).
I submit my life to You, Lord. Please use Your Word and this study to change me, all of me, forever.
Amen.

Please take the rest of this week to pray and think about this matter of unbelief.
Let the Holy Spirit speak to you about laying down all of your own striving to try and change this area of your life. When you surrender your struggle to God, He will show you through His Word which part you have to play in all of this, but it's important for you to know that you are not alone; the Holy Spirit has been given to you as your comforter and helper (John 16:4).

Day 2
Facing Denial and Pride

Are you maybe still in denial about your problem or at least the severity of it? I'm asking you this because denial is a universal problem for people with addiction. Most people only seek help after some strained relationships, problems on the job, or damaged physical health.

Why is denial such a problem?

First of all, people fear what others will think of them when they admit to having this problem.

Second, denial is Satan's oldest trick in the book. If people don't see their own sin, they don't repent, they don't receive God's forgiveness and help, and they stay in bondage.

Even right now the enemy might be telling you the following lies:
"You can stop this behavior anytime you want."
"It's not that bad, it's not like you have a real addiction."
"This is just nonsense, you've heard it all before."
"You just have to find a better diet."
"You don't need help with this, you should just get it together yourself."

Ask yourself this: If you could fix your way of dealing with food, wouldn't you have done so years ago? Would you hurt yourself and the people you love **on purpose**? Would you throw away your money, time, relationships and health **on purpose**? Would you live a life in chains of shame, anxiety, and self-hatred, if you could run free? **I don't think you would.**

I beg you to not be that person who goes down the path of denial for years and years. **EATING DISORDERS AND FOOD ADDICTION ARE BEHAVIORS THAT CAUSE SERIOUS PHYSICAL PROBLEMS, EVEN DEATH.**

How do you get rid of denial?

There is something that keeps denial alive: PRIDE
Pride is one of the biggest obstacles in our way. If pride is present we usually find it hard to admit that anything is wrong, or that we are dealing with a serious eating disorder. It might be that you grew up in a family where you always had to put on a "mask" in public, or pretend that everything was fine when you were in fact falling apart or hurting on the inside. **This behavior of "keeping up pretenses" or "wearing a mask" has pride at its root.** To pretend that your life is perfect keeps people at a distance and gives the message that you don't need anything from anybody.

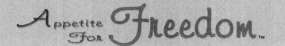

To really live free we have to come to a place where we admit that pride might have slipped in ever so subtly. PRIDE IS A SIN; IN FACT GOD CLEARLY STATES THAT HE HATES PRIDE

Please look up the following verses and write them in the spaces below:
Proverbs 8:13

_____

_____

Proverbs 16:18

_____

_____

These two verses talks about the other end of the spectrum, humility. Please summarize these verses in your own words.
Isaiah 66:2

_____

_____

James 4:10

_____

_____

Can you see how pride could be a huge obstacle in your pursuit for freedom while humility could benefit you greatly?_____

You may have laid down pride before, but it is unfortunately one of those things that can sneak back into our lives if we do not ask the Holy Spirit to search our hearts for places it might be hiding. In fact, we would be wise to do this on a *daily basis.*

One of the places pride hides is in low self esteem:
It doesn't seem possible, but the fact is that a person with low self esteem is always busy with herself in the same way as someone with a huge ego. She is painfully aware of her own behavior and any mistake is met with self loathing and shame. In a later week we will discuss the importance of having a healthy self image, and what that means. For now it is important to note that putting oneself down can be yet another form of pride and a way to stay self centered and self focused.

The sooner you get denial and pride out of the way, the sooner you can be on your way to freedom. If you are too proud to admit that you have a real problem, you might:
- Minimize it and think that you don't really need God
- You might harden your heart
- You might resort to your own will-power again
- You might end up denying this for another year, yet at some point find yourself back at this crossroad

Not sure if you have a problem with pride?
Pride tends to hide in corners where we least expect it, so have a look and see if you missed some pride hiding out in the corners of your life.

Please take a look at these questions and circle the ones that apply to you:

- Have you detected that you are overly critical of yourself and others? For example: Do you replay the behavior of yourself and others over in your mind and analyze every detail?
- Do you set high standards for yourself and others and do you feel guilt and shame (even on behalf of others) if these standards are not met?
- Do you find yourself putting others down or gossip in order to feel better about yourself or to make yourself appear better than others?
- Do you often control or manipulate other people and circumstances?
- Are you highly sensitive to the remarks of others and cannot stand being criticized?
- Is it hard for you to ask for help, or admit that you cannot do it all?
- Do you have to do things perfectly even at the expense of relationships and your own sanity?

I challenge you to let God into your "heart of hearts" today. Let Him put His finger on the very dangerous place where you might have hidden pride. The enemy hides pride behind all kind of "innocent" veils so that we don't recognize it in our lives and stay in bondage. Don't let him fool you any longer, please join me in this prayer of repentance today.
Pride has kept women, like you and I, from freedom, healthy family lives, great ministries, and above all, a deep and intimate relationship with Jesus.

PLEASE PRAY THIS PRAYER WITH ME

Jesus, I never meant for pride to slip into my life, but it did.
I wasn't even aware that I carried so much pride, but today I ask you to forgive me.
Come wash me from this sin of pride and please open my eyes to any hidden pride that can keep me from living life in abundance.
The enemy used pride to keep me from asking You to help me with my eating disorder.
I believed that I could stop any time and that I was in perfect control, while I was in bondage all along. Please show me all the places of pride in my life, daily.
I want to root it up for good.
Thank You that You love me, God. I accept your forgiveness and love.
Amen

Please take a few minutes and write your own prayer to God in the space below:

_____

_____

_____

DAY 3
A Testimony of Hope

How facing denial, pride, and unbelief helped me

It took me a while to get over my denial. Like most people I didn't even know or believe that I was in denial. I struggled with pride in my life that actually fed the denial, but I would NEVER for one minute think that I was prideful. I had such low self esteem and I always tried to keep everyone happy. How could I possibly be dealing with pride?

When I finally opened my heart to God and let Him show me the truth, I realize that I **turned my pain into pride.** It started when the sin of pride prevented me from looking at what was hurting me. I didn't believe anything was wrong with my past and I especially didn't want to let go of the "ideal childhood" that I had created in my mind. Pride kept me from looking back and facing the fact that things were in fact not so peachy.

By refusing to look back at my past, I was holding on to grudges against my parents and other people. These grudges and pain from my past kept me in bondage, regardless of my superficial efforts to deal with the symptoms. Unforgiveness was standing squarely between me and God, and God was the only One who could free me.

- **I was actually very proud that I "used" my past pain to become a perfectionist.** I was determined to control my life and everything in it. I now realize how much pride went into that one thought. I also know now that no one is perfect and that you cannot control anyone other than yourself (and even this can only be done through the power of the Holy Spirit)

- **When I saw that I wasn't in control of my weight, I simply had to find a way to control this area as well.** I refused to look at the danger involved in abusing diet pills. I just wanted to be thin at all cost. This prideful attitude also made me deny the fact that I was bulimic and that I could die from this disorder.

- **I cared more about what people thought of me than about my health, my loved ones, and my relationship with God.** I thought being thin would take away my pain and when it didn't, I just had to find another way to make the pain go away. I then had to have the perfect outfits, decorate my house perfectly, and be the perfect hostess. I was totally self-absorbed 24/7 and I couldn't even see it.

- **Despite the outward charades I always felt sad and hopeless, like I was crying on the inside.** I had a deep yearning for God that I kept trying to fill with other things, yet pride kept me all along from crying out to God for help, or asking people around me to teach me how to surrender to God.

- **Constantly pleasing the people around me turned out to be my prideful way of controlling them.** I was trying to control what other people thought about me, and how they felt about me. I wanted to have "perfect relationships" and I prided myself in the fact that I had no enemies, no one disliked me, and I always avoided conflict.

But this was an unnatural state of living. If we control others, we cannot grow in relationship with God and find self-control, which is part of the fruit of the Holy Spirit. So as long as I controlled others, I was not in control of myself. I was always anxious and my eating disorder prevailed.

My denial about having an eating disorder looked like this:

Denial: *"I don't have a disorder, I just need to find the right diet and lose some weight. I'll be fine."*
Truth: I could never find the right diet, because I was really trying to fill a deep longing inside of me with food. So I had to turn to dangerous methods (abusing diet pills and finally purging) to lose weight.

Denial: *"I don't have a disorder, the pills are just helping me to have more self control, and I can stop taking them any day."*
Truth: When I stopped taking the diet pills due to complications to my health, I couldn't stop binging and had to turn to more drastic measures (vomiting). The pills and vomiting gave me a false sense of "self-control". These dangerous methods became another god or idol I turned to instead of the only true God.

Denial: *"Okay, maybe I do have a problem, this can't be normal, but I'm sure I can stop this if I try harder."*
Truth: I couldn't stop it myself. It was only when I finally realized that all of my best efforts were useless that my denial finally fell away, and I started surrendering my struggle to God.

My denial about needing help looked like this:

Denial: *"I just need to read the right book; I don't need to let people into this."*
Truth: I didn't get any better; all the books just made me feel better for a little while. I needed others to hold me accountable and teach me how to have a daily relationship with Jesus.

Denial: *"I'm good at so many things, how could I possibly fail at this? I should be able to get this right if I try harder."*
Truth: I kept failing because I wasn't perfect, and I desperately needed God and other people to help me. I spent years trying to fix myself, without any success. I was ready to look for a helping hand.

Denial: *"Surely this isn't something I should ask from God, He would have healed me by now if He wanted to. This is probably one of those things that He wants me to do for myself."*
Truth: The truth was that I lost faith in God; I didn't think He could or wanted to heal me. In my eyes this eating disorder became HUGE, much bigger than my God. This was a sin and I had to repent from my unbelief.

My denial about the danger surrounding this problem look liked this:

Denial: *"This is not a real addiction. It doesn't affect me like alcohol or drugs would."*
Truth: I couldn't function normally in many areas. The food struggle became the center of my life and took up all my attention, it became gradually worse and affected all of my relationships. Most importantly, it diverted me from the very reason I was born: To glorify God in and through my life.

Denial: *"I can't die of this, it's just a problem with food."*

Truth: I started developing health problems from the pills, the vomiting, and the huge amounts of sugar and fat. Slowly my eyes opened to the many people around me who die every day from eating disorders.

When I finally worked through my denial, I knew that:

- This is definitely a problem in my life. I do not eat in a normal, healthy way.
- I needed help, not just a quick fix. I also knew I needed God and people in my life who would tell me the truth that I so desperately needed.
- I could lose my health if I didn't get help. Carrying on like this was not worth it. I could lose the people I love; in fact, I could lose the one precious life God gave me.

I finally came to a place where there was no more hiding behind denial. I was down and out. I repented from the sin of pride and unbelief that I let into my life. I asked God to help me trust and believe Him again. This was my first big step. I felt such relief when I took this step towards surrendering my life, and especially my eating disorder, to God.

Are you ready to take the first step out of the jungle of denial and pride? Please write down ways that you have been denying the existence or severity of your problem with food.

_____

_____

_____

Now write down ways that pride might have contributed to the problem and kept you from reaching out for help.

_____

_____

_____

PLEASE PRAY THIS PRAYER WITH ME

Lord Jesus, I admit today that you are all powerful and all knowing. The Bible says that we can ask you for wisdom when we need it.
I need your wisdom to see past years of denial and pride into what is really going in my heart. Please help me to find the truth through your Word and the power of the Holy Spirit in the days and weeks to come.

Please show me practical steps that I can take to start letting You and other safe people into this broken area of my life. Thank you that you Love me Lord! Amen

We will be talking more about these things in the weeks to come, but please take a moment now to write your own prayer in the space below. Also write down practical steps that you can take as it comes to mind during your time in prayer.

_____

_____

_____

Day 4
Journaling and Memorizing Scripture

I will be asking you to write things down in a journal as we move through this study together, and I hope to encourage you to make it a daily habit even after you've completed the 12 weeks. Please purchase a journal as soon as possible. It can be a fancy one or simply a notebook from a dollar store (I always buy these because I fill them so quickly). You can also choose to start a journal on your computer or iPad. If you are part of my online program, you can even journal on the private members' forum. Many ladies who journal on there told me that it has been a great accountability tool for them and they also receive encouragement from other women who struggle with the same issues.

Journaling is a very effective tool that I have been using for years, so please don't skip this step. Your journal can take on the form of a very private prayer journal where you write things down as God reveals it to you through this program and His Word, or it can be a journal where you simply write your thoughts down as you walk out this journey of freedom. It depends on your style and preference, but it is VERY IMPORTANT to do it. I know it might seem like something trivial, but it plays a huge role in identifying lies of the enemy that might be popping up in your head on a daily basis that you are not even aware of. Even more so, it is a constant reminder of the TRUTH of God's Word that we as Christians have at our disposal.

Once you're ready please write down the following verses in the front of your journal and take a minute to meditate on these. You can take one more step by writing these verses on note cards that you can take everywhere with you. The idea is to start reading these verses all the time until you've committed them to memory. If you are not familiar with memorizing Scripture, then let me encourage you that this will become one of your strongest weapons when the enemy comes at you with lies.

The Word of God is our sword, our offensive weapon, so don't be afraid to strap on your sword; you will be needing it on our journey together.

 Start today by writing down these verses in your journal.

Jeremiah 29:11 (NIV)
"For I know the plans I have for you," declares the LORD, "plans to prosper you and not to harm you, plans to give you hope and a future."

Micah 7:7-8 (AMP)
But as for me, I will look to the Lord and confident in Him I will keep watch;

I will wait with hope and expectancy for the God of my salvation; my God will hear me. Rejoice not against me, O my enemy! When I fall, I shall arise; when I sit in darkness, the Lord shall be a light to me.

God has good plans for your life! He cares so much about you and He wants you to have a good future. He wants you to let go of the past and start something new with Him TODAY.

These verses meant so much to me, because I was sure that I had failed too many times for God to forgive me. I was sure that there was no more turning back for me and that I had used up all of my chances with God.
I remember shouting these verses all the time when I first started this journey. I would literally shout, "You keep quiet, Satan! I might be doing this again and I might feel so gross about myself right now, but this is not where I'm going to stay. The Lord is my light in this deep pit. I am going to be free!"

It might be time for you to take a stand against the enemy who has been planting lies of guilt, shame, hopelessness, fear of failure, and insecurity in your mind. Please believe me when I tell you that it can only be done through the power of the Holy Spirit and by the truth of God's Word. We will be memorizing a lot of Scripture together in the weeks to come in order for you to have a weapon against the lies of the enemy.

Please write down one more Scripture passage in your journal for this week. Copying these verses into your journal is a great way to really hear it and receive it into your heart.

Isaiah 61:1-4 (NIV)
The Year of the LORD's Favor
The Spirit of the Sovereign LORD is on me,
because the LORD has anointed me
to proclaim good news to the poor.
He has sent me to bind up the brokenhearted,
to proclaim freedom for the captives
and release from darkness for the prisoners,
to proclaim the year of the LORD's favor
and the day of vengeance of our God,
to comfort all who mourn,
and provide for those who grieve in Zion—
to bestow on them a crown of beauty
instead of ashes,
the oil of joy
instead of mourning,
and a garment of praise
instead of a spirit of despair.
They will be called oaks of righteousness,
a planting of the LORD
for the display of his splendor.
They will rebuild the ancient ruins
and restore the places long devastated;
they will renew the ruined cities
that have been devastated for generations.

These words are referring to the One, Jesus, who came to set the captives free, heal the broken hearted, and bring good news to the poor. Jesus Himself confirmed that these words have been fulfilled in and through Him (Luke 4: 18-21).

I have memorized this passage and it has become such a source of encouragement and power to me through the years, especially on days when my flesh is weak and the attacks are fierce. JESUS HAS COME TO SET US FREE!

PLEASE PRAY THIS PRAYER WITH ME

Thank you Jesus that you have good plans for my life! Thank you that you don't give up on me, but that you are my light even if I find myself in a very dark pit right now. Please hear my cries for redemption and healing, and pull me out Lord. I can not do this myself, I need you desperately!

Thank you that you came to set the captives free and to bring healing to the broken hearted. I stand on your Word today and declare that there is healing and freedom for me in Jesus.
Amen

Did these verses encourage you? In the space below, explain what these verses meant to you, and be prepared to share it with the ladies in your small group.

_____

_____

_____

_____

_____

Day 5
Pin Down Your Dreams

I have a very important question for you: What does freedom mean to you, or in other words, what is it that you really want from God?

Here are some of the dreams I had:
- Clothes that actually fit. Forget about being super cute, I just wanted to feel comfortable in my own skin without having to keep buying bigger clothes
- Pictures of my family, with me actually in them
- Courage and ENERGY to pursue my dreams of writing and teaching
- Confidence in relationships (to trust some and let go of others)
- Playing, running, and swimming with my kids (without feeling ashamed about my body and physically unable to do some things)
- Getting rid of the condemning voices inside my head
- Loving God in a new way (not just me constantly begging Him to help me with the food)
- For crying out loud, just one Christmas without guilt about what I eat, and shame about how I look!

Many of these dreams of mine were purely self centered, and God gradually changed them to become more God-focused as I grew in relationship with Him. Others were truly things that the enemy had stolen through the years, and those things God restored to my life as I learned to surrender to Him (John 10:10)

I will encourage you today to make your own list and write down all those things Satan has stolen from you, as well as those long buried desires and dreams.
If you're like me, you'll probably start bawling at this point, and it's okay. I want you to know that you are surrounded in this moment by a cloud of witnesses who came through their own struggles, cheering you on to throw off those things that entangle you, and instead look to the purposes and longings God placed in your heart so that you can run the race He set before you.

Hebrews 12:1 (NIV)
Therefore, since we are surrounded by such a great cloud of witnesses, let us throw off everything that hinders and the sin that so easily entangles, and let us run with perseverance the race marked out for us.

Maybe you don't know what to write just yet, or maybe you only have one or two things you can think of. Whatever the case might be, I know God will reveal it to you now that we've stirred the water a little. Like my list above, your desires might mainly revolve around finding freedom from your food struggle, and that's okay too, because God also desires for you to be free. However, the more we grow in our relationship with God, the more He reveals our true purpose and desires.

There's a reason why we are alive and why He put us on this planet: It is to glorify Him. We glorify God by growing in relationship with Him, and allowing Him to work through our gifts and talents to reach a broken and lost world around us with His love. However, if we are so focused on SELF (weight loss, appearance, food addiction, eating disorders, etc) those deep longings to glorify Him are suppressed and we miss out on the very reason we were created.

So I'm here to remind you, dearest one: **THERE IS SO MUCH MORE TO YOU THAN THIS EATING DISORDER.** Hidden behind years of struggle and obsessing about weight, food, and diets is the TRUE YOU that wants to glorify God and truly live. I dare you to find her again. We will talk more about all of this in Week 2, but I want to encourage you to search your heart, start to think back when you were just a little girl, think of what you loved to do or the dreams you had. When last have you done something truly amazing? Not amazing to others, not something you did to impress or please anyone, but something you thought was truly amazing because you loved it. When last did you laugh out loud? When last did you feel the hours pass by like minutes because you were doing something that you felt really passionate about?

I know she's in there somewhere, the daughter of the King, and she wants to be free of her shackles and her years of bondage! Like me, you might have had a deep longing for years to just experience a little taste of freedom. That kind of freedom, joy, and fulfillment is only found in a close relationship with the King of all Kings.

PLEASE PRAY THIS PRAYER WITH ME

Lord, I know that you have put me on this earth to glorify You. Thank you for giving me talents and abilities to serve You and your people. Please remind me of those gifts and talents that I may have forgotten about. Please bring healing and freedom to my life so that I will be able to use those gifts for your glory.

Thank you for always loving me Jesus, even in my lowest state. Amen

Take today and the rest of the week to pray and meditate on what it is that you really desire and dream about. Keep adding onto your list, and be prepared to share some of your dreams and desires with the ladies in your group.

Please start making your list in the space below (and also transfer it to your journal so you can look at it daily):

_____
_____
_____
_____
_____
_____

Week 2
Surrender to God

Day 1
True Love Motivates

I trust that our previous week together helped you realize how important faith is on our journey to freedom. Many of us have been robbed from believing the truth that God is for us and that He wants to help us in our struggle with food.

It takes time to completely get rid of denial and pride. It also takes time to get to know God better and learn to trust Him with all of your heart. So please don't despair if you're not there yet. As we go through this study together I will be reminding you to lay down denial and keep trusting God more with this particular area of your life.

Today, let me ask you a question:
Do you know that Jesus wants all of your heart? Do you know that the desires and passions that we spoke of last week only come alive when we love God and fully surrender it to Him?

All of the Law is summed up in one very important command. Please write down Mark 12:30 in the space below:

_____

_____

_____

Let's delve a little deeper into this very important love-relationship between a girl and her God.
True Love Motivates
A deep love for God motivates true sorrow for our sin, true repentance, obedience, and permanent change. Nothing in life motivates us to change like true love. People with food struggles might change for a little while when they're faced with a health crisis or pressure from family members. However, if a change of heart doesn't occur, the best programs, support, counseling, or inpatient treatment will only bring temporary change. If you still love food, crave the approval of others, are obsessed with being thin, or love the feeling of "control" when you starve yourself, permanent change will remain an illusion.
Let me encourage you today to no longer settle for the fleeting pleasures your idols might bring. Don't settle for dining with the pigs like the prodigal son did, while your Father has prepared a feast for you. Your bridegroom is Jesus Christ. He is waiting to give you a crown of beauty, instead of ashes. He wants to give you the oil of gladness instead of this sadness and depression you have lived under, and instead of a spirit of despair, He wants to hang a garment of praise around your shoulders (Isaiah 61).

The ideal husband
The relationship between Christ and the church is compared to the relationship between a bride and bridegroom in Ephesians 5:22-32. Jesus Christ is not just any bridegroom, He is perfect.

Many of us have been blessed with wonderful husbands, but allow me to speculate for a minute what a *perfect* husband would look like:

- He takes care of me, financially yes, but also in all other areas. I feel safe with him and know that if things get rough, I can count on him to support me and get us through it.
- He is full of wisdom, especially when I'm not sure what to do. Sometimes he gives me an honest reproof when it benefits me, but he's never abusive, harsh, or mean.
- He wants to be with me and enjoys spending time together, without me ever having to ask for it.
- He knows everything about me - the good and the bad - and loves me unconditionally.
- He is passionate about me, and about life.
- He cares about other people, but never to the point where I feel threatened or doubt his love for me.
- He cares about my heart, my passions, and the things and people that are important to me.
- I am proud of him and the things he does.
- When I look at him, I'm amazed that he could even love a girl like me. Yet in his presence I always feel that I am beautiful, even though I'm not perfect.
- He appreciates all the little things I do.
- I tell other people about him and think about him all day long, knowing that he is thinking of me too.
- He fights for me, not just in times of physical danger, but also when he sees the enemy of my soul attacking my heart, and I start to drift into dangerous waters.
- He encourages all my dreams and helps me remember the person I am deep down in my heart.

Sound like a fairytale husband? Actually, Jesus is exactly that - the perfect husband! In the Bible you will find Him to be every one of these things I've mentioned and so much more.

Why then do we turn our back on this perfect bridegroom and cling to false lovers or idols (food, obsession to be thin, the approval of others)?
Maybe you haven't yet built a true love relationship with Jesus. Maybe you only know Him superficially through the words and experiences of others. Maybe you never really studied the Bible or opened your heart to God so that He could remove bitterness, unforgiveness, and pain. Maybe you've never experienced the power of the Holy Spirit in times of weakness and temptation, coming to your rescue when you are too weak to fight.

If we don't love God above all else and we don't know the truth of His Word, we can easily fall for the lies of the enemy and turn to idols.

 Please write down the following statements in your journal:

True Love will motivate me to...
- experience true sorrow for my sin
- truly repent from my sin
- surrender to God
- obey God
- change permanently

In her well-known Bible study *Breaking Free,* Beth Moore asks us to answer the following questions to determine if we really love God:

IDENTIFYING TRUE LOVE:
- Does God regularly circulate into my thoughts (Ps. 63:6)?
- Am I often drawn to spend time with Him (Ps. 27:4)?
- Does my life demonstrate a love for God (Rom 5:8)?
- Do I often enjoy God (Ps. 16:11)?
- Do I ultimately find relief or satisfaction in obedience (John 14:12)?[1]

I grew up in a Christian home and have loved Jesus since I was a little girl. For most of my life, if anyone would have asked me if I loved Jesus, I would have quickly responded, "Yes, I've loved Him all my life." Even now, when I see my sweet little girl praying to Jesus and hear her talk about Him, I remember myself at her age, praying to God in the same manner. However, through the years some questions formulated in my mind ABOUT my love for Christ: Do I love Him enough? Why do I still lack the fruit of the Spirit such as self control and patience in my life? Where is my joy and peace in trying circumstances? Why is it still so hard for me to obey? Why do I still turn to other things to satisfy me if I love God more than anything or anyone?

I think I will have to agree with Beth that we sometimes fool ourselves by thinking that we love God when we simply don't, or at least not enough.

If we look at the names of God and read the Bible, we see that He is everything we can ever need or desire. Life is not easy, and the truth is that we cannot handle many of the things that come our way in our own strength. **On any given day women are faced with stress surrounding marriage, children, friendships, ministry, career, household, extended family, health, and so much more. We fool ourselves if we imagine that we can just buckle-up.** The shock, pain, rejection, sadness, and stress that sometimes enter our lives unexpectedly needs an outlet. If we don't truly hide under God's everlasting wing during these times, we will have to find something or someone else to help us cope with life. The world would have you believe that you are strong enough and that you can depend on yourself, a mere flesh and blood human, to get through these times. It's simply not true. In fact the Bible warns us that if we put our trust in any human, including ourselves, we will end up like a dry bush in the desert (Jeremiah 17:5-6). In this Scripture passage we also see the other side of the story: Jeremiah 17:7-8 (NIV) "But blessed is the one who trusts in the LORD, whose confidence is in him. They will be like a tree planted by the water that sends out its roots by the stream. It does not fear when heat comes; its leaves are always green. It has no worries in a year of drought and never fails to bear fruit."

One of the names of God is *El Shaddai,* All Mighty God. He is all sufficient and through His Spirit He gives us everything we need to cope with life. However, if we became so accustomed to turning to idols instead of God, we may no longer believe that He can be all of that for us. Please take a closer look at your own life. Maybe you will find, as I did, that you don't know or believe that He can truly supply all your needs and desires. Maybe you keep turning to a false god (food or the approval of others) to satisfy your needs because you never found true satisfaction in the arms of God.

These questions are obviously for your own private reflection, so please answer them honestly before God:
Do you love God with all your heart, soul, mind, and strength?

Do you believe that God can supply your every need? In other words, do you believe that you can love God more than you love food or any other idol right now?

_____

Do you recognize that you might need to grow in relationship with God in order for you to change permanently?

_____

How can I love God more?
We will talk more about loving God in the weeks to come, but for now there are two things you can do to start growing in relationship with Him:

- **Ask God to give you a love for Him**. God is the source of love, and He is the only one who can give you true agape love for Him and for other people (1John 4: 7-8,19). Ask Him DAILY to increase your love for Him. Set an alarm on your cell phone to remind you to pray. Start off with short prayers at first where you simply ask God to give you a true love and desire for Him and His Word.

  Important: Ask with the right motive. See what the Bible has to say about it in James 4:2-3 (NIV): You want something but don't get it. You kill and covet, but you cannot have what you want. You quarrel and fight. ***You do not have, because you do not ask God.*** When you ask, ***you do not receive, because you ask with wrong motives, that you may spend what you get on your pleasures.*** (emphasis mine)

  You may have asked God in the past to set you free so that you will lose weight or so your life will be easier and more enjoyable. This time around, start asking God to give you a deep love for Him and His Word so that He can be glorified through your life. Freedom will come as a result of growing in relationship with God, but if you are seeking it INSTEAD of relationship with God, it won't work. **Lasting freedom and life in abundance is wrapped up in RELATIONSHIP with God the Father, Son, and Holy Spirit.**

  I love the way Max Lucado says this in his book *It's Not About Me:*
  "When our deepest desire is not the things of God, or a favor of God, but God himself, we cross a threshold. Less self-focus, more God-focus. Less about me, more about him."[2]

- **Be accountable**. Attend this study weekly, and keep up with the daily work, **even if you're still binging or purging**. Attending women's Bible studies is a great way to grow in your knowledge of God's Word and, as a result, grow in relationship with Him.
  Also find friends that will hold you accountable to grow spiritually, and surround yourself with people who obviously love Jesus. Attending this study weekly is a way to surround yourself with others who are seeking more of God.
  You see, the more we learn about God and open our hearts to Him, the more we love Him, and the more we love Him, the more we want to be in His presence where we are changed. Get yourself into that blessed upward cycle, girl!

 Please look up Matthew 7:8 and write it in the space below. Let this encourage you that to keep asking to love God more, and to keep knocking on heaven's door, is never a waste of your time.

_____

_____

_____

God loves you so much. Asking for more of Him in your life is Biblical and pleasing to God. Keep asking to love Him more DAILY!

I invite you to pray this prayer with me:

Jesus, I want to love you with all of my heart, soul, mind, and strength as the Bible commands. I need a love that can sustain me through difficult times, carry me through deep valleys, and satisfy me all the days of my life. I recognize that agape love originates with You alone God. It is a love that fills every crevice of my heart and spills over to the people around me. I won't settle for anything but the love that comes from you Lord. I repent of turning to false lovers and idols. Forgive me God and come fill me with your love Lord Jesus!
Amen

Please use the space below to write your own prayer to God. Ask Him to give you a deep love for Him, and a desire for His presence and His Word.

_____

_____

_____

_____

_____

Day 2
How do I surrender to God?

What does it mean to surrender?
Surrendering or submitting all of our lives to God plays a huge role in finding healing from food addiction or other food struggles. Surrender also goes hand in hand with learning to love and trust God more. The very act of surrender made such a difference in my life that I wrote an ebook[3] on this topic.

Please Read the following excerpt from my book *God Will I Ever Be Free?*

What is surrender? How do you do it?
I started looking into the word surrender. I know it means to give up, like in a war or a game. Giving the other party the right to say "I win." That doesn't sound so good, I know. Definitely not in our society where everybody encourages you to "go for the gold," "be your own person," or "don't let anybody tell you that you can not do something."

This is what I found in the Bible: Rom 6:16 (AMP) "Do you not know that if you continually surrender yourselves to anyone to do his will, you are the slaves of him whom you obey, whether that be to sin, which leads to death, or to obedience which leads to righteousness?"

This part of the verse jumped out at me;"**surrender YOURSELF.**" Wow, can it be that God actually wants me to surrender all of me?

Does that include my whole mind, body, and spirit? That would mean all of my time, my money, my relationships, my work, my interests and yes, my eating habits. I started thinking about this; how everything in my life works together and has an effect on each other. How many times have I shoved hand-fulls of potato chips down my throat after I had a stressful telephone conversation? And how about the times that I ate anything I could find after I spent money that I really didn't have?

Jesus said that if anybody wants to follow Him, they have to take up their cross daily, leave all of their own interests and desires behind and follow Him (Luke 9:23, my own words). I started to get the picture: If God would have just 'saved" me instantly from my eating disorder, I would still not have learned to surrender to Him. A miracle like that would have been wasted on me, seeing that I most likely would have picked up another addiction or harmful behavior to "help" me deal with the chaos in my life. The reason for the chaos was due to the fact that I wouldn't surrender MY LIFE to God.

Life is hard, make no mistake, this is why we desperately need God. But if we take up an idol, such as food, and put it in God's place, we make our own lives harder, in fact our lives become unmanageable. This is why, even at times when I lost weight through questionable means and looked great, I was not happy, and I found other harmful ways to try and fill my life. **So I have to choose; will I become a slave of Christ or a slave of this world, my own selfish desires, and ultimately Satan?**

The way to surrender is actually so simple, but somehow Satan has managed to make us believe that surrendering to God is only for a few fortunate souls and to the rest of us it would always be an unattainable mystery. This is simply not true. THEN HOW DO WE SURRENDER?
We simply have to make time for God, front and foremost. We have to worship Him by giving him our most prized possession: Our time.
In short: WE HAVE TO STOP, WAIT, LISTEN, AND OBEY.

So why is this so hard to do? Why do we avoid doing the thing that we need the most? I think the main reason is **continuous activity.** We live in a world where everybody is always busy with something, and nobody has any time for anything. This is a real problem, seeing that AS LONG AS I KEEP MY BODY OR MIND BUSY, I CAN'T HEAR GOD, AND AS LONG AS I CAN'T HEAR HIM, I CAN'T OBEY HIM, AND MY LIFE CAN NOT BE CHANGED.

It seems so easy; just settle down, just calm down, just listen. And maybe it is because of this simple truth that we tend to believe that it cannot be true. We want a deep theological explanation of how to draw near to God. There must be something more substantial that we can do. Do you know that stopping activity is probably the most difficult thing for people to do in our society? Satan obviously has a field day with this. As long as he can remind us of ten thousand things that still need to be done, he wins. If we are busy, his work is done, we can't hear God, so we can't obey Him and we're as good as dead in our bonds.

The truth that many Christians refuse to see is that we are at war; **there is a battle raging for our freedom and our hearts.** Satan has us in bondage and there is no way he would just willingly open up the prison door and let us walk free. But there is a key to our prison, and that key is **God's presence.** It is in His arms, on His lap, and at His feet where our chains start to break and fall off.

I believe we are all born with a yearning for His Presence. Sometimes I would have fought this yearning for so long that it literally died. I would still have the vacuum, the terrible thirst for something, but I wouldn't recognize it for what it was anymore. Days would go by, weeks, months, and years where I started to feel more frazzled every day. The pain would later be so fierce that I would cry while stuffing my face with anything from cereal to pork chops.
I also remember times when I just stopped listening to the voice of the enemy in my head and all the voices surrounding me. Times when I listened to my heart and started searching after God with my whole being. I would read *Jeremiah 29:13 (Amp)"Then you will seek Me, inquire for and require Me, and find Me when you search for Me with all your heart"* and it would always make me cry. I would cry because I had such a longing to find Him, and hearing this promise made me think that searching after God might just be worth it. These were times when I let down my guard of unbelief and started searching for Him with all my heart. It was in a time such as this, that my chains fell off and I could walk free.
How does one stop?
You have to stop the train that you're on, ON PURPOSE! Throw out the idols of busyness, TV, computer, food, cleaning, shopping, church activity, yes even those friendships that take up all your time. YOU HAVE TO STOP: SIT AT HIS FEET, SURRENDER, WAIT, LISTEN, AND OBEY.[3]

STOP, WAIT, LISTEN, AND OBEY

Let's talk about these steps for a minute.

What will your life look like if you actually STOP in your tracks? Stop the busyness and the craziness. Think about one day out of your life: During the course of one morning you may endure frustration, pain, and an enormous heap of stress. These things are not going to vanish, even if you deal with your past and relational issues. Your life will definitely become more manageable if you no longer carry around baggage, and for this reason we will address such issues later in this study, but you can never escape all the difficulties in life. You need to learn how to hide in God's presence where you can unload, refuel, and sort out lies from the truth.

Each one of us can find a time in our day to just STOP: No more excuses and no more running. If this is as hard for you as it was for me, start crying out to God for help. Cry out in the car, in the shower, at your desk, while changing the baby, or walking the dog: "God I need you. I want to surrender to You, but I don't know how to just be still. Please help me; show me how, when, and where." If you keep crying out for help you will hear the Holy Spirit calling you to a quiet place: A chair in the back yard, a park, the privacy of your bedroom, or somewhere you've never even thought of.

That said, I want to encourage you to **COME JUST AS YOU ARE.**

Don't wait to first "get your act together" or for the "perfect moment" when you have lots of time. It's never going to happen! Come to God right after you've binged and purged. He saw it all anyway and His heart is so tender towards you in this time of pain. Start calling out to Him while you are binging; you can cry, eat, and pray at the same time, He understands. Just come as you are and where you're at. Every time you stop to talk to Him, or invite Him into your struggle instead of shutting Him out, you are taking one step closer to freedom.
Remember how the prodigal son hesitantly came back to the father in his filthy rags, thinking that he will not be recognized or accepted as a son anymore? Great was his surprise when the father embraced him, gave him a new robe and a ring for his finger, and prepared a feast for him.

In these intimate moments with God, pick up your Bible or your note cards (more on this later) and start meditating on a few verses. Start with the Psalms or the gospels and while you read ask God to speak to you through the Holy Spirit. The Bible is God's spoken word to you, and the Holy Spirit lives in you as your helper and counselor to apply the Word of God to your specific situation and circumstances.

As God speaks to you through the Bible, start talking to Him as well. You don't need fancy words, He knows you so well, He is the only one with whom you can truly be yourself. Just talk, like you would to a friend, about your day, about how things have affected you, about your desire to love Him more. Talk to Him about the times you run to food. Open up to Him about the hidden places of pain and frustration in your heart. He has all the answers about your life, including your food struggle.

Of course it doesn't help to just hear the Word of God, in fact the Bible warns that we have to listen AND obey. Obedience and love actually go hand in hand. So you will be glad to know that as you grow in your love relationships with God, you will want to obey Him more. The more we get to know Him, the easier it becomes to lay down idols and false gods in our lives. The opposite is also true, sometimes we have to obey or repent simply because the Bible says so, and that step of obedience makes us grow in our love relationship with God.

Please write down these verses in the space below to see the link between love and obedience. Also note how JOY is linked to obedience. John 15:10-11

_____
_____
_____
_____
_____
_____
_____
_____

Remember	**STOP WHAT YOU'RE DOING AND JUST GO TO GOD. You might feel unable to control how you relate to food right now, but there is one thing you can control: You can make time for God.** Don't wait until you are "better" or "cleaner." He will make you clean and whole in His presence, you can't do it without Him. He is waiting for you with open arms.

Have you been making time for God in your life?

_____

You may be procrastinating because you have a set idea about how your time with God should look like as far as the perfect circumstances, Bible study, place, or length. The enemy might have kept you from God by over-complicating the process in your mind. Which simple steps can you take today to make time for God?

_____
_____
_____

Do you believe that surrendering your life, and consequently your time, can result in a love relationship with the God of the universe that will outrank any love you've ever felt?_____
Please write down Jeremiah 29:13 in the space below.

_____
_____
_____

My dearest friend, if you start surrendering your time to God today, and start searching after Him with all your heart, you WILL FIND HIM!

As we finish this day on surrender I can't help but think of that old song
I surrender all
I surrender all
All to Thee my blessed Savior
I surrender all

 I invite you to pray this prayer with me:

Lord please teach me how to be still in your presence. Please call me into that quiet place with you where I can hear your voice and where your Word and presence brings CHANGE to my heart. I'm calling on you Holy Spirit, my helper and counselor, to teach me how to surrender. I want to be still, listen, and obey, but you know that it doesn't come easily or naturally for me. Please show me moment by moment how to surrender this struggle to you
Thank you, Lord. Amen.

Please take a moment and write your own prayer to God where you ask Him to help you surrender this struggle to Him.

_____
_____
_____
_____
_____
_____
_____
_____
_____

Day 3
Resist the Enemy

In our quest to surrender our time and hearts to God, we will unfortunately encounter some resistance. Satan would love nothing more than to keep us from truly loving Jesus with all our hearts. You see, if he can get us to turn away from our true love and set our eyes on a different "lover" or idol that has no power to protect us, then we are just where he wants us: Alone, vulnerable, weak, and ashamed.

In this vulnerable place Satan can badger us with lies, because we no longer talk to Jesus and we no longer listen to the truth of His Word. In this isolated place the enemy pounds our hearts with so much guilt and shame that we can no longer see our true passions and desires. We then become so ashamed of our rotten state, that we believe Jesus could not possibly love us anymore.

So what are we supposed to do when we are attacked or tempted by the enemy?

 Please write James 4:7 in the space below

_____
_____
_____

Now write these specific instructions that we found in James 4:7 in your journal:
- **First: Surrender/Submit to God**
- **Second: Resist the enemy**
- **THEN he will flee from you**

According to this verse it's useless to try and resist the enemy in our own strength. A life that is surrendered to God and armed with the truth of God's Word is the perfect offensive weapon against the attacks and temptations of the enemy. We spoke about this yesterday, but I want to encourage you again to stop the fast train that you're on and keep surrendering your time and your life to God. The surrendered life not only brings us to a place of joy and fulfillment in the midst of trying circumstances, but it also brings protection.

It's time to strap on your armor and join the war.
Up until this point the enemy might have had a field day with your life. He would tempt you, and you would just give in, he would present you with lies and you would believe them, or he would present idols that harm you and you would reach for them.
I want to encourage you today that you no longer need to fear the enemy. When you gave your life to Jesus, Satan's hold on your life was broken forever. Make no mistake, he will try to harass you with lies and thoughts of fear, but it's exactly here where the surrendered life makes all the difference. **Once we start surrendering our hearts and thoughts to God on a daily basis, the enemy loses all footing in our lives.**

Do you fear the powers of darkness? I want to instill some faith in you today: Our God is stronger! He lives in you through the Holy Spirit, and that makes you so much stronger than Satan and all his demons. The reason we don't believe this is simply because we don't know or believe the truth of the Word. God has not given us a spirit of fear, it comes from the enemy.

Please look up 2 Timothy 1:7 and write it in the space below

_____

_____

_____

_____

How do you resist the enemy?

We will speak more about temptation in a later week, but for now I want you to know that when the enemy tempts you, God will always provide a way of escape for you. The problem, again, is that we don't always know or recognize the way of escape because we are not familiar with turning to God and His Word in trying times. If you are used to STOPPING and waiting to hear God's instructions, you will clearly see the way of escape that He has made for you in a certain situation.

Please look up 1 Corinthians 10:13 and write it in the space below:

_____

_____

_____

_____

God is indeed faithful, He will not let the enemy tempt you with anything that you cannot overcome through the power of the Holy Spirit who lives in you. Many times our way of escape is simply in drawing our sword, the Word of God, against the enemy. Jesus clearly demonstrates this when He was tempted by the enemy in the desert (Matthew 4:1-11). He resisted every single temptation by quoting Scripture.

Start practicing today to stand against the temptations of the enemy. When the enemy comes at you with temptation, ASK God to show you the way of escape.

Note Cards

I've asked you to start journaling in our first week together, and I now want to introduce you to another tool that will prove to be extremely useful in times of temptation: Memorizing Scripture.

Please don't get discouraged by the very thought of having to memorize verses. I have been encouraged by various Bible teachers to use a pretty simple, yet effective, method to get some Scripture written on my heart: Note cards.

If you are just starting to break out of a food struggle or any other addiction, you will most likely be very weak and vulnerable. Your spirit needs to be fed and your heart repaired by the truth of God's Word. Knowing the truth is the only way to spot the enemy's lies. Please believe me when I tell you that this won't just come naturally. What comes naturally to you right now is probably

self abuse, guilt, and shame. **Like me, you might have bought into the enemy's lies for so long that you can no longer distinguish between his lies and your own thoughts**. God's truth might not be familiar to you at all right now, and that is what we need to change.

I urge you to go out today and purchase a big pack of notecards, punch holes in them and bind them with a keyring or ribbon. In fact, you can get very creative with your note cards. Some ladies type them up and laminate them while others buy the pre-bound note cards. It really doesn't matter, as long as they can easily fit in your purse so you can take it with you wherever you go. As we've seen in 1 Corinthians 10:13, we are "seized" by temptation to turn to our idol. It could happen anywhere: At your workplace, the doctor's office, in the car, at a basketball game, and most certainly at the grocery store.

 Once you have those note cards ready, please start by copying James 4:7 and 1 Corinthians 10:13 (see above) on your very first note cards. Read these as many times a day as you can and start to memorize them. You will not believe what a difference it makes to fight off temptations with a real weapon: The Word of God.

	I invite you to pray this prayer with me:
	Lord Jesus, I am ready to live in the truth!
	I do not want to listen and live by the lies of the enemy. Please help me to pick up the Sword of your Word and start using it to defend myself against the lies of the enemy. Please remind me of your example of refuting the lies of the enemy with the truth of the Bible. Help me memorize Scripture and give me a greater desire to read the Bible. I don't have to fear the enemy, because you have given me a spirit of love, joy, and a sound mind, not of fear. I know that if I surrender myself to you, and resist the enemy, he will have to flee from me.
	Thank you Jesus for the truth and power of your Word.
	Amen

DAY 4
Identify the Idols

Food in itself is an innocent and good thing created by God. However, Satan has an age old plan: He loves to take something beautiful and convince us to worship the thing instead of the Creator. It then distorts the thing that we worship, because it was never meant to be worshiped. **Food was created to be delicious nourishment for our bodies. It's main purpose is to give us energy and help our bodies function well, but somewhere along the line it became the thing we worship.**

THE IDOL OF FOOD

Food was for years my number one idol: I would "use" food when I felt lonely, depressed, and sad. I would definitely "use" food when I was anxious or stressed. I would "use" food to fix relationships or smooth over difficult situations. I would also "use" food to comfort others or make people like me. On the flip side I sometimes refrained from eating to control situations or manipulate people. I hoped that food, or controlling my food intake, would fill the emptiness I felt inside of me.

It became unthinkable for me to celebrate anything without food.

A date with my husband became only as good as the restaurant we went to. A family movie or game night could only be enjoyed when there was a lot of unhealthy food around. Holidays could not possibly be holidays without stacks and stacks of food and PMS could only be survived with comfort food.

Times when I deprived myself from food by going on a diet would leave me cranky, sad, and angry. I couldn't stand being separated from my idol (food), and anyone who tried to keep me from it bore the brunt of my anger.

My heart was sold out to food 100 percent, and I didn't even realize how bad it was. The veil of denial was lifted during times when I hit an all-time low and acted in a way with my idol that was absolutely unacceptable, even to me (out of control binging and purging). **During these times I had to admit that this thing that I loved above all else could not help me, save me, or fill the emptiness inside of me. On the contrary, it was merely an object that harmed me when I used it to fill a void that could only be filled by God.**

Have you had times when you were so ashamed of how much you ate or what you've done to get rid of the food that you would give anything to be free?

_____

Maybe you're at such a place right now. It is a good place to start, but **remember that things will only change temporarily if you only look for a solution to lose weight and look good while your heart and mind remain in bondage to food.**

Exposing the Sin

The love affair with food is a sin: The Bible calls it **IDOLATRY** and we are warned against it throughout the Old and New Testament. Not only did I love food and exalted it above God and other people in my life, but my insatiable need for large amounts of food proved that the sin of **gluttony and lust of the flesh** were also prevalent in this area of my life.

By not calling it what it is, SIN, we can stay in this behavior for many years. If you see your food struggle simply as a physical issue or a disease, you may find yourself helpless to change and trapped forever. However, if you open your eyes to the fact that this disorder has sin at its root, then you can in fact agree with God that there is hope and healing for you.

Food might actually not be the only idol in your life. When I finally admit to myself and agreed with God that I was in fact worshiping food, I discovered a whole bunch of idols that were entwined with my food struggle. Truthfully, the Holy Spirit often gave me clues about these things in the past, but I sadly chose to ignore Him.

THE IDOL OF BUSYNESS

This idol totally alienated me from God. The enemy kept me busy all the time. I fell for his lies that to keep busy was to be successful and even "spiritual." But really all it did was keep me from surrendering to God. I was keeping busy every moment of every day and this became an addiction in itself. I couldn't stop, and resting was unthinkable.

This addiction was fueled by pride: I felt good about my busy-self in comparison to the "lazy slobs" around me. The truth is that continuous activity robs us from our relationship with God and the people we love. If you are always busy, you also ignore your body's need for rest and recreation. It's a vicious cycle really: If we're always busy, we are always tired and irritable. The only cure for this is to rest in God's presence and being washed by the water of the Word.

However, if we don't make time for God's Word and prayer we start to feel like we're losing our minds and we turn to dangerous substitutes such as food, sugar, caffeine, diet pills, and energy drinks. This gives us a fake boost, so we keep doing more and keep repeating the cycle of destruction.

We have to stop this cycle on purpose. Nobody can do it for us. Most mornings when I wake up, I feel the urgency of the day's responsibilities and tasks pressing upon me. My feet always want to start running, and my mind starts racing. I have to literally talk to myself: "You will sit yourself down and worship the Lord!" It never comes naturally. I have to turn on some worship music, take out my prayer cards and start praying the Word of God over my mind and my emotions ON PURPOSE. Then I will get my Bible study out and begin to study the Word to keep my mind from wandering.

It is definitely something to get used to if you have been running from God for a while. This will not feel natural or even comfortable at first, but believe me, when you have been doing it again for a while, your feet will start running to that quiet place with God. Your soul will start to respond to the Holy Spirit immediately.

Other things that I exalted above God in my life were: An obsession to be thin, shopping, mind-numbing activities such as watching TV or surfing the web, and pleasing other people. Each one of these idols that I had erected in my life were backed by sin such as pride, rebellion, disobedience, and the fear of man. God hates sin, so while I remained in this sin it was impossible for me to grow in relationship with Him.

I had to make a decision that, regardless of how difficult it would be, I had to remove these idols from my life. I wanted to start a life without idols, but I was terrified. I couldn't imagine such a life, but I asked God to help me fall in love with Him, at least as much as I loved food. For me this was a big step. Even today I have to stay diligent at keeping these idols out of my life, but it is not as hard anymore and loving God makes all the difference. If you ask me if I am totally free of idol worship today, I will tell you YES, but as with everything else in my life, I can only remain free if I keep up my surrender to God.

I learned the hard way that the void in my heart needs to be filled with God or it will be filled with something else.

I have been inspired by various Bible teachers through the years to literally "eat" the Word of God daily in order to satisfy my soul, and stop it from yearning for something else. Take a look at these verses in Psalm 81:10-12: "I am the LORD your God, Who brought you out of the land of Egypt; ***Open your mouth wide, and I will fill it.*** But My people would not heed My voice, And Israel would have none of Me. So I gave them over to their own stubborn heart, To walk in their own counsels." (emphasis mine)

Please look up and write down the following verses to see what the Bible says about idolatry:

Exodus 20:3

_____

_____

_____

Isaiah 44:9

_____

_____

_____

Colossians 3:5

_____

_____

_____

1 Corinthians 10:14

_____

_____

_____

IDENTIFY YOUR IDOLS

I want to ask you to write down the idols that have taken up the throne of your heart. God already knows about those so you don't have to feel ashamed in His presence. Some idols are obvious in our lives, but others have crept in almost unnoticed. God knows about every idol in your life, so go ahead and ask the Holy Spirit to help you identify those.
Jeremiah 33:3 (AMP)

Call to me and I will answer you and show you great and mighty things, fenced in and hidden which you do not know.

 Please write down the things that you think you have put above God in your life. It's between you and God and you will not be asked to share any of these things with your group if you're not comfortable doing so.

_____
_____
_____
_____
_____

Are you hesitant to lay down your idols?

It's really no use to try and fake repentance or surrender if you're not ready, because God already knows what goes on in your heart. I have learned to ask God to bring me, or "draw" me by His Holy Spirit, to surrender certain areas of my life to Him. If you desperately want to make this decision, but you're scared, then ask God to bring you to that point. He knows exactly what will get you there, He made you and He knows what it will take.

	I invite you to pray this prayer with me if you honestly feel unable to let go of food or other idols right now:
	Jesus, I'm not ready, I want to be ready, but I'm not. I still love food and I'm scared and not prepared to let it go. Will you please open my fingers one by one so I can let this false lover slide out of my hand. I know I am asking this according to your will, seeing that you command us to love YOU with all our hearts. Please teach me how to love you even more than I love food right now. This thing is too big for my human strength, I ask that you will help me get there because nothing is impossible with you. Thank you, Lord. Amen.

We will talk about true repentance tomorrow, but please take a few minutes to pour out your heart before God and ask Him to forgive you for letting these idols and sin creep into your life. Please write your own prayer in the space below.

_____
_____
_____
_____

God loves you so much dear friend. He has been waiting, like the father of the prodigal son, for your return.

Day 5
Remove the Idols

How do you remove idols from your life?

ONE: True Sorrow for Sin

There are two reasons why people experience deep emotional pain in this struggle:

1. Most people experience pain because of the symptoms and consequences of a food struggle such as obesity, clothes that don't fit, shame about their physical appearance, lack of intimacy in their marriage, illness due to the disorder, relationship problems and social isolation because of the food struggle.

2. Some people experience pain because of the spiritual problem behind their food struggle. They feel a deep pain about the distance it creates between them and God, and a sorrow for not being able to live a life of self control. They despise being mastered by food and they ache because they let pride, gluttony, and idolatry into their lives. They also have a deep sadness about grieving the Holy Spirit in the process and not fulfilling their main purpose: Glorifying God in and through their lives

You might actually experience all of the above, but only one of the scenarios that I've described can bring you to a place of permanent change.

If you just feel sorrow over the physical symptoms and consequences, you will keep trying to fix it with diets, drugs, surgery, purging, and excessive exercise, but you won't find lasting change. It's like putting a band aid on a deeply infected wound. The pain prevails...

However, if you feel true sorrow because you see how you have sinned against God, who has sacrificed His own Son for you, and you feel true sorrow for the distance it creates between you and the One who truly loves you, then it brings forth TRUE REPENTANCE, which results in permanent change.

I have never seen a woman overcome this struggle permanently without a TRUE CHANGE OF HEART. I know it's hard to hear, but if we desperately want to look good, but still want to overeat, still want to hang on to certain occasions where we binge, or still have our times where we just don't care, then the pain that we're feeling is only about the symptoms and we only want a band-aid, not true healing.

The difference between SORROW FOR THE CONSEQUENCES and TRUE SORROW FOR THE SIN can clearly be seen in bulimia. When I struggled with bulimia I couldn't bear being overweight and judged by others. I felt a deep sorrow and shame for the symptoms of binging (extra weight) and wanted desperately to be free from it, but I didn't feel sorrow for my sin (gluttony and idolatry). I didn't want to give up my favorite piles of comfort food, so I settled for a quick fix (purging and diet pills) instead of God's healing power. This plan proved to be destructive and deadly!

Take a minute and let the Holy Spirit search your heart before honestly answering this question. Do you feel sorrow for the consequences of your sin, or do you feel deep sorrow for sinning against God?

_____

_____

God hates the sin of gluttony, pride, and idolatry in our lives. His Son paid the ultimate price to cleanse us from our sin. However, even though God hates the sin in our lives, He loves us and keeps drawing us by His Spirit to turn again to Him, repent of our sin, and let His love soften our hardened hearts.

TWO: True Repentance

Repentance is one of the mightiest tools and most wonderful gifts God has given us.
Let this verse sink in and be new to you today as you write it down.

Please write I John 1:9 in the space below.

_____

_____

_____

There is only one way to get rid of sin in our lives: Repentance.
I want to remind you that true repentance also means turning from the sin and accepting God's forgiveness. The enemy likes to come back and accuse us of things God has already forgiven. Please take a look at this verse in Rom 8:1-2 (NIV): *Therefore, there is now no condemnation for those who are in Christ Jesus, because through Christ Jesus the law of the Spirit who gives life has set you free from the law of sin and death.*
After repentance we are forgiven and there is no more condemnation for us if we no longer remain in that sin.

THREE: Change takes time
You will quite possibly feel relieved and experience the joy of repentance when you repent from the sin of idolatry. Now I wish I could say that this would be the end of it, but that is not true. Turning away from your idols will mean deliberate choices and changes to your life.
Many times we've worshiped these idols for such a long time that they became part of who we are. This idol might be so woven into your life and personality, that you might have to put a few more things into place. We will be talking about all the practical steps you can make to remove these idols from your life in the weeks to come.

Expect grief
I had to deal with a great deal of grieving when I first repented from the sin that fueled my idols. I started laying them down one by one, but I was sad, angry, and confused at times. I was also disappointed in myself that I couldn't just let it go. Grief is a natural process that we all go through if we lose something dear or familiar to us. So don't deny it and don't beat yourself up about it, just go through it. God never said that we will not experience difficult emotions such as anger and sadness. He did, however, promise to be with us through it all and get us safely through it, if we will let Him.

Isaiah 43:2 (Amp) "When you pass through the waters, I will be with you, and through the rivers, they will not overwhelm you. When you walk through the fire, you will not be burned or scorched, nor will the flame kindle upon you."

 Do you experience sadness or anger when thinking about laying down idols such as junk food, shopping, TV, pleasing others, or the obsession to be thin?

_____
_____
_____
_____

Recognizing these feelings is actually a good thing. If you feel sad or angry when you have to give these up, it points more clearly to the fact that these idols have been filling a void in you that can truly only be filled by God. Let me encourage you that this grief process will be behind you before you know it, and you will be so glad that you stuck it out, because the freedom that comes from leaving an idol behind and the true satisfaction of turning to God is priceless!

	I invite you to pray this prayer of repentance with me: **Lord Jesus, I'm so sorry that I've put food and other idols before you in my life. I repent today from the sin of gluttony, pride, and idolatry and I ask that you will help me turn away from these for good.** Jesus, thank you that you promised in your Word to be with me even if I go through difficult things. Laying down these idols that I held dear for years will not be easy Lord, but I stand again on your Word and declare that nothing is impossible with You! Please teach me in the coming days and weeks how to draw closer to you and fill this void inside of me with a deep desire for You and your Word. Amen.

Please take time today to repent from any form of unbelief, pride, idolatry, or gluttony that might have kept you in this place of bondage. You can write your own prayer of repentance in the space below.

_____
_____
_____
_____
_____

NOTECARDS

I have made note cards with corresponding Scripture verses indicating the sin I let into my life. I keep them close in order to be on the look-out for it, and to make sure I confess any of these if I let them slip back into my life. Please copy these onto your own note cards as they apply to your life.

Confess UNBELIEF and accept God's forgiveness
Matthew 21:22 (NIV)
If you believe, you will receive whatever you ask for in prayer.

2 Corinthians 5:7 (NIV)
We live by faith, not by sight.

Confess PRIDE and accept God's forgiveness
Isaiah 66:2b (NIV)
This is the one I esteem: he who is humble and contrite in spirit, and trembles at my word.

Proverbs 11:2 (NIV)
When pride comes, then comes disgrace, but with humility comes wisdom.

Confess BUSYNESS and accept God's forgiveness
Isaiah 30:15 (AMP)
For thus said the Lord God, the Holy one of Israel: In returning [to me] and resting [in me] you shall be saved; in quietness and in [trusting] confidence shall be you strength. But you would not...

Isaiah 64:4 (NIV)
Since ancient times no one has heard, no ear has perceived, no eye has seen any God besides you, who acts on behalf of those who **wait** for him.
Also see Isaiah 40:31

Confess IDOLATRY and accept God's forgiveness
Jonah 2:8 (AMP)
Those who pay regard to false, useless, and worthless idols forsake their own [Source of] mercy and loving-kindness.

Mark 12:30 (NIV)
Love the Lord your God with all your heart and with all your soul and with all your mind and with all your strength.

Confess PEOPLE PLEASING and accept God's forgiveness
Gal 1:10 (NIV)
Am I trying to win the approval of men or of God? Or am I trying to please men? If I were still trying to please men, I would not be a servant of Christ.

Please keep adding onto your note cards as we move through the weeks together. It is important for you to keep memorizing Scripture and to have these verses close by.

Week 3
Physical Ramifications

Day 1
Food Addiction

Is this an addiction?
Good question! There are a wide variety of opinions and scientific findings when it comes to the issue of food addiction. A number of psychiatrists and doctors believe that food addiction is at the heart of eating disorders and obesity. According to them some people are more susceptible to food addiction because of hereditary factors and genetic makeup, in similar ways that some people are more inclined to have a drug or alcohol addiction than their peers.
Others have written books about food allergies. They claim that when some people eat certain food (the food they are allergic to) it causes them to spiral into a binge episode.
Some experts shun the whole idea of food addiction and say that overeating cannot possibly be compared to something as severe as alcohol and drug addiction where brain alterations occur. There is still a lot of research going on surrounding this subject, so I guess time will tell what really happens biologically when people eat certain food.

However, seeing that I am not a doctor or researcher in the field of addiction, I can only speak from my own experience and my observation of the women in my support groups.
I cannot recall meeting one lady with a food struggle who didn't have some family history of eating disorders, obesity, or other disordered ways of relating to food. In most cases their children were already carrying the burden as well. This is heart breaking for moms, and one of the main reasons why they are so desperate for change is to also help their children.
I am of the opinion that hereditary factors may play a role, but I also believe that most disordered eating patterns are due to learned behavior. This means that these behaviors can be changed or un-learned, but *only* by the power of the Holy Spirit.

Please look up Ephesians 4:22-24 and write it in the space below. These verses illustrate the part we have to play in our journey to freedom.

_____

_____

_____

There is complete freedom for you in Christ! The Holy Spirit can teach you day by day how to "put off" the old you, and "put on" the new woman who has been bought by the blood of Jesus Christ.

As born-again Christians, we are NEVER simply victims or the product of our genes and urges. We can walk in victory over food addiction, even if we are more susceptible to it than others. In this very moment people are breaking free from addiction and sin that have been part of their families for generations. **It really doesn't matter if something came through genetic**

disposition or learned behavior, the only thing that matters is that you can change the heritage of your whole family line by repenting from sin and surrendering your struggle to God.

Have you seen signs of food addiction or a disordered way of relating to food in your family? Please explain.

_____

_____

Do you believe that God is bigger than any hereditary disposition or learned behavior?

_____

Whether you believe that food addiction is for real or not, there are some physical ramifications that occur if we consume high amounts of fat, sugar, white flour, and caffeine that can simply not be ignored.

What is the solution?

You have probably heard some experts say that you will no longer crave certain food if it's not forbidden. This is definitely true for some people, so I recommend testing it if you suspect that the idea of "forbidden food" makes you want them even more. However, if you decide not to restrict any type of food in order to gain freedom, I still advise adding foods that are high in nutritional value to compensate for the unhealthy food you are allowing yourself to eat. Not all foods are created equal as far as nutritional value is concerned and we build up an appetite for the food we eat on a regular basis. So if you only feed your body the food that you "feel" like eating, you might end up with a body that is totally depleted.

According to others, and my own experience and observations, the remedy for addiction usually involves some sort of abstinence (even if just for a period of time). This helps to curb strong physiological cravings for certain food (usually food that are high in calories and low in nutrients).

In my own life I've found that I truly do "crave what I eat." At times when I've latched on to food to help me cope with life, I kept craving more of the unhealthy food. I would promise myself after an evening of binging that I would never touch that kind of food again, just to wake up the next morning with a very real craving for more deep-fried sugary desserts.

Once I gave my heart back to God and started "eating with my head," that is eating the food I knew my body needed to have energy to function well, I actually started craving healthier food. It took a while of course, but it confirmed to me that we really do develop an appetite for the things we eat regularly.

Before simply dismissing the idea, I want to encourage you to think about the possibility that you too might need to refrain from certain food for a period of time in order to remove it from the place you've exalted it to in your heart.

Do you feel that strong cravings for certain food held you back on your journey to freedom in the past? Please explain how.

_____

_____

Have you let God heal some of the deep seated emotional issues in your life, but still find it easier to just numb yourself with food when you're stressed, angry, sad, or bored?

_____

_____

How do you feel about getting rid of certain food (even if only for a period of time)? Please circle your choices.
- Excited
- Ready
- Scared
- Hesitant
- Skeptical

During the next few days I'm going to suggest a four-point plan to you. This plan has helped me many times to get out of a downward spiral of binging and compulsive overeating:
1. **Nurture your body**
2. **Choose a plan of action**
3. **Reach for ONE sober day**
4. **Break the power of a binge**

I invite you to pray this prayer with me:

Lord Jesus, I want you to rule and reign in my heart, but I still have cravings in my body that make it very difficult to not obsess and think about food.
I need to be honest with you about all this Lord, because I know that you see it all anyway.

Thank you that you bought me with your blood and that I no longer have to be a victim of my past or the product of my genes and environment.

I don't want to be mastered by anything Lord. I want to be completely sold out to you. Show me during this week how to take charge of my eating habits, and how to get rid of the cravings in my body.

Thank you for caring about me and all these areas of my life Jesus.
Amen.

Day 2
Nurture Your Body

Are you familiar with the effects that eating disorders have on your body? The list below was given to me by a doctor friend and he assured me that it is by no means a complete list.

1. Skin rashes and dryness (dehydration due to vomiting and starvation)
2. Tender and painful salivary glands (due to frequent vomiting)
3. Constipation (due to poor and irregular eating habits)
4. Water retention (due to malnutrition, vomiting or excess laxatives/diuretics)
5. Bloating (due to over or under eating, vomiting or excess laxatives)
6. Abdominal pain (due to over or under eating)
7. Heartburn (due to eating large amounts of food)
8. Rotten teeth (due to vomiting)
9. No menstrual period (due to lack of body fat)
10. High blood pressure (due to excess weight)
11. Serious lung and stomach problems (due to vomiting)
12. Raw, bleeding sore throat (due to vomiting)
13. Coronary artery disease (due to obesity)
14. Orthopedic problems (due to excess weight)
15. Hyperglycemia and diabetes (due to compulsive overeating)
16. Depression and mood swings (due to over or under eating)
17. Weak bones (lack of calcium due to malnutrition)
18. Low potassium levels that can cause sudden cardiac arrest (caused by vomiting)

The ladies in my support groups also mentioned symptoms or side affects such as tiredness, irritability, insomnia, and anxiety. These were very familiar to me as well.

Our bodies are temples of the Holy Spirit. God made us stewards over our bodies and He expects us to take good care of this great gift of life that He has given us.

Please look up 1 Corinthians 6:19-20 and write it in the space below.

_____
_____
_____
_____

We cannot expect our poor bodies to suddenly be on board after years of abuse. Your body needs nurturing at this point, not more deprivation. The simple act of nurturing your body before you start removing binge foods is one of the sure ways to make permanent changes. Submitting your already depleted body to a rigorous diet or abstinence can intensify the cravings and make you fall back into patterns of binging and purging.

Please write down the 10 main points below in your journal. Some of these issues will be covered in the weeks to come, however, others might need some action on your behalf right away. Please circle the ones you can commit to doing today or this week. Then come back as we go through our weeks and circle something else that you might be ready to commit to.

Commit to start nurturing your body in the following ways:

1. **Spend time with God EVERY DAY**
   I've talked about this in our previous week, but wanted to remind you once more that staying healthy spiritually will be the driving force behind all of the other 9 points below. Anything that seems too difficult or daunting to you right now can *only* be accomplished by the power of the Holy Spirit in you.

2. **Make an appointment to see a physician.**
   If you've suffered from an eating disorder for a while it is crucial for you to see your physician for a well check. Be sure to talk to him/her about possible physiological issues caused by eating disorders and ways to treat those problems.

3. **Make an appointment to see a Christian counselor.**
   If you've been dealing with issues such as depression or deep-seeded pain due to abuse in your past, you may need more than this program can offer. Don't let pride or denial keep you from seeing a Christian counselor or pastor who can help you work through these issues and find healing. These ongoing problems can keep you stuck in the downward spiral of an eating disorder.

4. **Drink at least 64 oz of water and take vitamins daily.**
   Water and vitamins are two simple ways to start building up a depleted body. I have a huge jug of water and a bottle of gummi vitamins by my computer where I work. Ask God to show you how you can start incorporating these simple, yet very important, habits consistently into your life.

5. **Find a food plan that fits your life and has both accountability and support in place.**
   We will discuss this in detail in week 4.

6. **Make time for rest and recreation DAILY.**
   Are you taking care of everybody but yourself? It's not uncommon among moms to put the needs of everybody in the family above their own, but this might be contributing to your eating disorder. You might feel that junk food is the only "good" thing you give to yourself and that you cannot possibly give that up as well. Make time to breathe in some fresh air and feel sunlight on your skin (hiking, gardening, just being outside) and get enough sleep. Our bodies need oxygen and sleep to function properly, but some of us are so busy with life and our food struggle that we've forgotten how to

breathe deeply and sleep soundly.

7. **Exercise 3-5 times a week.**
   We will discuss this in detail in week 5.

8. **Make time for the people and things you love, DAILY.**
   Hidden passions, long forgotten hobbies, or healthy friendships can bring joy back into your life. There is a huge link between your emotional, relational, and physical well-being. Reach out to a friend or pick up a hobby you love, even if it's just for 5 minutes a day.

9. **Look for opportunities to laugh.**
   Laughter brings healing and relieves stress, so invite laughter into your life. What makes you laugh? Maybe a funny movie, playing with your dog, or swimming with your kids. Ask God about ways to enjoy the life He gave you again.

10. **Take care of your body TODAY, at your current weight.**
    Get a massage/facial/manicure/pedicure or just treat yourself to a relaxing bubble bath and face mask.
    We tend to hold off with these things until we lose weight. Many of us have detached ourselves from our bodies (we ignore our own bodies) because of the weight we've gained. However, taking taking care of your body at your current weight will become a huge part of your journey to freedom.

A few words about commitment:

Most of us have found it hard to keep commitments to ourselves and to God over the years. The fear of failure might make you cringe back from making a fresh commitment. The enemy might be presenting you with thoughts of shame and guilt about previous commitments to God and yourself that you didn't keep. **I want to encourage you that the most important lesson I have learned on this journey is that victory lies in getting up every time you fall, it's not in walking without falling.**

So the only appropriate action for me and you is to COMMIT AGAIN, in fact God is calling us to do just that.

Please look up Romans 8:1 and write it in the space below to remind you that you no longer have to feel guilt, shame, or condemnation about your past sins and broken commitments:

_____

_____

Take a look at Proverbs 24:16 and explain in your own words how falling down might NOT be our greatest challenge on our journey to freedom.

_____

_____

Did this verse encourage you to make a fresh commitment? If so, take a minute to write down the steps you commit to doing to better nurture your body.

_____

_____

_____

_____

_____

_____

_____

_____

 I invite you to pray this prayer with me:

God please forgive me for not being a good steward of my body. Forgive me for not properly nurturing this great gift of life that you have given me.

Please guide me to the right physician who can help me restore the damage that's been done in my body. Also show me in the weeks to come if I need the help of a Christian counselor, and give me the strength to take the necessary steps forward if I do.

Thank you that your mercies are new every morning and that You have given me another chance to regain my health. I'm so sorry about the commitments that I've made to you in the past that I didn't keep. Please forgive me and help me to not feel any more shame and guilt about those. I commit again Lord, but I want to admit from the start that I can only keep my promise to take good care of my body if you help me. Please help me Lord, I am desperate for your intervention in my life.

I want more of you Jesus.
Amen

DAY 3
Choose Your Plan of Action

Making a List

We are going to start by making an honest list of the food that have been a huge stumbling block for each of us. This list is very specific to every individual. It has to do with the food that you use as a crutch and especially those that are habit-forming and that seem to produce insatiable cravings in your body (food that makes you lose all self-control). It will typically be food high in fat, salt, and refined sugar and flour, but it is not always limited to these foods. I will refer to these as your "binge" foods.

A quick word about "bad" and "good" food: God created food for our nourishment and enjoyment, so there are truly no "bad" or "good" food. However, if we have exalted food to a place of worship, then we may have formed emotional and physical ties with these specific kinds of food. **Abstaining from these, even if just for a season, is a good way of breaking at least the physical stronghold it has over us.**

God does not want you to be mastered by food or any other substance. Please look up this verse and write it in the space below: 1 Corinthians 6:12

_____

_____

Please write down the foods that usually get you in trouble in the space below and copy it to your journal. You can add onto this list later as you come across more food that are obvious triggers for you. Be very aware of **denial** while doing this. Here are some clues for you:

- Think about the food you "need" when you are nervous, angry, sick, bored, depressed, exhausted, or hurt
- Also think about the food you simply have to eat when you're happy or celebrating

_____

_____

_____

_____

_____

Choose your plan of action

Struggling with food through different seasons in my life, and also listening to the feedback I've received from ladies through the years, made me realize that there is no "one-size-fits-all" approach to eliminating binge foods. You may be in a season where you cannot possibly take the time to prepare menus and slowly eliminate binge food, or you may be in a place where eliminating binge food fast will throw you into immediate binging and purging. For this reason I'm presenting you with different options below.

Option 1 and 2 (slow approach) worked best for me most of the time. However I have recently found myself in a place where the "slow approach" didn't make any sense for the season that I was in, but the "fast approach" worked immediately.

Please read carefully over the three options below, then stop to pray and ask God which approach will be best for you at this particular season of your life.

Option 1: Let the light push out the darkness

I believe we are changed as we FOCUS ON GOD, instead of on trying to change ourselves. "... our lives gradually becoming brighter and more beautiful as God enters our lives and we become like him" 2 Cor 3:18 (The Message). As we focus on Him to help us bring good things into our lives, the negative habits that we couldn't change by ourselves for years, start to fall off.

The principle of letting the light push out the darkness can clearly be seen in this verse "Do not be overcome by evil, but overcome evil with good" Romans 12:21

This principle has helped many ladies get rid of binge food. As they start to grow in relationship with God, they ask Him to help them add healthy food to every meal, and habits such as Bible study and mild exercise to every day. Many of them have emailed me to say how their lives changed and deep ingrained habits were broken off, as they kept focusing on the Bible and falling in love with Jesus. Some have kept their Bibles in the kitchen, or note cards in their refrigerators to be reminded to turn to the "bread of life" instead of junk food during times of stress, pain, anger, sadness, and anxiety.

This is the best option for you if...
- You are scared to stop eating any of your favorite foods right away
- You are mainly dealing with binge eating, or compulsive overeating tendencies WITHOUT PURGING
- You have tried many times in the past to stop eating your binge food "cold turkey" but always ended up binging even more
- You eat huge amounts of food before starting any kind of detox or food plan because you feel that this will be the last time you ever get to eat your favorite foods
- Even the idea of any meal replacements such as bars, drinks etc. makes you panic

Plan:
- Don't focus on eliminating anything at first but FOR NOW focus on ADDING HEALTHY THINGS to your diet and be sure to make time for God DAILY
- Let the "light" start pushing out the "darkness" by adding salads, fruit, whole grains, and lean meats to every meal
- Ignore the fact that you're still eating unhealthy things at first and only focus on the good things you're adding
- As we go through the weeks, start eliminating your binge foods one by one and replace them with healthier options that will not make you binge. Make sure that you are honest with yourself about replacements. Some "healthy" items may contain ingredients that keep your food addiction going and will make you binge anyway

A program such as Weight Watchers or First Place might be a good choice for you

Option 2: Stop the cycle at the purge/starvation

This is the best option for you if...

- You are binging and purging (through vomiting, laxatives, or excessive exercise) several times a day
- You are starving your body to rid it of calories
- You are mainly purging/starving because you feel unable to stop binging
- You have tried many times in the past to eliminate your binge food "cold turkey" but always end up binging even more
- You eat huge amounts of food before starting any kind of detox or diet because you feel that this will be the last time you ever get to eat your favorite foods
- Even the idea of any meal replacements such as bars, drinks etc. makes you panic

Plan:

- **Start by making a commitment to yourself and to God to STOP THE CYCLE AT THE PURGE or STARVING. If you keep trying to stop it at the binge you may never stop**
- Ask God to help you "close the backdoor" Start by taking baby steps, you may only be able to NOT PURGE ONCE today, or go one day without starving yourself. That's okay, just keep adding onto that number. Take practical steps as well, such as throwing out all your laxatives, and eating with a friend or spouse who can keep you accountable..
- It doesn't matter how many times you have to "re-commit," what matters is that you arrive at that FIRST DAY and then keep adding onto it. Remember that falling is not your enemy, **not getting up is!**
- You may be gripped with the fear of gaining weight. Fear, according to the Bible, is not of God, and in this case the fear of losing the perfect appearance and the admiration of others has pride at its root. I want to encourage you to get additional counseling while going through the program if you feel consumed by fear of gaining weight. Have a pastor or counselor pray with you on a weekly basis to uproot the lies of the enemy and declare the truth of God's Word over your life. You may in fact gain some weight, but if you shut the back door of purging and starving, you will finally get out of the cycle of trying to erase the consequences of your sin (weight gain) and instead deal with repenting and turning from the actual sin (gluttony, idolatry, and pride). Make no mistake, this is not easy, but it is possible with God and the help of others. Keep reaching out for help.
- ONCE YOU HAVE FIRMLY CLOSED THAT BACK DOOR for at least a few weeks, you can start eliminating your binge foods one by one and replace them with healthier options that will not make you binge. Make sure that you are honest with yourself about replacements seeing that some "healthy" items may contain ingredients that can keep your food addiction going.

IMPORTANT: If you have Anorexia it is best to ONLY eliminate food under the supervision of a nutritionist. You will be needing the accountability to not fall back into obsessive or rigorous eating patterns.

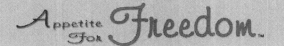

Option 3: Cold turkey

This is the best option for you if..

- You DO NOT have anorexia or any form of anorexia
- You have tried the things I've mentioned above and still find yourself unable to stop binging and purging, and unable to focus on anything. Huge amounts of sugar and carbohydrates in our diet can create a type of "brain fog." This means that the food we eat not only numbs our emotions in times of pain and stress, but we also find ourselves unable to concentrate on anything. Even ONE "sober" day away from your binge foods will make you realize how much this may have influenced you in the past
- You have tried "taking it slow" in the past and only succeeded for a little while
- You feel ready and motivated to give up all your favorite binge foods, but also know now that you can only do it by the power of the Holy Spirit
- You don't usually binge out of fear before starting a restrictive program
- You prefer meal replacements due to your hectic schedule

Plan:

- Start today (with the prayer and support of others) by eliminating all or most of the food on your list from your diet (usually white flour and sugar). IMPORTANT: Do not attempt this without finding healthy replacements for those foods. However, these replacements should not contain white flour and sugar and you should keep a close eye on how your body reacts to these. If you binge on replacement food, it defeats the purpose
- Stop all forms of unnatural diet patterns and periods of starvation, but rather start eating 3 meals with snacks or 6 small meals which include fruit, vegetables, dairy, protein, and whole grains, and a little healthy fats daily.
- Note that some healthy food might even be triggers for you, avoid these for now
- If white flour is your biggest trigger, you might have to back away from all kinds of wheat and gluten for a while
- IF YOU FOLLOW THIS CLOSELY AND TAKE OUT ALL SUGAR AND WHITE FLOUR FROM YOUR DIET, YOUR CRAVINGS WILL START TO DISAPPEAR AND THE "BRAIN FOG" WILL LIFT IN AS LITTLE AS 7 DAYS. Make sure that you set yourself up for success, especially for the first week when you will still have intense cravings for your binge food. Rid your home of all these food, and avoid situations where you are tempted
- A meal replacement program or food plan that is high in protein, medium in carbohydrates, and low in fat might be ideal for you (more of this in week 4)

IMPORTANT FOR ALL 3 OPTIONS:
REPLACING your list of binge food with healthier options is key to stay healthy and satisfy cravings when you first start detoxing. This in turn can prevent binging.

WARNING:	You can expect the following withdrawal symptoms when eliminating food that contains high amounts of sugar, white flour, fat, salt, and caffeine. • Headache • Fatigue • Irritability • Depression • Upset stomach • Just not feeling well in general **Drink enough water and rest often to help counteract these. Hang in there, it will only last a few days. Please keep in touch with your doctor throughout this process, especially if your symptoms are severe and/or abnormal.**

 Which plan to eliminate binge food seems best for you?

_____

Do you feel that you may only need to abstain from some of the food on your list for a short period of time to "reset" your system and get on track again, or does it seem like something you will have to do for a longer period of time?

_____

Do you recognize that you need the help of the Holy Spirit to lay down binge foods or keep to any kind of food program?

_____

	Please pray this prayer with me: Lord Jesus I admit today that I desperately need you to change this area of my life. Please show me which steps I need to take to break the physical hold this food struggle has on my body. Please forgive me for turning to my own will-power and futile methods so many times in the past. Please draw me closer to you, and help me grow in relationship with you so that I can bear fruit, including self control (John 15). I recognize today that ONLY YOU can change my heart and behavior, and I believe that you want to help me change these destructive patterns in my life. Thank you for leading me every step of the way Lord. Amen

DAY 4
Reach for One Sober Day

Once you've decided on a plan of action you are obviously faced again with the HOW. How does the plan on paper become a reality in your life?

It all starts with ONE DAY. Today is all you have. Today will shape your tomorrow and as a result, your future. Once you feel the victory of being able to, if only for one day, say NO to some of the food and activities that obviously harm your body and YES to those that promote physical well-being, you would have taken the first step on your journey to finding freedom.

What is a "sober" day?
Many people are crying out to God this very minute to help them not take another drink, smoke another cigarette, or log onto a porn website. In a similar fashion you and I have to cry out to the Holy Spirit to help us not open that first bag of chips that might send us into a mindless spiral of binging. We need a few victories strung together into one "sober" day. It's simply a day where you eat food that are high in nutrients every time you're hungry while avoiding your binge food. If you have 21 of those days stacked on top of each other, your body will not be craving the binge food anymore and your need to binge will have diminished greatly. We will talk more about the emotional issues that drive a binge in the weeks to come, but once you dealt with the physical cravings you are already half way there.

I never cease to be amazed by the testimonies I receive from ladies who have had ONE SOBER DAY. These girls are coming out of hiding. Even after one day, they feel as if they can breathe again. They are able to better cope with the stress surrounding parenting and other relationships, they are taking steps to nurture their bodies, they start talking to God, and they are feeling a glimmer of hope returning to their lives...

YOU TOO CAN HAVE THAT FIRST "SOBER" DAY, AND THE NEXT ONE, AND THE NEXT ONE, UNTIL YOU WALK FREE FROM THIS DEVASTATING STRUGGLE WITH FOOD.

How do you have ONE SOBER DAY?

You need God.
You can NOT do it on your own. We have times when our will power is a little stronger and we temporarily take control or our eating, but it usually doesn't last. However, when God comes through for you, it's different. The fear that "this will not last" is gone, because you know it is no longer up to your fickle will-power, but what you're experiencing is a true miracle.

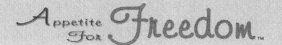

You need to get through your weak moments:
I want to tell you about the one thing that helps me when I get to those moments where I find myself at the cookie jar or with the candy bar half way to my mouth. I've learned to recognize my thoughts of *"just this one time"* or *"what difference does it make"* in those weak moments. Those thoughts are **LIES OF THE ENEMY**. He knows my weakness and he will present those lies to me every time when I feel stressed or weak, for as long as I believe it to just be my own little innocent thoughts.

Please look up 1 Peter 5:8 and write it in the space below.

_____

_____

_____

Now back up a little and read 1 Peter 5:6-7. According to these verses how can we resist the enemy or be protected from the prowling lion?

_____

_____

_____

So when that weak moment hits, there are only two things to do:

1. **Recognize the lies of the enemy and**
2. **Remove yourself from the situation**

Believe me if I tell you from painful personal experience that you will only find victory in those weak moments if you IMMEDIATELY get out of that place or situation. Find a quiet spot to pray, worship, pour your heart out before God, or read the truth of God's Word out loud so your ears can hear it. The Bible says that in God's presence the veil is stripped away, and as we look into the truth of His Word, we are changed (2 Corinthians 3:16-18). You may have to do this 20 times a day at first, but don't worry, it will become easier. The more you submit to God and resist the enemy, the more he will have to flee from you (James 4:7).

I found it necessary to avoid certain activities, places, and people in order to reach my first sober day. Please have a look at the list below and let the Holy Spirit search your heart and highlight the things that feed, or people who enable, your food obsession.

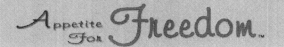

MIND-NUMBING ACTIVITIES:
TV and movies
Computer (especially social media sites)
Reading fiction

PLACES OF TEMPTATION
Buffets
Grocery and candy stores
Fast food restaurants
Food court in the mall

PEOPLE
Eating buddies
People who press your buttons
People who enable your food problem

 Please write down the mind-numbing activities, places of temptation, and people who might keep you from reaching your first sober day.

_____
_____
_____
_____

Please pray this prayer with me:

Jesus, I'm asking according to your Word for faith to believe today that, with your help, I can have that first sober day.

Please help me through my weak moments Lord. Make me aware of the lies I encounter in those moments, and help me run to your presence to refute those lies, instead of giving in to temptation.

I ask you to help me get through the withdrawal symptoms in my body, and also help me with the emotions of sadness that I might feel. Please show me which places and activities I need to avoid, and also help me set-up healthy boundaries with the people in my life who might enable me.

Thank you Holy Spirit for helping me.
Amen

DAY 5
Break the Power of a Binge

In order to build onto that first sober day, you also have to learn how to overcome the power that overeating or binging might have on your life.

Food addiction causes huge cravings in our bodies, and where cravings are present, binging or compulsive overeating can usually be found. Getting rid of the binge food is one key element in reducing cravings and as a result, reducing binging. However, eliminating cravings might not necessarily prevent binging.

If you are on a journey of finding healing for the root issues behind your eating disorder, you might not quite be at the place where you recognize the early signs of a binge (starting in the thoughts and emotions) and therefore find yourself often in the downward spiral. You can easily undo all the progress you've made with one lousy binge!

So how do we prevent a binge from turning into a whole day (or month) of overeating?

The answer lies in permanently shifting our focus from:
- **WEIGHT LOSS** to **HEALTH** and
- **PERFECTIONISM** to **CONSISTENCY**

HEALTH versus WEIGHT LOSS
Weight loss is not a big enough motivator for permanent change. We may be motivated by special occasions, but as soon as we reach our goal and the occasion is behind us, we plunge right back into unhealthy habits. Following a balanced food plan for the sake of GETTING HEALTHY is a long-term motivator that can produce permanent change. Reading books about the nutrients in different food and how those benefit your body can make you more aware of your choices and help you make the switch from "eating for health" instead of "weight loss." DECIDING not to eat something because it's not beneficial for your physical well being is very different from the deprived feeling of "I'm not allowed to eat that because I have to lose weight."

CONSISTENCY versus PERFECTIONISM
We will speak in a later week about the huge link between perfectionism and food struggles. For now I just want to explain the difference between a "sober" day and a 100% perfect day. People who have perfectionism tendencies have an ALL or NOTHING outlook on life. If they cannot follow a program perfectly, they swing to the other extreme of throwing everything out the door and binging.

When I refer to a "sober day" I'm referring to a 90 - 99 percent successful day. It's a type of day that you can do over and over again because it's not unattainable and unrealistic. On a sober day you will replace the unhealthy food and habits in your life with healthy ones, **and IGNORE the inevitable slip-ups along the way.**

We are so scared of those binges because it make us spiral down, but if you throw every binge or overeating in the 10% "failure-basket" and just get on with doing the 90% of healthy eating, exercise, rest, drinking water, and making time for God, our lives will look totally different. 90% successful days will give us 90% successful months, which in turn will produce 90% successful years. That, in my book, is a huge victory for anybody with a food struggle! Please start asking God today to help you change your focus FOR GOOD.

How can focusing on HEALTH and CONSISTENCY help you deal with the panic surrounding a "slip-up" and prevent it from turning into a binge?

_____

_____

You and I need the Holy Spirit desperately in our journey to freedom. We cannot get through our weak and tough moments without the Holy Spirit. He knows what you need to do to overcome, and he can help you spot the lies of the enemy. You have your own personal Counselor 24/7, and this Counselor knows you better than you know yourself.

Please copy this very important verse to your journal and note cards.
Zechariah 4:6b (NIV) "Not by might nor by power, but by my Spirit, says the LORD Almighty"

Please read Romans 8:5-6. Explain in your own words why you think having the Holy Spirit as your daily companion is crucial in this struggle

_____

_____

_____

_____

Inviting the Holy Spirit into your life is as simple as asking! I challenge you to ask Him today to lead and guide you through the moments of your life.

Please pray this prayer with me:

God, thank you so much for giving me the Holy Spirit to guide and counsel me moment by moment. Holy Spirit I give you full control of my life today. Please come fill all the empty places in my heart (Ephesians 5:18). I repent of sin in my life that may have grieved you Holy Spirit (Ephesians 4:30-32). Please forgive me.

Please help me change my focus to health and consistency instead of weight loss and perfection. More than anything help me set my eyes on You Lord Jesus, my Savior and Deliverer. Remind me that permanent change happens as I learn to love You more every day of my life. Amen

Ladies, I know this week's information might seem daunting and overwhelming, but let me encourage you that NOTHING is impossible with our God. He is calling you, just as you are. You might be dealing with incredible pain, shame, or anxiety at this very moment. You might have just eaten so much food that you are in physical pain. Maybe you just purged and you feel shame hanging like a cloak around your shoulders. Maybe you are past all these feelings and you just feel a great numbness inside of you, and yet, God is calling you. He saw everything you did and He is still drawing you by His Spirit. Don't wait any longer, open your heart to Him, let Him be strong in the areas where you are weak.

Week 4
Finding a Food Plan

Day 1
Dangerous Methods of Weight Control

I pray that God will use the information presented in this week to help you turn your back on dangerous methods of weight control and embrace the right program He has for you in your specific situation and season.

Please read carefully through the following dangerous methods of weight control. I have added my own experience in the hope of making you aware that these cannot only destroy your health, but ruin your life on so many levels.

FASTING (Full fast or liquid diets)
Let me first of all say that I DO BELIEVE in fasting as the Bible recommends. However, if you are suffering from an eating disorder I would recommend that you tread very carefully around this topic. The enemy will try to twist this Biblical discipline and use it against you. A clear indication that you are on the wrong track is when you start off by fasting in order to humble yourself before God, but somewhere along the way it turns into a form of weight control.

If you have a history of anorexia, fasting can be especially dangerous because it might trigger old obsessive patterns of food control which can turn into full blown anorexia. A friend who struggled with anorexia told me that she used to love fasting because it was a great way of "legalizing" her disordered way of eating while people would believe her to be so spiritual. Also, she could get away with her disorder for a while without any questions being asked.

Fasting can also trigger old feelings of deprivation which in turn can result in binge episodes, especially if you have a history of using fad diets to control your weight. I still fast, but only when I'm sure I heard from God and that my motive has nothing to do with pleasing others or controlling my weight.

RESTRICTIVE OR FAD DIETS
Fad or restrictive diets are diets that cut out certain food groups **permanently**, or restrict you to only a few items with very little nutritional value. These types of diets are accidents waiting to happen for the following reasons:
- It puts your focus on food and the scale (feeding the obsession with food and your body)
- It usually deprives your body of a much-needed food group (such as carbohydrates or fat)
- Deprivation and lack of proper nutrition causes cravings and a nagging fear that you are harming your body
- The above mentioned cravings are inevitably followed by binging on the "forbidden food"
- After a binge the vicious cycle of guilt and shame commences: You feel like a failure and this causes you to binge even more and quickly pick up all (or more) of the weight you've lost.

Note: Certain well-balanced food plans temporarily eliminate SOME carbohydrates (such as fruit). This can actually help you get rid of sugar addiction and can be especially helpful for people with Type 2 diabetes. (More on this later)

DIET PILLS (prescription, over-the-counter, and herbal)
- Diet pills only work while you're on them
- Losing weight this way is usually at the cost of your health. When you have NO appetite you are tempted to skip meals or only eat a few bites of your favorite binge food, instead of eating regular, balanced meals. This can bring your metabolism to a halt and deprive your body from much needed vitamins and minerals.
- It provides you with a false sense of "control." You might get so swept up in your weight loss and buying new clothes, that you neglect your relationship with God, which is a trap of the enemy to keep you enslaved to the appetite suppressants.
- The biggest problem with these pills is that they all contain addictive substances so in order for you to maintain the lack of appetite and high energy caused by ephedrine, caffeine, and other ingredients in the pills, you will have to increase the dosage which can cause serious health problems and even death.

Note: Do not be fooled by the "natural" substances in herbal medicine. Some of these can have exactly the same harmful effects and complications. Test herbal appetite suppressants by the symptoms you have. If you experience a lack of appetite, jitters, much more energy than usual, dry mouth, irritability, and insomnia the ingredients in those "natural" pills are most likely habit-forming and will lead you down the same dangerous path.

Please take a look at the unique set of complications brought on by diet pills:
Seizures, headaches, heart palpitations, dizziness, anxiety, irritability, insomnia, loss of libido, blurred vision, dry mouth, menstrual irregularities, paranoia, cardiac arrest, stroke, and even death.

Unfortunately, I abused diet pills for many years. This was during the 80's and 90's when diet pills were still widely available over the counter and before the ephedrine scare. The pills worked great: I wasn't hungry and didn't have any cravings, so it was easy to simply say NO to food. I loved the feeling of "control" and the attention the weight loss brought on. I had so much energy and stamina. I exercised every day of the week for hours and I almost felt invincible.

However, the "control" was short lived and food cravings returned with a vengeance. This was devastating to me: How could I go back after I've tasted the feeling of absolute control? So I kept increasing the dosage. I ignored the warnings and possible side effects. My top priority and desire was TO BE THIN AT ALL COST.

I can now see how dangerous this all was, but when you're protecting an idol in your life (in this case my desire to be thin), it trumps all common sense. All along the enemy fed me lies: He told me that I could be god over my own life, I could decide how much I weighed, I could decide how much I slept, and I could sculpt my own body and my own future. I felt such contempt for the people that couldn't get a grip on their own weight and lives. I felt so proud that I was not like them, and yet, I didn't think I had any pride in my life...

The reality was that my health deteriorated every day. The large amount of pills harmed my body in ways I can still not fully comprehend. I started suffering from issues with my digestive track, stomach, kidneys, and skin. I also experienced anxiety and depression due to the lack of sleep. I finally hit rock bottom after a big health scare and a wake-up call that my marriage was falling apart. I had to get "sober" to save my life. This was probably one of the most difficult things I ever had to do. Withdrawal consisted of food cravings, fatigue, weight gain, and depression. I had to start from scratch and pick-up the pieces.

All of this happened while I was actively involved in church and went through all the motions of living a holy life. The truth was that my personal relationship with Jesus was almost non-existent. **Today I know that nothing matters as much as having a relationship with Jesus. It's in that real, love relationship where we find truth, break free, and learn to live in victory.**

PURGING (Vomiting, Laxatives, Diuretics, Ipecac, and Excessive Exercise)

Desperate people use desperate measures, and purging is one of them. We usually turn to purging when we cannot let go of the idol of food, but at the same time nurture the desire to be thin at all cost. It is really an attempt to "have the best of both worlds." This is an extremely dangerous method of weight control that can cause serious health problems and sudden death due to potassium deficiency.

There is also a great deal of shame involved with purging, especially through the use of laxatives and vomiting, and for this reason people who struggle with bulimia tend to alienate themselves from everyone they know, which leaves them vulnerable to the lies of the enemy. I was only able to get rid of this dangerous method in my life when I broke the secrecy and told people about it. They counseled me and prayed with me until I recognized the truth of God's Word and broke the vicious cycle.

STOP THE LIFE OF PANIC

Fad diets and dangerous methods are sometimes the things we grab onto in moments of panic when we're faced with a birthday, a wedding, a Christmas party, a church picnic, a graduation, a funeral, a family reunion, etc. These things happen ALL THE TIME, so if you don't find a program that you can follow consistently, you will always be in some state of panic, going around in circles of madness, and losing the same twenty pounds year after year.

 What kind of "magic diets" or dangerous methods did you use in the past?

_____

_____

How did these work out for you?

_____

_____

The enemy does not want you to give up dangerous methods and fad diets, in fact he is the mastermind behind all forms of destructive methods and substances.

Please look up John 10:10. What does the Bible say about the enemy's "plan" for your life?

_____

Now also jot down the reason that Christ came, as found in the second half of this verse:

_____

 I invite you to pray this prayer with me:

God, please forgive me for turning to dangerous methods and fad diets through the years. I admit that I have not been a good steward of my body, and I ask you to forgive me.

Holy Spirit, I need your help to let go of the secrecy around this behavior. I need to speak the truth and accept the love and support of others. Please show me who I can trust with these secrets.
Please help me identify the lies of the enemy that is keeping this behavior going, and help me to accept your truth and turn from the lies.

God, thank you so much that you came so that I can have life in abundance. Thank you that you love me. Amen

DAY 2
Laying Down the Crutch

Your body might go through withdrawal when you lay down dangerous methods. You might need the help of family, friends, or a Christian counselor to get you through this. Don't try to do this on your own. ASK PEOPLE TO PRAY WITH YOU. There is power in prayer!

IMPORTANT	This program can be very beneficial in taking care of your spiritual, emotional, relational, and to some degree, physical needs. However, this course is not sufficient to help you deal with severe physical ramifications. I strongly urge you to see a doctor if you have developed serious medical problems.

What can you expect when you stop taking diet pills?
- You can expect an increase in appetite and a loss of energy when you stop taking diet pills. This will only last a few weeks, but in the meantime you want to build up your body with lots of healthy food, water, and rest.
- Eat six small meals a day, even if you don't feel like it and even if you binged on unhealthy snacks earlier. Skipping meals is part of the problem. If you skip a meal you will just make up for it in an hour or so with more unhealthy snacks. Give your body what it needs until you develop an appetite for the healthier options. Your body is literally starved for nutrition and care, yet it is addicted to junk food, so you will have to give it what it "needs" instead of what it "wants" right now. You have to train your body again, like you would a young child who keeps on asking for candy; as the parent you would ignore the request and keep introducing healthy food so that she can build an appetite for it.
- You might feel sick, shaky, exhausted, and have headaches as your body withdraws from the pills for the first two weeks. Keep at it though, it is so worth it. I reminded myself in the past that others before me went through withdrawal of heavy drugs and alcohol by the power of the Holy Spirit. If they could survive that, then surely I can survive withdrawing from addictive foods.
- Make sure to use a multivitamin or vitamin-enriched shakes to supplement your meals.
- Sleep enough and take naps until you start to feel less tired. The superficial energy high that your body was on for so long would have left you sleep deprived, so you need all the sleep you can get to bring your body back into balance.
- Exercise moderately even though you might feel too tired. Just go for a walk, the fresh air and exercise will help you feel less tired and it will also relieve possible depression. If you used diet pills for a long time, chances are that you might suffer from severe depression due to the lack of sleep over a period of time. You might have to speak to your doctor about medication (if only for a period) to help you. If these issues go untreated you may very well go right back to abusing diet pills.
- Talk daily to God about your fear of gaining weight. You will gain weight initially, but if you build your body back up and keep to a healthy eating program your weight will

stabilize. More importantly, you will get your life back and start remembering the things you used to love before food addiction and diet pills. You will also not have the irritability, depression, nervousness, and moodiness that were brought on by the diet pills.

What can you expect when you let go of purging?
- You will experience anxiety and fear of gaining weight. So please get support from your friends and family, especially to get you through the first three weeks. You need the truth of God's Word to break through the fear, because the only way out is to **stop the cycle at the purge.** You need to make a commitment to yourself and before God to not purge again EVEN IF YOU STILL BINGE. Remember what I said earlier about commitment: Keep committing as many times as you have to and keep getting up when you fall. Your victory lies in GETTING UP - not in never falling.
- You used to plan everything so that you can purge easily, now plan it so that it is difficult for you to purge. Don't eat where you're alone or where there's a bathroom close by, eat food that's hard to purge, throw out your laxatives, diuretics, and ipecac, and give your husband or roommate your car keys for the first week.
- You will still experience the craving to binge, partly because of a totally-depleted body that is crying out for nutrition. This is why you have to close the back door, and first deal with stopping the purging and immediately start building up your body with a balanced food plan so the cravings can stop (more on this in Day 3).
- Your digestive system will most likely be out of balance because of the purging. You may experience bloating and gas. Eat yogurt with acidophilus daily to get this balance back naturally, or speak to your doctor about medication. Yeast infections might occur too, so be sure to speak to your doctor about that as well (acidophilus will also help with yeast infections)
- If you are letting go of laxatives you will have to add a lot of water, fiber, fresh fruit, and vegetables to your diet to bring your elimination system back to normal.
- Vitamins are very important. Make sure that you especially take **potassium and zinc,** as purging depletes the body of these and it can lead to cardiac arrest.
- Exercise mildly. Do not use exercise as a form of purging, but as a way to care for your body. A low-impact walk will do it, because your body will also benefit from the fresh air.
- Sleep and naps are crucial. Your body will be sleep deprived because of getting up at night for the binging and purging. Depression is very likely, also due to lack of sleep over a long period of time and vitamin deficiency. So see a doctor and make sure to get the right medication for you (if needed) to get out of this cycle of sleepless nights and days filled with lethargy and depression.
- You might have to be hospitalized, depending on how far along your bulimia is. This can actually be very beneficial for you, especially if you don't have any care at home, so don't fight it. Getting your vitamins through an IV can help you recover faster. Please take every hand that is extended to you, your life depends on it.
- Also make an appointment to see your dentist to discuss ways to treat your tooth decay due to the purging. All of this can be very humbling, but it is very necessary to regain your care and love for your body, which is a temple of the Holy Spirit.
- Plenty of water, fruit, and vegetables will also bring your hydration back and help with your dry skin and other skin-related problems. For some rashes you might have to see your doctor or dermatologist so you can get prescribed treatment.
- Make time for God. He wants to talk to you about how valuable you are to Him. Keep calling out to Him even when you have just purged and you feel totally disgusted with yourself. Even in that moment God sees you perfectly redeemed, washed in the blood of

His Son. In that moment he also sees you as you will be, freed from the chains that bind you and healed from the pain that drives you

What can you expect when you let go of starvation?

- Almost all of the things mentioned in bulimia will apply to you. Chances are that you might be dealing with both disorders anyway.
- As far as meals: Fear of losing control will be prevalent for you. Start with small portions, just a hand-full, eight times a day. Pray before you eat, and pray especially when you are tempted not to eat. Many women that I've counseled found that they had to eat at first with the Bible open next to them. They would be "eating" the Word of God (reading it) as part of their daily meals, so that they won't experience the panic and fear that the enemy had them associate with eating.
- Shakes that are packed with nutritional value, at least three times a day, will be very helpful to build up your body.
- You really need to be under the care of a physician, especially if you have been starving for a while, your life depends on it. Many things can go wrong in your body when you don't feed it, and only a physician can tell you what the physical ramifications are and what can be done about it. Again, seeing a doctor is humbling, but crucial.
- You might very well need hospitalization or might have to be enrolled in an impatient program where you can receive care around the clock.
- Time with God is crucial for you. Learning to trust Him and to give control over to Him can change your whole life. Your relationships and home life might have been traumatic and painful and you might have sold out your heart to control and starvation during this time. It is time to learn how to deal with relationships and receive healing from the past. God and other caring people can help you with all of this, **but you must take the first very scary step to give up the control and start to take care of your body, one bite at a time.**

Please note that I don't mean to oversimplify this whole process. Some ladies will not be able to break free of the above-mentioned dangerous methods without the proper care from a team of specialists. If this is you, please don't hesitate to get help as soon as possible. Tomorrow might be too late!

When you give up dangerous methods, it will get worse before it gets better, but hang in there, you will never be sorry that you did. Also, keep going through the weeks of this program even if you're still struggling with laying down dangerous methods. When our bodies are weak, we are by far the most willing to open up our hearts to the Holy Spirit.

TWO OBSTACLES
There are many things that can drive us to keep using dangerous methods and ignore the warning signs; however the two most common reasons are a desire to be thin at all cost, and the fear of losing control.

1. The desire to be thin
This desire can become an idol in our lives that drives our every decision, consumes all reason, and numbs us to the voice of the Holy Spirit.

Please look up Jonah 2:8 and write it in the space below.

_____

_____

_____

If you're still holding on to the idol of wanting to be thin at all cost, you will find it very difficult to lay down the dangerous methods you've been using to control your weight.
Please ask the Holy Spirit today to search your heart to see if you might still be holding onto this. He is willing and able to help you open your hand and let go of this idol you're clutching. Please write your own prayer to God in the space below if you still "want to be thin" more than anything.

_____

_____

_____

_____

_____

2. Fear of losing control

Fear is a tool that the enemy uses. God gives us a spirit of love, power, and a sound mind (2 Tim 1:7). Memorize this Scripture and use it often when you are gripped with fear.

Please read 1 John 4:18. What is the one thing, according to this passage that drives out all fear?

_____

As you can see LOVE, perfect agape love that comes from God, does not only motivate us to change, but it drives out all fear, including the fear of gaining weight.
If you want to walk free from these dangerous methods, then you will have to make time for God FIRST AND FOREMOST in your life. Even if you don't "feel" like it yet, make a conscious decision to show-up and quiet your spirit in His presence DAILY. If you keep showing up, your appetite will grow, and God will fill your heart with a deep love for Him.

Will you keep asking God today to give you a deep love for Him and His Word?

_____

_____

_____

_____

I invite you to pray this prayer with me:

God, I'm sorry that I have allowed the *desire to be thin* to become an idol in my life. I repent from idolatry and ask you to forgive me.

Please open my eyes to the lies of the enemy. My worth is not wrapped up in my appearance, but it is in being a daughter of the most high King.

Please show me in the days to come how to turn from this idol for good and help me lay down the fad diets and dangerous methods.

I stand against the fear of the enemy in Jesus' name. Please give me a love for you that is bigger than my desire to be thin, the kind of love that will drive out all fear.
Amen

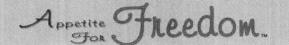

DAY 3
Choosing the Right Food Plan for You

Please remember that the best food plan in the world won't do you any good if your heart is still sold out to idols and you have not dealt with denial and pride before God. Please go back over the material of the previous three weeks and get your pastor or small group leader to pray with you if these issues are not yet resolved between you and God.

That said, choosing the right food plan is a very important step on your road to freedom. The structure, accountability, and support that can come through a well-balanced food plan can greatly benefit you in this struggle.

God created our bodies with certain SIGNALS to tell us when we need nutrition and when we are full. Most people with eating disorders have lost touch with these signals such as a stomach growling, etc. We may eat to fill up an emptiness inside of us, so we keep on eating long after we're full. We may eat when we're really thirsty, tired, or when we're tempted. A sound food plan can help you get in touch with "real hunger" again so you will know when you're eating for other reasons.

What does a good food plan look like?

- It is a plan that you can follow CONSISTENTLY for years (not a quick fix)
- It has proper SUPPORT and ACCOUNTABILITY in place
- It takes your focus OFF food (after the initial period of getting used to the plan)
- It is high in nutrients and supplies you with energy and a feeling of well being
- It gives you peace about your health (it's not dangerous to your health)
- It fits your economic situation
- It fits your family and work situation
- It has been proven and trusted by people you know

Is this checklist helpful? What would you have liked to add to this list when looking for your ideal food plan?

_____

_____

CREATING A CUSTOM PLAN

I recognize that some of you may be in a situation where it is impossible for you to follow a set plan or program due to financial difficulty or food allergies. For this reason I will give some tips

and ideas below to help you create a custom plan before we start reviewing different programs. Let me assure you that our God is not limited to a certain plan or program. If you surrender your life to Him, develop your own healthy menus, consider portion sizes when you eat, and keep to this consistently, you can have the desired results: Freedom from the idol of food.

MENUS and SHOPPING LISTS

Putting together menus and shopping lists can help take your focus off food, minimize the time you spend thinking and preparing food and save you money. It can also help you incorporate healthy food into every meal and keep variety going.

Things to consider when creating menus

- Be sure to avoid your binge food when creating menus, as well as food that are obviously high in salt, fat, sugar, and caffeine.
- **If you have been binging, purging, or grazing you need 6 small meals a day (or 3 meals and 3 snacks).** It is crucial to eat regularly in order for your metabolism to kick in again, but it is just as important to give your body a break in between meals. If you have been grazing all day long you may be totally oblivious to your body's hunger signals. Also, if you're prone to night-time eating, your body never gets a chance to rest and recuperate which can cause depression, lethargy, illness, and food cravings.
- **If you have been starving your body, you need to incorporate 6-8 small meals.** Introduce a variety of food and keep them small (a handful of nuts, half a cup of oatmeal, etc) to keep anxiety under control. A meal replacement program can actually help you with this, but it should be done under strict supervision of your doctor or a nutritionist to make sure you get enough calories. If you surrender your life to God on a DAILY basis through Bible study and prayer, and you turn to a doctor, nutritionist, or Christian counselor for accountability with your food plan, you can be free from this devastating disorder for good.
- **Variety is important.** Your body needs a variety of food to function properly, so you want to make sure to incorporate protein, grain, fruit, vegetables, dairy, and healthy fat on a daily basis.
- **Keep your schedule in mind** and plan accordingly. Be realistic about your body's needs: If you crave protein in the morning, put scrambled eggs or oatmeal and nuts on the menu, or if your are tired at 4 o'clock in the afternoon be sure to put down a small meal that can boost your energy level at that time.
- **Be realistic when choosing meals.** Be sure to incorporate food that you enjoy and go out of your way to make it enjoyable and presentable. You can't fool yourself by putting salad on the menu for every meal, it will just cause you to abandon the menu idea and binge on unhealthy food.
- **Keep your budget in mind and shop at appropriate stores.** Healthy food is more expensive, but it is possible to feed even a big family healthy meals if you plan ahead, stick to a shopping list, and buy at discount food stores.
- **Create different menus.** Be sure to have at least five or six menus that you can rotate throughout the year. You can of course be creative and make menus for different seasons and holidays as well.
- **Turn to the Internet for healthy recipes** that are high in protein, medium in carbs, and low in fat. You can also look for menu templates online to save some time. Search for "food to boost energy" or "food high in fiber" to find lists of food you can add to your menus that will help you regain your health and build up your body.
- **If you are single,** consider cooking big meals and freezing the leftovers. Remember to incorporate these into your menus.

Tips on portion control

The need for piles of rich food are fueled by an emptiness inside of us that can ONLY be filled and satisfied by God. People with eating disorders are often anxious about not having enough food for a certain meal or occasion, even though there's clearly enough to go around. Your stomach is roughly as big as your fist. It takes a while for your brain to register the full feeling after you've eaten only a small portion, but anything you "need" beyond that is in fact no longer stomach hunger but a deep insatiable hunger that cannot be filled with all the food in the world. **If you've ever binged you know exactly what I'm talking about: You keep eating and eating until you are physically sick, but the emptiness just doesn't seem to go away...** Have a look at the serving sizes on food packaging to know how big one serving is

ACCOUNTABILITY AND SUPPORT

Support and accountability are CRUCIAL elements in creating healthy habits. If you want to follow your own custom plan I would strongly recommend that you do it with an accountability partner that you see at least once a week. Make sure this is not an "eating buddy" that will sabotage your progress, but rather someone that will inspire and motivate you when you feel weak. Another tool to use is a free online food tracker and support groups such as www.Sparkpeople.com. You will find many Christian groups on there as well. **Please note that these online communities should not be your only source of support. One-on-one, flesh and blood accountability is still the best and most reliable form of support.**

Please read the following verse and explain why you think accountability and support are crucial elements in your journey to freedom.

Ecclesiastes 4:12

"Though one may be overpowered, two can defend themselves. A cord of three strands is not quickly broken."

_____
_____
_____

What kind of accountability and support do you plan to bring on board to make sure you succeed? Beware of pride. It's not easy to ask for help, but it a very important step to move out of your food struggle for good.

_____
_____
_____
_____

I invite you to pray this prayer with me:

Lord Jesus, please search my heart and remove all traces of pride that might hold me back from asking for help. I recognize that you have given us each other, as different parts of the body, to help one another.

Your Word says that if we lack wisdom we can ask You (James 1:5). Please show me how and to whom I should reach out for help and accountability in order to keep to a food plan.
Thank you that you care about all these details of my life Lord.
Amen

Day 4
Food Plan Reviews

Note: I will briefly review some of the programs I am familiar with and that worked well for me and most ladies I've counseled through the years. However, this does NOT mean that I recommend these exclusively, or condemn other programs that are not mentioned here. Please evaluate any program you consider against the points I've mentioned in Day 3 and be sure to take your own medical history, financial position, and season of life in consideration. Also pray about the program you're considering and seek counsel from safe people in your life before simply jumping in.

IMPORTANT	Please check with your doctor before starting any new food program, especially if you have certain medical conditions.

WEIGHT WATCHERS

I don't think this very popular program needs much introduction, so let's have a look at the pros and cons that other ladies shared with me and that I've experienced myself:

PROS:

- It is online-accessible so you can quickly track your points on your computer or iPhone.
- It allows you to eat everything, so you don't experience that panic of impending deprivation before you start this program. The fact that you can eat everything in moderation can help you turn your back on the "all or nothing" mentality that feeds binging.
- The tracker reminds you to drink water, exercise, take vitamins, and add important food such as vegetables, dairy, and healthy fat to your diet. Having this visual in front of you daily is a powerful reminder and motivator.
- It takes just a few weeks to get used to the points and then you pretty much know how much everything counts and you don't have to think much about food. If you are online, you just type in the food that you are about to eat and it tells you exactly how many points it is.
- It has menus and recipes that you can use or just add to your own weekly menus and shopping lists so you don't keep thinking about food all day long.
- Attending a Weight Watchers group can be the make-or-break factor when following this program. Research has shown that 80% of people drop out of diet programs that don't offer some kind of coaching or accountability. Fortunately, Weight Watchers has support in places all across the country. There are groups in shopping malls, churches, maybe even at your workplace. So be sure to check online for a group close to you, and show up. It might be uncomfortable at first, but it's part of laying down your pride and asking for help on this journey, plus, it could help you stick to the plan and lose your excess weight.

CONS:

- This program doesn't deal with letting go of binge foods, which can actually keep your food addiction going, even if you lose some excess weight. It does encourage you to eat healthy, but the extra points each week can tempt you to also add foods high in sugar, white flour, and fat while still staying in your points range. This might fool you into believing that you're doing okay while your cravings are still hiding under the surface, ready to pounce on you in a weak moment. However, if you deliberately stay away from your binge food (or starting cutting them out one at a time as we've mentioned earlier in this program) it will be easier to stay inside your points, and your chances of success on this program will increase dramatically.
- Weight loss on this program can be pretty slow and even though it is considered healthier to lose slow, it can also be very discouraging. Some people end up returning to their unhealthy habits before they reach their goal weight, simply because it takes a long time. That said, if you're truly after a change of heart not just appearance, you will find it easier to be patient with this process.
- If you can't join a group for some reason, you may not have success on this program for long. Online accountability is just not as potent and hands-on as face-to-face encounters with a coach or group leader. I have a few friends who have found great success and freedom from the physical ramifications of food addiction on this program, however, they all have one thing in common, they attend a group in their area at least once a week. I tried "doing it myself" online for a long time but I could never quite get below a certain weight and found myself losing and gaining the same 20 pounds for many years.

Remember: Cutting back on binge food is not the same as deprivation. When you deprive your body you take away food or food groups that are important to health and well being. When you cut out binge food, you take out foods that are extra (not essential), have almost no nutritional value, and can even be harmful to your body.

TAKE SHAPE FOR LIFE

This program consists of Medi-fast meals and free health coaching. I was very skeptical about meal replacements when I first started this program and many ladies on the forum where I was journaling about it were concerned that this is simply another fad diet or dangerous method. However, this program has helped me get rid of food addiction and has been one of the best food plans I have ever used. I have also received countless testimonies of ladies with binge eating disorders and compulsive overeating who found this to be a powerful tool to get rid of their food addiction and lose their excess weight, especially if combined with my 12 week program. Here are the basic pros and cons for you:

PROS:

- **After a few days on this program you feel the "brain fog" of food addiction lift and the anxiety subsides.** This is mainly due to the reassurance that you're feeding your body six meals a day that are high in vitamins and minerals, but also because you can think clear as your body gets rid of all addictive foods and starts to function properly (the meals contain very little sugar and no white flour).

- **It gets rid of cravings.** After 21 days most people have no more cravings and can walk into a store without the anxiety and strong desire for their binge food, but you already start to feel stronger in resisting temptation in as little as 7 days.

- **It takes your attention off food** (after the few days that it takes to get used to preparing the packaged meals). You literally go into autopilot about food and meal preparation. This has been a tremendous help for me at a time in my life where I was so overwhelmed with our businesses, housework, and homeschooling my kids. It is a fact that most of us moms will make sure that our children eat healthy (even if we are stretched to the limit), but then we have no time left for ourselves and tend to just grab junk food or bread. This plan helped me make sure that I'm also taking good care of my children's mother. I had a great knowledge of nutrition when I started this program, and I knew exactly what to eat, but the problem was that I never got around to preparing those things for myself on a regular basis, because of the demands of life. These packages became my "healthy fast food" that I could just grab and go.

- **I was amazed at the difference support from a health coach made AFTER I laid down my pride.** Many people with long-standing food issues are very suspicious of food programs, and rightly so because they have been disappointed by fad diets so many times. I too felt myself suspicious of this program and the coaching. I already knew so much about nutrition, so what could a health coach teach me, right? There was actually pride hiding in my heart, I was still convinced that I didn't need anyone and that I knew all the answers, and yet... I was struggling. A compassionate coach who was supportive and who walked this journey herself turned out to be exactly what I needed to break out of food addiction.

- **Fast and safe weight loss.** I was especially skeptical about the "fast weight loss" because I've always equated that to fad diets and dangerous methods. I changed my mind though when I actually kept the weight off and met other people who kept their weight off for years through this program. The biggest benefit I found from losing weight fast, IT'S A HUGE MOTIVATOR! I became more and more inspired every day to keep

going on the program and to start exercising MAINLY BECAUSE OF THE FAST WEIGHT LOSS. Seriously, is there anything more devastating than working your best at a program, giving it all you've got for weeks, and not losing anything?

- **I thought that it would be difficult to incorporate this program into family life, but I was surprised at how easy it was.** Eating my own six small meals a day made me more aware that my kids also need small fuelings of food that are high in vitamins and nutrients throughout the day. Also, on this program you have one meal a day that you have to prepare yourself (consisting of low-fat protein and vegetables), so we ate that together as a family. Having vegetables and low-fat protein every night proved to be beneficial for our whole family and I simply added a whole grain for the children.

CONS:

- **One can get pretty sick of the same food.** There are 70 different foods to choose from, but even with that variety it can start to get old. However, I have to add that the makers of this program hinge some of their success on the fact that "our cravings diminish when we have limited choices."
- **The cost can be an obstacle for a bigger family where everybody needs to eat healthier.** It costs about $11 a day per person, which is less than the average $16 that most Americans spend on food per day. However, if you have a big family and you have been shopping carefully and planned your meals frugally in the past, this might jack your budget for groceries. I found that it cost our family of six a little more when my husband and I first went on this program. However, after a while our budget went back to normal, simply because I didn't go to the store that often anymore and I actually stuck to my shopping list when I went.
- **You can get stuck in a cycle of eating the meal replacements for years.** If you don't work the program, lose the weight, and transition into "normal" eating with the help of your coach, you can stay stuck in eating Medifast meals for years on end. Some people keep eating *only* the packaged meals years after they've lost the weight because they fear they might gain it back. This is the same fear we spoke about earlier this week. Fear of gaining weight can make you abuse this program and turn it into a dangerous method. However, if this program is not abused, but actually used in the way it was intended, it is a powerful tool to regain your health.
- **This kind of program is not for everybody.** If you have bulimia or anorexia you cannot follow this kind of program. You may be able to benefit from this program AFTER you've stopped the purging cycle in bulimia for a few months. Please have a look at the other two programs I recommend if you're struggling with these types of eating disorders. There are also certain medical conditions that might prohibit you from following a low-calorie program such as this, so make sure you have a look at the contraindications on the Take Shape for Life website.

FIRST PLACE 4 HEALTH

An excellent and well laid out Christian weight loss program with basically all the same advantages and tools as Weight Watchers (on a smaller scale). You count calories on this program and it uses the "whole person approach." However, you get so much more than just a food plan as it includes Bible studies, memory verses on CD, daily planners, and support. This program has been around for quite a while and they have many groups around the country, so if you can find a strong group close to you, with a knowledgeable and compassionate leader, you can reap spiritual, social, and accountability benefits from it.

You can also start your own First Place Group and help others. You will find their material at most Christian book stores or look for them online. They now also have "The Live It Tracker" which is a tool (similar to that of Weight Watchers) where you can keep record of your nutrition and physical activities as well as your spiritual disciplines.

All of the above mentioned programs, if used correctly, are excellent methods of getting your metabolism running again, lose excess weight, and supply your body with nutrients. However, it's only a small piece of the puzzle, and can become an idol in itself if it's not surrendered to God (like anything else in our lives really).

 Have you thought about a plan to follow?

Look back at the criteria for a good plan in Day 3. How does your plan or program measure up especially in the area of CONSISTENCY and SUPPORT?

I invite you to pray this prayer with me:

Lord Jesus, thank you that you care about my eating habits and that I can ask you to be involved in this process with me. Please help me choose the program that will work best for me in my season of life and my unique circumstances.

Please show me where pride might be keeping me from trying again, or trying something new.

Please use the program and support I choose to help me break free from my food struggle for good.
Amen

Day 5
A Shift in Focus

Before choosing a food plan, it is of great importance for you to ask God to help you shift your focus to HIM instead of food, a food plan, weight loss, or your appearance. If you TRULY want to change PERMANENTLY in the area of food, you need a change of heart and focus. God specializes in changing our hearts, but you and I have to recognize where our focus has been, and change it.

Warning: If you harden your heart and refuse to let God help you change your focus, you will most likely start up a program, have some success on it, and fall right back into binging, purging, or starvation in a few months. I have lost weight just to gain it back more times that I can remember. ONLY A CHANGE IN FOCUS and HEART made the changes permanent in my life.

Get your focus off the FOOD
In order to break your love relationship with food, you have to get your attention and thoughts off food: No more thinking about food all day long, hanging out in the kitchen, or going to the grocery store every day. The food plan you choose should not consume your thoughts and have you pour over recipes for hours.

A clear indicator that I have picked up my idol again is when I just want to "hang out" in the kitchen. I'm referring to preparing elaborate meals for everybody just to be close to the food. Sometimes I would prepare rich meals for my family because I'm already secretly in the middle of a binge. I was not really treating my family to a great meal, but I was preparing binge food for myself before "starting over" on my diet the next morning. The sad part is that I dragged them down with me, because they didn't need all that excess fat and sugar either. Other times I would pride myself in my strong self-control to abstain from food while cooking rich and unhealthy meals for guests. However, hours spent planning, cooking, cleaning, and storing food was all an attempt to be around food, even when I wasn't necessarily eating it. I was all along trying to fill a void inside of me that could only be filled by God.

Please be honest with yourself when choosing a food plan. You may be choosing a particular program where you can be pouring over healthy recipes and keep cooking all day long, simply because you want to stay close to your idol. This is obviously not a good choice for you.

Be careful not to worship the FOOD PLAN
GOD ALONE CAN SAVE US, NOT A FOOD PLAN! Some food programs are sound and can be greatly used by God if we surrender these to Him. However, if we exalt any type of food program to a place of worship, we are simply trading idols.

A very good indication that we started worshiping a program is when we find ourselves pulling away from God while feeling so proud of ourselves for finally "getting a grip" over our eating. We might feel so wonderful about how well the program is working for us, the new clothes we get to buy, and the compliments we're getting, while we know that we have not even cracked our

Bibles in weeks. This "freedom" will only be temporary, and even if the weight loss sticks, we might end up picking up another idol to fill the growing emptiness inside of us.

Don't get me wrong, **clothes that fit and the ability to enjoy certain activities are spoils we should take back from the enemy, and God wants us to have these**. However, if it takes center stage in our lives we are simply busy with SELF again, just in a different form than the previous self-hatred and low self esteem.

People have in fact created religions around the adherence to specific food programs. Anybody who doesn't eat in a specified way or maintain the boundaries of the program is cast out of the order of "holy ones." This is a very dangerous practice and a trap of the enemy to enslave people to a food program instead of being yoked with the ONLY TRUE SAVIOR: Jesus Christ.

Ask yourself these questions:
"Does this program take my attention off food and cause me to lean heavily on God?"
or
"Does this program give me a feeling of pride in my own great will-power, and do I find myself slipping away from spending time with God while being consumed with the rules of my program?"

 Have you exalted a food plan above God in the past? Please explain:

_____

Do you recognize that any balanced food plan can be beneficial if we surrender it to God and ask the Holy Spirit to help us?

_____

Get your focus off WEIGHT LOSS and APPEARANCE

An emphasis on weight loss and appearance revolves mainly around SELF and how we are perceived by others. This is a hard truth to hear, but it is the main driving force behind almost every failed diet. Wanting to look good and be complimented by others is a vain and self-centered motive that is INSATIABLE. We can never get enough compliments and we will always have someone prettier or skinnier to compete with. The number on the scale is never quite low enough if weight loss and appearance is our motive. We believe that if we can only reach a certain number or look a certain way we will be satisfied, but IT IS A LIE FROM THE ENEMY, because we will never reach that "magic place."

This lie stands in stark contrast to the Word of God. Jesus calls us to humble ourselves and serve one another as He models. **Galatians 5:13** "You, my brothers and sisters, were called to be free. But do not use your freedom to indulge the flesh; rather, **serve one another** humbly in love."

If our focus is rightly on *serving* the body of Christ instead of *impressing* the body of Christ, we will reach for healthier food to give us energy, we will make sure that we exercise and keep our bodies strong so we can serve, and we will make sure we get enough sleep and recreation so God can use us in our families and the world around us. We will also be free from the "brain fog" and depression surrounding food addiction that keeps us from reading the Bible and praying.

 Do you see the difference between focusing on health and energy to glorify God instead of weight loss and appearance to glorify ourselves?

_____

What does Jesus say about those who wish to be His disciples? Please write Luke 9:23 in the space below:

_____

_____

The only way to get our focus OFF food, a food plan, weight, and appearance is to SET OUR FOCUS ON GOD! This is not a popular idea in the culture we live in. Do you know someone who truly has his/her focus on God?

_____

_____

Can you think of practical ways that you can set your focus on God daily (even hour by hour)? Please be prepared to share this in your group.

_____

_____

_____

_____

I invite you to pray this prayer with me:

God, please forgive me for setting my eyes on food, food plans, weight loss, and my appearance.

Please help me set my eyes again on you Jesus. Show me how to surrender even the food plan I choose to you and not let it become my focus or savior. I admit today that only you can set me free, and only by the power of the Holy Spirit will I be able to benefit from any program or food plan.

Please take all selfish desires from me, and help me to guard my heart, because everything in my life flows from it (Proverbs 4:23).

I want to love you with all my heart, soul, mind, and strength Lord, please give me that deep love for you.
Amen

Week 5
Exercise:
A Sacrifice of Praise

DAY 1
God and Exercise

I'm excited for our week together on exercise. I know this is not a very popular topic for most of us, but let's find out together what role exercise plays in our journey to freedom. My prayer is that you will put exercise in it's rightful place; as a tool in the hand of our Savior, to bring healing to your body and emotions.

 Please read 1Timothy 4:8 out loud:

"...for while bodily training is of some value, godliness is of value in every way, as it holds promise for the present life and also for the life to come."

Did you notice that bodily training is of "some value"?

_____

Did you also pick up on the fact that it should not have center stage in our lives?

_____

For someone with a food struggle, exercise can be another dangerous method of weight control:

- **People sometimes use exercise as a form of purging.** After binging or eating what they perceive as too much, they might exercise for hours on end to get rid of the unwanted calories.
- **Exercise can be despised by others, mainly because it has been used along the same lines as fad diets.** In other words, in the midst of a binge and downward spiral people with binge eating disorder will usually not exercise at all, but during the "panic times," before some event or important occasion, they will pick-up an extreme exercise routine usually combined with a fad diet. This type of exercise, just like the fad diet, can not last because it exhausts the already-depleted body and can even cause serious injuries. Every time I used exercise to get rid of some unwanted pounds, I found myself despising it with a passion. I looked forward to getting to a certain weight so I could be done with the torture of exercise, very much in the same way that I couldn't wait to return to my binge food.

Identify your Motive

Please answer the following questions to identify your motive. Be honest, these questions are for you personal evaluation:

- Do you exercise or plan to exercise to look good, even "feel" good, and lose weight?
- Or do you exercise, or plan to exercise, to bring health to your body and emotions so that you can glorify God and serve others?

Exercise for the wrong reasons or with the wrong motive has the same effect as following a food program for the sake of appearance and weight loss: It keeps us going around in circles of captivity. Exercise as a form of weight control can in fact be a very dangerous way of purging calories, mainly because people using this method don't easily turn from it. Some of them have even made it their profession and justify it as a way to "stay healthy" year after year while they remain in denial about the severity of the problem.

So should someone with an eating disorder exercise at all?
The answer is YES. Exercise plays an important role in your physical and emotional healing if you do it with the right motive: FOR THE GLORY OF GOD.

 Please read 1 Corinthians 6:19-20 and describe in your own words what these verses teach you about your body:

_____

_____

_____

Now let's take a look at the "some value" part mentioned in 1 Timothy 4:8. Here are just a few of the amazing benefits of exercise:

1. If you have been struggling with food, you may experience a disconnect from your body (ignoring your body). Exercise will help you re-connect and as a result, become a better steward of your body.
2. When you exercise your brain releases endorphins, a feel-good chemical that helps with depression. It can also help you get rid of stress and anxiety.
3. Aerobic exercises are known to keep your heart healthy, and a stronger heart can pump blood more efficiently, which is good news for your whole body.
4. Exercise can reduce the risk of heart disease, high blood pressure, type 2 diabetes, stroke, obesity, breast cancer, and colon cancer, to only mention a few.
5. Aerobic exercise activates your immune system, making you less susceptible to viral illnesses such as colds and flu.
6. Aerobic exercise is also known to help with a lack of energy and fatigue. Although it might not feel like it at first, it will increase your energy over time if you keep doing it consistently.
7. Incorporating weights with your aerobic exercise can reduce your risk of osteoporosis.
8. Exercise builds and maintains healthy muscles, bones, and joints.
9. Exercise helps you work better, play better, and become better at sports because it makes you more agile and it increases your strength and stamina.
10. Exercise can help you maintain a healthy body weight (of course not if used for purging or as a quick fix).
11. Exercise actually improves digestion.
12. Exercise can enhance your quality of sleep, providing you don't exercise right before bedtime.

God obviously made our bodies to move, however, this area of our lives should also be surrendered to Him in order to restore it to it's rightful place.

I invite you to pray this prayer with me:

Lord, thank you for reminding me today that my body is a temple of the Holy Spirit, bought with a price, and it's not my own to abuse or neglect. Forgive me for not being a good steward of my body by either depriving it of exercise for years or harming it through extreme exercise regimes.

Please change the motive of my heart so that I will no longer strive for the perfect appearance and the recognition of men, but rather exercise to glorify you through a healthy body.

I surrender my body to you Lord Jesus.
Amen

DAY 2
Simply Show Up

Most people with food struggles tend to not live in the present moment.
Does the following statements sound familiar? "As soon as I lose weight I will invite people over, buy better clothes, go to women's retreats, reach out to friends, join the worship team, work with the elderly, go to my kid's soccer game, attend the prayer meetings, launch my ministry." We convince ourselves that we are going to exercise and eat healthy after Christmas, after our birthday, after this cold spell, or after this stressful situation.

Putting life off like that is in fact putting off living. TODAY IS ALL WE HAVE. Look at your day today and you have a glimpse of your future.

Procrastination
We will speak more about this topic in a later week, but for now I want you to consider that you might be procrastinating in the area of exercise. People who want to do things perfectly tend to procrastinate until they have it "all figured out" or because they are afraid they will never do it perfectly. Procrastination and excuses go hand in hand, and the enemy can use these to keep you in bondage for the rest of your life.

These are common excuses not to exercise:
- I don't have money right now to join a gym
- I don't have money right now for the right shoes and outfit
- I have to first lose a few pounds
- I cannot appear in public like this
- If I can just convince my husband/friend to go with me, I will go
- I will wait until summer, it's too cold now
- I will wait until winter, it's too hot now
- I am just not an athletic person
- I just have to deal with this crisis in my life first
- I simply hate exercise, it's just not me
- I will start tomorrow...

 Which excuses have you been using not to exercise?

_____

_____

_____

Please know that I am not minimizing your situation; on the contrary, my heart goes out to you and I know it's not easy. I have gone through times in my life when my excuses were very real and difficult issues. For the longest time I didn't have any money to join a gym, buy exercise equipment, or even buy decent sneakers. When my kids were all little, we were in a foreign country with very little money, no family or babysitters around, and my husband worked 12-hour days. Those in my book were valid excuses. However, even though you and I might be tempted to let each other off the hook, God has an answer for each of us. Through the years I've received amazing testimonies of how God showed ladies ways to get moving, even in the midst of physical handicaps and difficult situations.

Life is hard, but God is faithful! He will meet you wherever you're at, and show you a way to get your body healthy and moving. Just ask Him.

The habit of showing-up:
One of the things that probably benefited me the most in my search for freedom was to simply show-up. This principle does not only apply to exercise, but in any other area of our lives where we need help to "put on" new habits, as the Bible commands. We really can't do it, it is God who does the work and changes our hearts and desires, but we can do something and that is to SHOW UP.

Many times I would go to the gym, or get up early to go for a walk, just because I promised God and myself that I would show up, never mind how pathetic the effort. Sometimes I would show-up on my knees or with my Bible open on my lap, not because I'm "feeling" any deep yearning or experiencing fireworks, but because I promised God that I will do the one thing I can do, and that is to obey Him and show-up.

Please look up Galatians 6:9. What does the Bible say about those who do not give up?

_____

Showing up is really our faith in action. A sure knowing that we can't change anything, that things might be looking very bleak right now, BUT THAT OUR GOD WILL COME THROUGH FOR US.

Please read Heb 11:1. According to this verse, what is faith?

_____

Can you see how showing up for prayer, Bible study, and even moderate exercise can be an act of faith, especially when you don't see any changes in your struggle with food yet?

_____

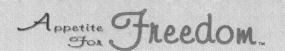

The following verse has always been one of my favorites. Please read it aloud.
Heb 11:6 (NIV)
And without faith it is impossible to please God, because anyone who comes to him must believe that he exists and that he rewards those who earnestly seek him.

 What does the above verse say about faith?

_____

What does it say about those who earnestly seek God?

_____

Can you see that "earnestly seeking God" can start by simply showing up at first?

_____

Please write this verse on a note card and keep it close so you will be reminded that simply showing up is in fact a step of faith that God will honor.

If you keep showing up in God's presence, the Bible that's now just lying open in your lap will come alive to you through the power of the Holy Spirit, and it will reach into every corner of your heart. If you keep laying on that carpet morning after morning, surrendering your heart to God, you will see Him take the wheel of your life in the most amazing way. Even better, you will get to know Jesus personally and never be the same again!

If you keep showing up at that gym, tennis court, swimming pool, or for that early morning walk and you have no great expectation other than making it a sacrifice unto the Lord, you will reap the benefits in your body. Not only will you overcome the physical ramification of this food struggle, but you will be able to glorify God through your body, and love him with all your heart, soul, mind, and *strength.*

Just show up, dearest woman of God. Always expect a miracle, but please don't give up if it doesn't happen on your timetable. We don't see the whole picture, but if we just keep showing up, God will change us from glory to glory (2 Cor 3:18).

If you want a different future it has to start today, and the only way to change today is through the power of the Holy Spirit.

So even in this very practical and physical area of exercise, we need God to come through for us, and He will if we ask.

 I invite you to pray this prayer with me:

Lord Jesus, please forgive me for procrastinating and putting my life on hold when you have given me today. This very day is the day that You have made for me to receive freedom, and leave the chains behind that bound me.

Please show me where I have just been making excuses, and also show me how to deal with the very real issues that I have in my life. I know you care about my circumstance, and I know that you have a way for me to exercise in the midst of difficulties and responsibilities. Please show me how I can overcome these hurdles Lord. I'm asking according to your Word that says if we lack wisdom we can ask You. I believe that You, the Maker of Heaven and Earth, has the answers for my situation.

I want to become a good steward of my body Lord, please help me to simply show up, even if it's difficult.
Amen

Day 3
Choosing the Right Exercise for You

IMPORTANT	Please see your doctor before starting a new exercise routine, especially if you have existing medical conditions.

Involve God in the process of choosing the right exercise for you. Ask Him to help you take that very scary first step to get started. Ask Him what, how, when, and where. God knows you, He knows your situation, and He knows how to help you get past your excuses.

Here are some things to consider when you're choosing the right exercise for you:

1. **If you're a night owl and you try and run with the early birds you are setting yourself up to fail.** Gyms are open late, in fact some are open 24 hours. You might want to join another night owl to stay consistent. Of course the opposite is true as well - if you're an early riser, you will probably fall asleep on the workout bench at night and be frustrated with your own lack of energy and motivation.
2. **Don't "spice things up" if you're really a routine person, even if your trainer/friend insists you do.** Rather, work out your own routine and stick to it. If you know exactly what to expect, you might not be so reluctant to go. However, if you get bored easily, you may need some variety. How about doing a different type of exercise on different days.
3. **If music is your thing, then it would be worth your while to invest in an iPod.** You can have your own worship session by listening to worship music at the gym or on your hike.
4. **If you are inspired and energized by other people,** then you will greatly benefit from having a friend join you on a walk or join an exercise group where you can make new friends. Actually most people find it much easier to exercise consistently if they do it with a friend who keeps them motivated and accountable
5. **Coupling things together might take the exercise load off your shoulders.** Combining your exercise time with something else can take your mind off the "pain" and make time fly. You can literally make your exercise time a sacrifice of praise unto the Lord. Drag your stationary bike over to the TV and watch a praise and worship DVD or listen to your favorite Bible teacher early in the morning on TV.

6. **Prayer walking** is another coupling of two very important things for both your body and spirit, especially if you're breaking free from an eating disorder. Take your note cards for a hike and read the Word out loud while you walk. God will meet you right there where you are.

7. **If you love nature,** get out there, come rain or sunshine, you will be thrilled anyway. Also, if you love nature you probably find it easy to connect with God through nature anyway, so hikes might just turn into your own personal worship sessions. Naturally the opposite has to be noted as well: If nature is not your thing, how about walking the mall for exercise?

8. **Exercise should be fun!** If exercise becomes a competition it creates stress, which can be more harmful to you than not exercising at all. If you find something that you enjoy, or better yet, that makes you laugh, you will get the most out of it by far. Fun exercise helps your body, mind, and spirit, and the best part, if you love it you will want to keep dong it.

Try to expand your horizon when it comes to exercise. For most people the word exercise is pure evil. They cannot get the picture of sweaty-people-running-like-maniacs out of their heads when they think of exercise. Don't get stuck in that rut, ask the Holy Spirit to help you think outside the box and give you fresh ideas that will fit your personality and situation.

I've written down a few ideas to get you started. You can also search online for more ideas and share your findings with the ladies in your small group:

Aerobic Exercise
Walking: inside, outside, trails, malls
Dancing (get hubby or a friend in on it)
Biking: Mountain, street, station, spinning, tandem
Exercise videos
Kayaking
Swimming
Organized sports
Dance Dance Revolution (a dance-game, ask your kids about it)
Aerobic or step classes
Running: Marathons or just for fun
Skiing, snowshoeing, or snowboarding
Rollerblading, in-line skating, or ice skating
Skipping jump rope
One-on-one basketball
Kickboxing
Working with a personal trainer
Gardening

Strength and Flexibility
Weight training
The Bar Method
Pilates

It is important to find a type of exercise that you will be able to do **CONSISTENTLY.** Please answer the following questions to help you figure out which exercise will fit your lifestyle and personality best.

When is the best time for me to exercise?

_____

Would I like to have someone to talk to, or would I rather listen to music?

_____

Could exercise be easier if I distract myself with something else like prayer or reading?

_____

Could I somehow kill two birds with one stone by combining exercise with something I never get time for such as memorizing Scripture or reading a magazine?

_____

Do I want to exercise indoors or outdoors?

_____

Am I too embarrassed right now to exercise around other people? Which exercise will help me avoid the crowds right now?

_____

How can I manage to exercise with my young children around?

_____

Which kind of physical activity do I enjoy (it will be fun for me and even make me laugh)?

_____

Which kind of physical activity will I be able to do consistently?

_____

How much money will it take to get involved in this exercise, and can I afford it?

_____

If not, what else can I do that will fit my budget?

_____

Can I do this physical activity with my kids, husband, or a friend?

_____

Is this a realistic option for my schedule?

_____

After answering these self evaluation questions, are there a few types of exercise that come to mind? Write them here if you can think of some:

_____

_____

_____

 Please be prepared to share some of your answers with your small group. Your small group is a safe place to bounce ideas off each other and pray for wisdom regarding these matters.

It is crucial that you start to exercise as soon as possible. You can always try out a few things and change your mind again. The most important thing is to SHOW UP and start with something.

Still not sure? Why don't you pray about it?
I remember being discouraged and tired of trying to incorporate exercise, especially during seasons of change in my life. During these times, I prayed and asked God to show me a new way that would make sense in my situation and that could also be enjoyable to me, and He did.

There is an exercise for you, something that will keep you motivated. I know that the Holy Spirit will help you find it. Keep asking and looking.

I invite you to pray this prayer with me

Lord Jesus, thank you that you care about the practical things in my life. I believe that you can and want to be involved in every decision I make to bring health to my body.
Please show me which exercise would be best for me. You know me better than I know myself Lord, and your Word says that you can show us great things we never knew before if we call to you and ask (Jer 33:3).
Please show me what I can do to get moving consistently.
Amen

DAY 4
Fight for Your Heart

When it comes to exercise, I have to fight off the enemy and my own flesh daily. Even though I have gone through the whole spectrum of figuring out which exercise I enjoy the most, what time of day is the best for me, and how I can work my exercise time around most of my family's emergencies and needs, it's never easy.

Resist the flesh
The truth is that I don't even need enemy attacks to keep me from exercising. Most mornings I already have a fight going on in my head, and just a little push can make me quit on the spot.

 Please read James 1:14. According to this verse, how are we tempted?

Our flesh is weak, and after years of giving in to our own desires for junk food and comfort, we need to re-train it to develop an appetite for God's presence and for positive habits such as eating healthy and exercise. This is where showing up is so important. I have to remind myself many days that I'm showing up to create new appetites for things that can bring me freedom, regardless of the intensity or duration of the exercise. If we keep our focus on glorifying God instead of weight loss, then no amount of exercise will be "useless" or "pathetic."

Resist the enemy
The Bible also warns us to be cautious, we have an enemy who goes after our time with God and the desires and dreams God has put in our hearts to glorify Him.

Please look up 1 Peter 5:8. What does this verse compare the enemy to, and who is he looking for?

Every morning, from the moment I commit to exercise, the enemy will try every trick in the book to block me. He will use family, friends, acquaintances, clients, and if this doesn't work, he will throw in busyness, finances, crisis, sickness, weather, celebrations, discouragement, the list goes on. It's the same kind of battle that goes on surrounding my time with God every day.

Do you find it difficult to commit to exercise consistently every day?

___

Have you been distracted or stopped in your tracks by people or circumstances in the past?

___

Have you thought that some of it might be the enemy trying to distract you from keep your commitment to God, even in the area of exercise?

___

Consistent exercise in moderation is an important element in overcoming food struggles and staying free. **So PLEASE don't give up when spending time with God or exercise becomes challenging. It's only so very difficult because it is important.**

James 4:7 remains a key verse when dealing with the enemy also on this front: "Surrender to God, resist the enemy, and He will flee from you." He might not give up the first time you resist him, but if you keep surrendering by making time for God first and foremost, it will get easier to sit down with your Bible, or lace up those running shoes, and in the end, according to the Bible, the enemy will have to flee. Every time you bow low before your mighty God, and flex that "NO" muscle against the enemy's attacks on your time and your own flesh, you will grow stronger spiritually and physically.

- **Sometimes we just have to raise up our own flesh to glorify God through physical activity.** So stop thinking about the "how" and just get on with doing it. At times the only way to break the cycle of procrastination is to simply get up from the couch and DO IT! As soon as you start DOING some exercise, your body's dopamine and energy levels start to rise and you start to feel better about it and even begin to like it.

- **Other times we have to "surrender to God, resist the enemy, and he will flee from us."** You may have to put up boundaries with some people, push through some difficult situations, and ignore some distractions. If you keep honoring your commitment to God to be a good steward of your body and glorify Him, you will reap victory in this area as well.

- **When it comes to exercise, I tend to do both, just to make sure**

Will you take up the challenge to start fighting for your time and as a result your freedom?

___

Which practical steps can you take daily to fend off your own flesh and the enemy? For example: A note card on your mirror to remind you that you're fighting for your freedom, or an alarm on your phone to remind you to go for a walk.

_____
_____
_____
_____

Next time you just give up when the kids interrupt your exercise video, or don't feel like getting up to go to the pool, or walk circles around your treadmill in the family room, or think that it's too cold to go for a run, or want to call your friend to cancel your afternoon game of tennis, remember that you are most definitely NOT ALONE in this fight. **In that very moment when you are having that fight with your flesh and the enemy, know for sure that other ladies are fighting the same fight, and you too CAN BE VICTORIOUS.**

Please look up 1 Corinthians 10:13 and write it in the space below.

_____
_____
_____
_____

This is going to become a key verse for you during times of temptation. We will talk more about getting through our weak moments in another week, but please write this verse on a note card and start memorizing it to arm yourself with the sword of the Spirit.

I invite you to pray this prayer with me:

Lord Jesus, thank you that according to your Word I am not tempted by my own desires or the enemy beyond what I can bear. Please help me in those moments when I am weak. Please remind me to cry out to you so that you can be strong in and through me.

Thank you Jesus that it is possible for me to overcome my own flesh and the enemy if I keep my eyes on you. Teach me how to surrender to You and keep my focus on You every moment of every day so that I will be able to resist when temptations arise.
Amen

Day 5
Consistency is Key

Just like with eating healthy, if your focus is on weight loss you will always have a short-term mindset without real commitment and consistency.

SLOW AND CONSISTENT

Slowly introduce exercise, little at a time, so your body can get used to it and keep up, not for the sake of weight loss, but with the intention of doing it forever.

Your goal, according to most professionals, should be aerobic exercise at least 3 times a week for at least 30 minutes at a time. Adding strength training to this is always highly recommended. My personal take on this: Opt for at least 5 times a week. Things always come up, life happens, and if you opt for 5 times then you have that 2 day cushion to absorb "life." It can be very discouraging and demoralizing if you keep on making it only once or twice a week. This is one of the reasons people quit. That said, if you shift your focus to health instead of weight loss, you will know that even once a week is better than nothing!

I recently picked up the challenge to exercise CONSISTENTLY for one year. Not the kind of exercise where you work out like crazy for 3 days and then take a break for three months (been there, done that). No, rather the kind where you exercise 5 to 6 times a week, NEVER MIND HOW MEDIOCRE THE EFFORT.

I agree that merely walking slowly for years on end will not get you super fit, but it is really consistency that will make this a life-long habit, not the intensity. If you don't associate exercise with pain, you will also be much more likely to do it. After six months, I wanted to up my work-out efforts. I was tired of walking on the treadmill, I wanted to start running! I never thought I would actually like exercise. However this would never have happened if I didn't FIRST make it a part of my life CONSISTENTLY.

Make no mistake, when I just started I felt sorry for myself EVERY DAY for at least the first few months. I had to call out to God every day to help me because I didn't think I could keep showing up, and He did indeed help me. It didn't always go according to my plans, but God's plans for me to exercise, spend time with Him, and eat healthy turned out to be much better than anything I could plan anyway.

I love this passage, especially when I start to feel sorry for myself on this journey. I read it out loud and remind my own flesh and the enemy that this journey of surrender is not just some silly thing that I'm doing, this is me getting out and staying out of the pit of food struggles:

Psalms 40:1-3 (NIV)

I waited patiently for the LORD; he turned to me and heard my cry. He lifted me out of the slimy pit, out of the mud and mire; he set my feet on a rock and gave me a firm place to stand. He put a new song in my mouth, a hymn of praise to our God. Many will see and fear and put their trust in the LORD.

We cannot do it on our own

Again, with exercise, as with eating healthy and making time for God, we cannot do it on our own. If we could, we would have done so a long time ago, and we would not have had this struggle with food.

Please read this quote from Andrew Murray's book "Absolute Surrender" carefully:

"... we are some of us **wanting God to give us a little help while we do our best,** instead of coming to understand what God wants, and to say: "I can do nothing. God must and will do all." Have you said: "In worship, in work, in sanctification, in obedience to God, **I can do nothing of myself, and so my place is to worship the omnipotent God, and to believe that He will work in me every moment**"? Oh, may God teach us this! Oh, that God would by His grace show you what a God you have, and to what a God you have entrusted yourself — an omnipotent God, willing with His whole omnipotence to place Himself at the disposal of every child of His! Shall we not take the lesson of the Lord Jesus and say: "Amen; the things which are impossible with men are possible with God?" (emphasis mine)[4]

Have you been able to make exercise, healthy eating, or spending time with God a consistent habit in your life?

_____

_____

According to this passage from Murray's book, why do we struggle to overcome things?

_____

_____

Please be encouraged today, that you and I cannot overcome our weaknesses (food addiction or any other struggle) by ourselves. We have one job in all of this, and that is to SURRENDER our hearts to God, and to ask Him to help us do the rest.

Please read this well known verse in Matthew 6:33 (NIV) out loud

But seek first His kingdom and His righteousness and all these things will be given to you as well.

According to this verse, how can you receive all these "other things" such as the desire to exercise, eat healthy, etc?

_____

Which practical steps can you take to "seek the kingdom of God first"?

_____

_____

_____

Living for God, and surrendering to Him are foreign concepts in our society? Have you also been lured into the "I can do anything I put my mind to" idea?

_____

If so, you might have endured a lot of shame and guilt for not being able to get it together in areas of weakness in your life. Are you ready to surrender to God and give Him full control of your life?

_____

I invite you to pray this prayer with me:

Lord, I repent today from trying to "fix things" in my own strength. Please forgive me for not believing that you want to be a part of every detail of my life, including something as practical as exercise.

I admit today that my best efforts to make exercise and other healthy habits a part of my life failed or only worked temporarily. I'm taking my hands off the wheel of my life and giving you full control Jesus. Please help me to surrender again in the coming days, as I might be tempted to take back the control.

Show me how to walk with you daily and seek your Kingdom first Lord. I believe that the things which are impossible with men are possible with you God. Even in our society, where people live lives that are totally focused on "self," I believe that you can teach me how to stay focused on you Jesus.

God, thank you for sacrificing your Son so that I can be free, and thank you for giving me the Holy Spirit as my helper so that I can live free every day of my life.
Amen

Please use the space below to tell God in your own words that you cannot make these changes in your life stick, and that you need Him to take over.

_____
_____
_____
_____
_____
_____
_____
_____
_____
_____

WEEK 6
A Godly Self-Image

DAY 1
Seeing Yourself Through God's Eyes

Most women with food struggle also struggle with their self image. They know something is wrong, but they don't know what exactly, and they don't know how to change it. They just know that they feel horrible about themselves and have huge issues with insecurity. God made us wonderful and unique and he wants us to view ourselves as He does, but unfortunately, after years of living with our idol and focusing on our bodies and food, we have drowned out the voice of the Holy Spirit. **We now only hear the loud lies of the enemy, the media, and the world around us. All off this can severely distort the way we see ourselves.**

Please join me on a quest to find out how the truth about us became so distorted and how we can change the way we view ourselves.

Why do I feel so bad about myself?
You are not alone in this: Every other woman on this planet struggles with insecurities. Some hide it well, others deny it, but we all wear this cloak of shame at one point or another. Confidence and outward things such as beauty or appearance are very fickle, and many women who seem to have it all together have deep-seated insecurities, just like the rest of us. In fact, many times people hide a very broken and empty heart behind a seemingly perfect career, body, family life, or house.

 **Please read Proverbs 31:30 out loud**
"Charm is deceptive, and beauty is fleeting; but a woman who fears the LORD is to be praised."

Have you found charm to be deceptive and beauty to be fleeting in your own life, or the life of someone you know? Please explain:

_____
_____
_____

How do I change the way I see myself?
First of all: We have to drown out the lying voices of the enemy and society ON PURPOSE! This war is mainly going on in our MINDS. The enemy, the media, and the world around us present ideas, and in that moment we have a choice to make: Will we accept it and let it shape our future, or will we take the thought captive, as the Bible commands, and weigh it against the truth of God's Word first?

Please look up 2 Cor 10:5 and write it in the space below. This will also be an excellent verse to copy to your note cards.

_____

_____

_____

It is only the truth of God's Word that sets us free from the lies of the enemy. "Then you will know the truth, and the truth will set you free." John 8:32 (NIV)

If you start to read and meditate on the truth of the Bible DAILY, you will not only recognize the lies when they are presented to you, but your faith in God will grow.

Please look up Romans 10:17 (NIV). According to this verse, how do we receive faith?

_____

_____

Hearing the Word of God can cause faith to rise up in our lives, so that we will not only ASK for the things that we need God's help and provision with, but we will take Him at His Word and start to EXPECT a miracle.

Please look up the very familiar verse in Psalms 139:13-14 (NIV). According to this verse, how does God see you?

_____

_____

_____

Regardless of how you see yourself and your body, you are God's creation and He made you wonderful! You are no accident, on the contrary, God planned for you to be here on this earth this very minute.

What is a godly self image?
We often hear the word "self-image" being thrown around in our society, and there are many books on the market about improving ourselves. However, a focus on "self" is never the answer.

Only a total focus on God can restore a healthy self image. Let's have a look at what the Bible has to say about this subject.

 Please read Paul's words in Romans 12:3 (NIV) out loud.

For by the grace given me I say to every one of you: Do not think of yourself more highly than you ought, but rather think of yourself with sober judgment, in accordance with the measure of faith God has given you.

What does a healthy and godly image of self look like according to this verse?

_____

_____

_____

Our self image should be based on "sober judgement" or in other words, that which is realistic and true about us. Thinking too highly about ourselves or putting ourselves down keeps us busy with "self" all day long, but if we use sober judgement we see things simply how they really are. For example "I might not be a superwoman, but I'm not a worthless slob either." Paul further encourages us to also view ourselves in accordance with the faith God has given us. In other words, we have to look at what is true and real about us, and mix it with who we can be if we rise up in faith, and allow the Holy Spirit to work in and through us.

The search for a healthy or godly self image involves two things:
1. **Taking our focus 100% off SELF and putting it on GOD**
2. **Refuting the lies of the enemy and society with the TRUTH of God's Word**

We will take the rest of this week to refute some lies of the enemy, society, and the media, with the truth of God's Word. We will also turn our focus again on our God.

I invite you to pray this prayer with me:

Thank you God for knitting me together in my mother's womb and creating me in exactly the right way for me to glorify you on this earth. My skin color, hair color, eye color, body shape, and unique set of circumstances were all part of your master plan for my life.

Please help me this week to bring my self image in alignment with the truth of your Word so that I will no longer be surrounded by insecurities and lies.

Thank you for giving me your Word as a guidebook for my life and a lamp for my feet.
Amen

DAY 2
Distorted by LIES of the Enemy

Please get out your note cards and write down some of the lies of the enemy we encounter in this struggle. **More importantly, write down the TRUTH OF GOD'S WORD that stands against it, and start reading it today to increase you faith and change you.**

The lie: You are guilty and shameful

	The lie: You are guilty and shameful **The truth:** Romans 8:1 (NIV): Therefore, there is now no condemnation for those who are in Christ Jesus, because through Christ Jesus the law of the Spirit who gives life has set you free from the law of sin and death.

We often hear the gentle voice of the Holy Spirit calling us to repent when we have sinned, and we should welcome His call to repentance so that we can be free and forgiven.
However, condemnation is that guilt and shame we feel, **after we repented from our sin.**The enemy knows that if he can get us to believe that we are guilty and shameful we will be haunted by a distorted self image and live lives of defeat.

Carefully read the questions below and circle the ones that apply to you.

	Have you experienced the following: • A nagging feeling that you did something wrong, you're not sure what, but it bugs you? • Feelings of utter failure after an encounter with certain people? • Feelings of despair over your less-than-perfect performance? • Shame after you spoke to someone of "position" such as a pastor? • Do you sometimes replay every word you've said (in your thoughts) after you had a conversation with someone? • Do you sometimes feel like slapping yourself because you are so "stupid" when you make an innocent mistake? • Do you feel waves of guilt or shame wash over you when you think of past sins or mistakes? • Do you find it hard to forgive yourself for past sins and mistakes? • Do you retreat from God when you fail? • Do you retreat from people when you fail? • Do you eat and turn to mind-numbing activities to block out the shame and guilt you feel after a perceived failure or mistake?

What is going on? Why do we feel so ashamed and so guilty? Are we guilty? The answer is NO. Jesus died for our sin and if we confess our sin and ask for his forgiveness, we GO FREE! We feel so ashamed and guilty because we **believe** the enemy who tells us constantly, every day, at every opportunity that we are guilty: Guilty of failure, guilty of past sins, and guilty of not measuring up. It is time for us to start believing the truth of God's Word instead of the lies of the enemy.

Please read Isaiah 53:5 (Amplified Bible) out loud:
But He was wounded for our transgressions, He was bruised for our guilt and iniquities; the chastisement [needful to obtain] peace and well-being for us was upon Him, and with the stripes [that wounded] Him we are healed and made whole.

Did you notice in this verse that Jesus also died for your guilt and iniquities? If Jesus died for your mistakes and failures, are you still guilty after you've repented from them?

Has the enemy been using guilt and shame to keep you stuck in a place of a low self esteem and insecurities? Please explain.

_____

_____

Also read Romans 8:1 as written in the Amplified Bible out loud
Therefore, [there is] now no condemnation (no adjudging guilty of wrong) for those who are in Christ Jesus, who live [and] walk not after the dictates of the flesh, but after the dictates of the Spirit.

Would you take a few minute to write your own prayer in the space below? Give God your guilt and shame, and thank Jesus for dying for your sins, and also setting you free from guilt and shame:

_____

_____

_____

The lie: You must have done something to deserve abuse

The lie:
You must have done something to deserve abuse

The truth:
Nobody deserves to be abused. The people who abused you will have to answer to God.
Matthew 18:6 (NIV): But if anyone causes one of these little ones who believe in me to sin, it would be better for him to have a large millstone hung around his neck and to be drowned in the depths of the sea.

Many ladies who suffer from eating disorders have been verbally, physically, or sexually abused at some point in their lives. The enemy might use situations from their past or present to load false guilt on them:

- Satan will tell a woman who has already suffered deeply at the hands of an abuser that she is somehow to blame for what happened to her.
- He will tell a woman who was abandoned as a little child that she was unlovable and that no one will ever love her.
- He tells a woman whose husband cheated on her that she is somehow to blame for his infidelity, that she fell short somehow
- He tells a woman whose husband left her for another man that her body must be so hideous that it gave her husband a disgust in women.
- He tells a woman who endured physical abuse as a child that she was so bad that she deserved it, and that she still deserves to be punished.
- He tells a woman whose parents got divorced when she was just a child that she was somehow responsible for their break-up.
- He tells a woman who was born out of wedlock that nobody wanted her, that she was just a burden, and that no one will ever want her.

 Have you heard some of these lies?

_____

Please let me assure you: YOU ARE NOT GUILTY and YOU ARE NOT RESPONSIBLE FOR THE SIN OF OTHERS. If someone else hurt you and sinned against you, then you need Jesus to come and heal your broken heart and help you to forgive. The enemy's plan here is to keep you in false guilt and shame, so that you will feel that you don't deserve God's love. This way you don't come closer to the only One who can truly heal you and give you new life.

Our God does not sleep. He sees when one of His own is abused and hurt, and He will not let this sin go unpunished. Come to God so that He can heal your broken heart and help you forgive those who hurt you. If you received healing and find the truth about who you truly are in God's Word, you will be able to move on, and Satan will lose his grip of shame and guilt on you.

 Please look up Isaiah 61:1. What did Jesus come to do for the broken hearted?

_____

Also read **Isaiah 57:15 (NIV) out loud**
For thus says the One who is high and lifted up, who inhabits eternity, whose name is Holy: "I dwell in the high and holy place, and also with him who is of a contrite and lowly spirit, to revive the spirit of the lowly, and to revive the heart of the contrite.

Do you find comfort in knowing that God is very close to those of us who are in a deep valley of pain and sorrow? If this is true for you, please write a prayer in the space below where you ask

God in your own words to come and revive your heart and spirit. Tell God the lies the enemy has spoken to you and ask Him to replace each lie with His truth. Write down what God says to you about how He sees you.

_____

_____

_____

_____

The lie: You cannot possibly come to God in your filthy state

The lie:
You cannot possibly come to God in your filthy state
The truth:
Hebrews 10:22 (NIV):
Let us draw near to God with a sincere heart in full assurance of faith, having our hearts sprinkled to cleanse us from a guilty conscience and having our bodies washed with pure water

The enemy knows that once we turn our focus COMPLETELY to God, he has lost His grip on us.

Be encouraged by the truth today:
- If you come to God, just as you are, He will do that which is impossible for you: CHANGE you permanently through the power of His Word and the Holy Spirit.
- If you cry out to God even while you overeat, while you lust for food, while you purge the food, or while you refuse your body nutrition, He will stretch out His mighty hand to help you.
- If you, like the prodigal son, will run to the Father, even in your dirty state, and let Him embrace you, He will fully accept you.
- He is very close to you in your broken state, and if you let Him in by opening your heart to Him, He will tell you His truth about you, and heal your broken heart.
- He has been waiting for you, just like the father of the prodigal son, to return to Him. In fact that small still voice that's calling your name, is the voice of the Holy Spirit, drawing you daily to return to the Father.

Will you come to Him today? Come just as you are...

I invite you to pray this prayer with me:

Dearest God, thank you for your amazing love for me, even in my bondage. Thank you that I can come to you in my most broken or humble state, and you embrace me with love, ready to set me free and heal my broken heart.

Please help me to forgive those who sinned against me. I believe today that I didn't do anything to deserve abuse, and that vengeance belongs to you Lord. I repent today from bitterness and hatred. Please help me to trust again through the power of your Holy Spirit.

I'm asking you to also help me take every thought of guilt and shame that comes up in my mind captive to the obedience of Christ. You have forgiven me and washed me clean and there is no more condemnation for me. I no longer have to believe the lies of the enemy. I choose to believe what You say about me.

I love you Jesus
Amen

DAY 3
Distorted by LIES of the World

Please get out your note cards and write down some of the lies of our society that we encounter in this struggle. **More importantly write down the TRUTH OF GOD'S WORD that stands against it, and read it daily to increase you faith and change your life.**

The lie: You should be suspicious and fearful of other women

	The lie: You should view other women with suspicion and fear The truth: John 13:34 (NIV): "A new command I give you: Love one another. As I have loved you, so you must love one another."

One of the most important elements of healing in this struggle is breaking the isolation that the enemy kept us trapped in, and reaching out to others for support and accountability. The best people to support women are other Godly women.

Have you noticed how our society and the enemy plays women against each other? God gave us sisters and friends as allies against the enemy. God commands us to love one another and bear each other's burden with love that comes from Him. This love includes trust and drives out all fear (1 Corinthians 13). The enemy knows that women can motivate each other to shine forth the Glory of God and search after God with all our hearts, and this is why he whispers this lie of envy and distrust in our ears. The media and society in general chimes in with this lie that you cannot trust anyone, not even your best friend.

If we believe this lie, every woman who is thinner, prettier, smarter, taller, more spontaneous, more talented, more successful, more spiritual, or frankly more *anything* than us, becomes our enemy.

The enemy has a field day in the lives of the following women:
- **Women who feel insecure and envious of other women.** If thoughts of fear and envy are not taken captive and weighed against the truth of God's word, it can cause us to strike out and hurt our own sisters and best friends. What started out as a thought can give birth to sin: Gossip, cheating, lying, and back-stabbing.
- **Women who chose to turn their backs on God.** Many of us have been hurt by women who bluntly turned their backs on God, or who have never been saved. These women have become callous towards God and play in the hand of Satan, but they forget that there is a God who sees them, who fights on our behalf, and who will avenge us. Each of us will have to answer to God for our words and actions.

Cycle of Destruction

Research has shown that people who were scarred in life, and have not received healing, become perpetrators themselves. If you fell victim to the sin of another woman, and you refuse to forgive her, you are on dangerous ground. Bitterness can make you paranoid: Fearing and suspecting every woman, and as a result striking out and hurting another lady in a similar fashion.

How do we stop this cycle?

We have to intercept the cycle by forgiving those who hurt us, and resisting the enemy's lies of distrust and fear, but instead chasing hard after Godly love towards one another. Building each other up, encouraging each other to follow our dreams, and living in a way that attracts other women to God, not makes them envious, helps stop the cycle.

Have you been hurt or disappointed by another woman, or fellow sister?

_____

Please read Colossians 3:13 in the Message translation

So, chosen by God for this new life of love, dress in the wardrobe God picked out for you: compassion, kindness, humility, quiet strength, discipline. Be even-tempered, content with second place, quick to forgive an offense. Forgive as quickly and completely as the Master forgave you. And regardless of what else you put on, wear love. It's your basic, all-purpose garment. Never be without it.

You can ask God to help you forgive someone if this is still very difficult for you. We are commanded to even forgive our enemies, so that Satan would not have any foothold in our lives. Would you please use the space below to write your own prayer at this time. Forgiveness is the only way to find healing and open your heart again to receive the love and support of other sisters in Christ.

_____
_____
_____
_____
_____

The lie: You have to perform in order to have value

The lie:
You have to achieve high standards of excellence to have value

The truth:
Luke 12:24 (NIV)
"Consider the ravens: They do not sow or reap, they have no storeroom or barn; yet God feeds them. And how much more valuable you are than birds!"

Many of us have decided early on that if we cannot get our value from being thin and beautiful, then we will have to find our value somewhere else. So we become dutiful and hardworking to the point of depriving our bodies of much-needed sleep and recreation. **We believe the lie that we have to achieve value in the eyes of society through our performance and our constant busyness. If we bought into this lie, then we have really just found another crutch or idol.**

Have you tried to obtain value through performance or high standards you uphold in your workplace, church, school, or home? If so, please explain:

_____
_____
_____
_____
_____

Our value lies in the fact that we are children of God. You are valuable to God even if you do not accomplish one more thing in your life. On the contrary, the more we try to "boost" ourselves in the eyes of society and the world around us, the further we move away from the heart of God. We are encouraged in James 4:10 and many other passages throughout the Bible to humble ourselves before the Lord and He will lift us up.

Think about people with physical or mental disabilities, the elderly, moms with newborn babies, and people in hospitals. Everyone of these individuals are so valuable to God, despite the fact that they may not be able to "perform" according to society's standards.

God loved you long before you accomplished anything and He will still love you even if you are not able to do one more thing for the rest of your life. Let's repent from pride and humble ourselves before the almighty God so that He can raise us up.

Would you please use the space below to write your own prayer to God and repent from pride (trying to find your value in accomplishments in order to impress others).

_____
_____
_____
_____

Fear of lack

This drive to perform can have fear at it's root: We may fear that we will not have enough if we don't keep going. God instructs us to work and to provide for our families, however, we should also rely on Him in the area of finances, instead of relying on our own performance and abilities. One of the names of God is Jehovah Jireh, our provider. He provides for His children regardless of what's going on around us and what state the economy is in.

 Please write Psalms 27:1 in the space below and copy it to your note cards to memorize:

_____

_____

_____

_____

Please use the space below to ask God to take away the fear of lack, and replace it with faith that He is your provider.

_____

_____

_____

I invite you to pray this prayer with me:

Lord, please help me to identify the lies of the world around me. Please remind me that my security is wrapped up in relationship with you, nothing else. Help me to forgive the women who have hurt me in the past and teach me to trust again and open my heart.
I'm asking you to send friends into my life, Godly women, who will encourage me to search after you with all my heart.

Jesus I also need your help to truly believe that my worth has nothing to do with my performance, but that you love me regardless of what I do or don't do. Teach me to humble myself daily before you, so that you can lift me up in a way that brings glory to your name. Also take away all fear of lack or poverty, and replace it with a great faith that you are Jehovah Jireh, my provider.

Amen

DAY 4
Distorted by LIES in the Media

 Also write down the lies that the media presents to us on your note cards, **but more importantly write down the TRUTH OF GOD'S WORD that stands against it, and start reading it today to increase you faith and change you.**

The Lie: You need to be thin to have value

	The lie: You need to be thin to have value The truth: Proverbs 31:30 (NIV) "Charm is deceptive, and beauty is fleeting; but a woman who fears the LORD is to be praised."

We see pictures in magazines and on TV of women with perfect bodies and perfect faces, which can cause us to be dissatisfied with our own bodies. Magazine pictures are in fact unattainable for the simple reason that it is not real: These pictures are airbrushed and computer modified. Also, the "perfect" bodies we see in TV shows can usually only be obtained through dangerous methods such as eating disorders and vigorous exercise. No wonder so many girls and women throw themselves into the hands of these dangerous methods; they would rather die than be overweight.

Research shows that most women complain of feeling inadequate, insecure, and depressed after watching TV programs. There is a proven link between watching TV and certain eating disorders such as binge eating disorder and obesity. It's not just the lack of physical activity that causes weight gain, but the food commercials trigger cravings, and the images of perfect bodies can create feelings of dissatisfaction and inadequacy which in turn are "medicated" through binging.

Body obsession can take on the following forms:
- We may be so proud and protective of the body we've sculpted that we simply have to maintain our low weight at all cost. As a result all of our time and energy goes into controlling our weight.
- On the flip side, we may hate our bodies because of the excess weight and as a result spend our days trying to find a quick fix and making plans to lose weight.

124

Society constantly pushes us to "stay in control" of our weight or "find a quick fix" if we are overweight. Both of these things are in tune with the times we live in, but in stark contrast to the Bible. God calls us to give control over to Him, surrender our lives and struggles to Him, and to let Him do a deep lasting work in us that will affect everything in our lives instead of reaching for a quick fix.

 Please read Matthew 23:27 out loud:
" You are like whitewashed tombs, which look beautiful on the outside, but on the inside are full of dead men's bones and everything unclean."

How do these words of Jesus to the Pharisees also point to the shallow value system of our society and even people inside the church?

_____

Have you experienced the desire to find a "quick fix" or stay in control of your weight no matter what the cost?

_____

Please write a prayer to God where you repent from needing "a quick fix" or trying to take control of your life through dangerous methods. Ask Him to take control of your life today.

_____

_____

_____

_____

The Lie: Beauty brings happiness

	The lie: Beauty brings happiness **The truth:** Psalm 16:11 (NIV) "You have made known to me the path of life; you will fill me with joy in your presence, with eternal pleasures at your right hand"

The media paints this picture that we have to be thin to be beautiful and that all beautiful woman are incredibly happy. True love and joy are part of the fruit of the Spirit, and has absolutely nothing to do with how we look on the outside. Yet, this false portrayal makes anyone who doesn't fit the profile (most women) feel inadequate and unhappy with their "lot" in life. They will do anything to change their outward appearance, hoping that it will also bring them love, success, and happiness. Young girls are on diets, they too got the distorted message that to be beautiful is to be thin, and that all of this brings happiness.

I can't help wondering how many women would never have struggled with food if the media didn't turn the human body into an idol, and made us all join the rat race to sculpt the perfect body.

When is a woman truly happy and beautiful?
Only when she radiates the glory and peace of God by FOCUSING on Him daily. We're made to show forth the glory of God, so that people will be attracted to the light of God in us.

Please read 2 Corinthians 4: 7 (Amplified) out loud
However, we possess this precious treasure [the divine Light of the Gospel] in [frail, human] vessels of earth, that the grandeur and exceeding greatness of the power may be shown to be from God and not from ourselves.

I know women who truly radiate the glory of God. They never make me feel threatened or small, on the contrary, they are the ones I turn to when life falls apart, and the ones I look up to. They come in all shapes and sizes, and they all carry the heart of Jesus. Do you know women like that?_____

Would you please use the space below to write your own prayer to God and repent from making your body an idol by obsessing over it instead of focusing on God

_____
_____
_____
_____
_____
_____
_____
_____
_____

I invite you to pray this prayer with me:

God, I repent today from believing the lies of the media, and buying into the prideful method of trying to find my value through appearance.

I surrender my need for "a quick fix" and my need to make a new plan to gain control of my weight and my eating. I surrender this whole struggle with food to your timetable Lord. I want to find true healing this time by stepping into an authentic relationship with you.

Please help me to take my focus off myself and instead place it on you, so that the greatness of God can shine through me, and attract people to You.

Thank you for your amazing love for me Lord. Amen

DAY 5
Worship and Focus

Beth Moore says in her book *So Long Insecurity* that worship in it simplest form is FOCUS, or in other words, **the thing we focus on is the very thing we worship.**[5]

I have encouraged ladies through the years to change their focus from **WEIGHT LOSS to HEALTH** if they ever want to get out of this nightmare of food struggles. However, after reading this book and looking at my own life, I realized that there is more. There is a deeper level, if you will. **Our focus will probably never shift permanently from WEIGHT LOSS to HEALTH if we don't first move our focus from OURSELVES to GOD.**

Beth speaks about a deep insecurity that plagues the lives of so many. I've known this to be true in my own life and almost every lady I've encountered that has a struggle with food. Deep down at the bottom of our beings lays an insecurity that drives us to please others, to strive for perfection, to stay in control of our surroundings and the people we love, and to maintain or reach a certain weight AT ALL COST!

The vicious cycle of food struggles literally gets fueled by insecurity day after day. Looking for security in a mate, in appearance, in status, in marital bliss, in education, in family, in children, in financial stability, in position at church, in fame, in the perfect job, in beauty, or in a thin body are all futile! In chasing after any of these things our focus remains on OURSELVES and not on GOD. **A FOCUS ON SELF can take on the form of too much self confidence or self loathing.**

Focusing on God by making time for Him daily and surrendering our lives to Him is the best way to take our focus off ourselves. Here are a few other things we can do:

1. Purposefully steer away from the focus on appearance in the media
- **Teach your children the truth:** Point out how the media distorts the truth by implying that a certain body type and good looks equals love, popularity, and happiness. Teach them how the advertising industry is set up to make us want things we don't really need, or things that are really unattainable and that leave us with a feeling of inadequacy. Most diet products are a hoax, yet people spend millions on these, trying to change themselves.
  Also point out the link between television viewing and body dissatisfaction.

- **Don't buy magazines that focus on weight and promote fad diets:** Research studies have shown a strong relationship between reading fashion magazines and certain eating disorders.
- **Give up media for a week.** Try going without magazines, watching TV, and surfing the Internet for one week. Look for other things to do such as visiting friends, having dinner in the park, go to a museum, or read together as a family. At the end of the week, notice if you feel differently about yourself. Especially note if you had more time to spend in the Word and prayer, and how this has helped you refute lies of the enemy and the world around you.

2. Face your own prejudice

Prejudice toward people based on their appearance can keep you stuck in self absorption. If you are prejudice toward overweight people you may become obsessed with not gaining weight or keeping your family healthy. On the flip side, prejudice towards thin people might leave you envious and bitter, and the low self esteem that usually accompanies this might keep you focused on self all the time.

A person with weight problems has this particular area in her life where she is in need of God's healing power to set her free. This is no different from the thin person, who has other areas in her life where she desperately needs God to change her. Neither one of them deserve to be judged or labeled.

Unfortunately this kind of prejudice based on appearance is prevalent in our society. Please challenge your own beliefs by honestly answering the following questions (this is for self evaluation only):

- Do you believe that a beautiful, and especially thin person, matters more, has more value, is happier, and will be more successful than other people?
- Are you prejudice towards people that are overweight and therefore rigidly try to control your family's weight and calorie intake? This could be true for you even if you are overweight yourself.
- Do you pay more attention to and have more respect for people who are slender and good looking?
- On the flip side: Do you feel inferior and self conscious in the company of "good looking" people, and tend to avoid them as a result?

How can you change this behavior?

- Awareness of the destructive nature of prejudice, and especially an awareness of this in your own life, is the first step to find healing in this area. You can be prejudice toward overweight or thin people, it goes both ways.
  Repentance is crucial, because prejudice is sin.
  James 2:1 (Amplified) *My brethren, pay no servile regard to people [show no prejudice, no partiality]. Do not [attempt to] hold and practice the faith of our Lord Jesus Christ [the Lord] of glory [together with snobbery]!"*

- Change your behavior by being attentive to all people. Ask God to help you look deeper, beyond the physical appearance. You'll discover that the most interesting, funny, loving, and Godly people are not limited to a specific look or appearance.
- Raise your children with an awareness and disgust for any form of prejudice, and help them understand their responsibility as children of God to fight against it.
- Reach out to people of all races, age groups, sizes, and abilities.
- Complement friends and family based on qualities that do not necessarily place the emphasis on appearance. Our children pick up on what is important to us in what we say, so ask God to change your heart so that your speech will authentically change as a result of a heart change. **Matthew 15:18** *"But the things that come out of a person's mouth come from the heart, and these defile them."*
- Teach your children to never participate in name calling or labeling

3. Take the focus off your body

- Stop obsessing about your weight and shape, this self focus feeds food struggles. On the other hand, stop ignoring your body, it is part of you, God made it wonderful. Find a healthy balance where you appreciate your body, and treat it well. Focus on **what it can do to help you glorify God, not on what it looks like.**
- Exercise moderately to help you reconnect with your body as well and make you more aware of what your body is capable of doing. Pampering your body is also a good way to reconnect and care for it, as opposed to obsessing over it and abusing it.
- Learn to appreciate your uniqueness. There is no one exactly like you on this planet. God took special care to create you. He knew exactly why He made you the way you look and why you are here, right now, in this moment in time, at this specific location, surrounded by the people you know. Trying to be like others will keep you focused on yourself.
- Surround yourself with people that don't judge others on their physical appearance and who have a healthy Godly, self image. Avoid those who are obsessed with beauty and thinness, but be sure not to hang out with people who abuse their bodies with junk food and unhealthy habits either as it is just a different form of focusing on self.
- How do you talk to and about yourself? Do you berate yourself in a way that you would never talk to anyone else? Be very aware of this bad habit, it is not God honoring. Talk to and about yourself in the same respectful and nice way that you will use when talking to others. We sometimes berate ourselves because we're so focused on our own mistakes, instead of thanking God for using mistakes and imperfections in our lives to keep us humble before Him.
- Carry yourself with confidence, you will be surprised how different you feel if you start to walk and smile with confidence, simply because you are a daughter of the Most High King and you have the fruit of the Spirit in you. You can be confident in Christ without being prideful.
- Stop putting off living. Live in the present. Do the activities you always wanted to do and feel called to do, regardless of your current shape or weight. Get rid of the "perfect image" of how you should look before you can start living. Accept and love yourself the way you are right now, God loves you exactly the way your are. This will set your feet on the path of freedom and healing, and take your focus off yourself.

4. Become a servant

I love the song *Hosanna* by Hillsong. One sentence in particular always touches my heart: "Break my heart for what breaks yours." Once we start growing in relationship with Jesus, much of the selfishness and self focus starts to fall off us, and we want to know more about His purpose and calling for us on this earth.

If you daily make time for God, ON PURPOSE, things start to change in your heart, and you start to care about the things God cares about. You will want to give to others instead of trying to impress them or compete with them.

All of this may start off by you simply obeying God and committing to, for example, reading a passage from the Bible every day. Before you know it, this simple act of obedience starts to change your heart and you want to DO SOMETHING.

GIVING OF YOURSELF TO SOMEONE ELSE brings great fulfillment and takes your eyes off yourself and your own problems or struggles. It's really tapping into the heart of God, and it helps us deal with our own discontentment and gives us a spirit of thankfulness instead.

 **Please read Isaiah 58:10-11 (NIV) out loud**

"..and if you spend yourselves in behalf of the hungry and satisfy the needs of the oppressed, then your light will rise in the darkness, and your night will become like the noonday.
The LORD will guide you always; he will satisfy your needs in a sun-scorched land and will strengthen your frame. You will be like a well-watered garden, like a spring whose waters never fail."

What will your life look like, according to this verse, if you spend yourself by caring for the hungry and the oppressed?

_____

_____

_____

Why don't you give it a try? Next time you feel that you are sinking into despair over your food struggle and your own failures, try volunteering at a soup kitchen or a shelter. Seeing others in need of something as basic as food makes us look at our problems in a very different light.

Take some time today to ask God how you can give of yourself and your talents to others. He knows exactly where you are needed and it might even tie in with the purpose He has for your life.

Please scan over the four main points of ways to take your focus off self again. Which few simple steps can you take in your life today to start taking your focus off self, and focus in on God instead?

_____

_____

_____

_____

I invite you to pray this prayer with me:

God, I repent today from any form of prejudice regarding people's appearance that I may have allowed into my life. Please help me focus again on that which truly matters: Loving you and loving others.

Please help me treat my own body with respect and be a good steward of it, but also keep me from obsessing about it and making it an idol. Only a focus on you can bring me into that balance, God, so help me truly let you into every part of my life.

Lord Jesus, I want to be a servant like you. Show me how I can touch the lives of others around me that might be in more need and pain than I am. As I give, will you meet my needs, and give me a greater love for You.

Thank you that I am acceptable and loved by you, exactly the way I am right now Lord.
Amen

Week 7
Victory Over Temptation

DAY 1
Truth About Temptation

We've already touched on the subject of temptation in a previous week, but we really need to delve a little deeper. According to Scripture there is a spiritual war raging for our freedom (Ephesians 6:10-18), and it continues whether we engage in it or not. If we simply ignore it, we don't find victory over our daily battles and weak moments. I want to make sure you are prepared to face temptation so you can be victorious during times of temptation.

Let's have a quick overview

Who tempts us?

 Please take another look at this passage in James:

When tempted, no one should say, "God is tempting me." For God cannot be tempted by evil, nor does he tempt anyone; but each one is tempted when, by his own evil desire, he is dragged away and enticed. Then, after desire has conceived, it gives birth to sin; and sin, when it is full-grown, gives birth to death. James 1:13-15 (NIV)

According to this verse how are we tempted?

_____

_____

Can it be that we actually *desire* to do all the things we have been doing up until now?
Let me answer this for you: YES! We sure have messed-up desires. In fact some of our desires are in direct contrast to one another simply because some are still driven by our sinful nature and other desires are driven by the Holy Spirit who lives in us.

The Bible speaks about this.

 Please read Galatians 5:17 (NIV) out loud.

For the sinful nature desires what is contrary to the Spirit, and the Spirit what is contrary to the sinful nature. They are in conflict with each other, so that you do not do what you want.

Let's take a look at this conflict.

Do you have some of the following desires: To have a close relationship with God, have healthy relationships with others, have a healthy body that glorifies God, have a Godly self

image without insecurities, and a desire to see God's purposes fulfilled in your life?

_____

Now, do you also have the following desires: To eat whatever you want, turn to mind-numbing activities such as TV when you're stressed and tired, be in control of your life, have a perfect body that others admire, have a perfect life, and live on an island away from people and their issues?

_____

Which of these desires are still the strongest in your life?

_____

Can you see that when the desire of the "flesh woman" is still stronger than the desire of the "Spirit woman" in us, we will keep turning to the former?

I wish there was an easier way to say this, but the bottom line is that we will keep giving in to temptation if we still love the idol, or the sin, more than we love God. I've heard a pastor explain it like this: If we still have the desire for the sin in us then there is a "hook" in our hearts. All Satan then has to do is throw out a noose of temptation and it will latch onto the hook every time, without fail. You and I need to make sure we remove the hook of evil desires from our hearts if we want to run free from temptation.

You may be checked into an inpatient program where you are monitored day and night until you are seemingly healed from your food struggle, but as soon as you step out of that clinic, you can go straight back to starving, binging, and purging if you still have the desire to control your life at all cost.

You can have the best counselor that money can buy, be under the care of the best physician, and have your whole family support you, and still never break free from your food struggle if you still hold on to the idol of food in your heart.

Please be honest with yourself and God about the desires of your heart. God already knows what's in your heart, and He knows how to change your desires so they line-up with His purpose for your life. **We can trick others and tell them we are free while our hearts are still bound, but we can't trick ourselves, and we certainly cannot trick God.**

How do I get rid of these evil desires?
God created us to be motivated and directed by our desires. We are supposed to trade in the evil or destructive desires in our hearts for God's desires. Some of His desires are already very evident in our hearts, and others will start to surface as we get to know Him more and understand that the purpose of our lives is to glorify Him. The problem is that those desires, driven by the Holy Spirit, may be very faint and in the background right now.

So how do we get those "good" desires to override the bad ones?
We will take the rest of the week to discuss the things you and I can do to change our desires
- Choose a relationship with Jesus
- Live by the Spirit
- Protect your mind
- Get through your weak moments

 I invite you to pray this prayer with me:

Lord Jesus, thank you for making me aware of the "hook" of evil and selfish desires that might still be in my heart and cause me to fall for temptation.

I know that your Word says if I surrender to You and resist the enemy he will have to flee from me, and I can be victorious over temptation. Please help me to surrender these desires that I still secretly nurture to You, God. I don't want to leave any foothold for the enemy in my life.

Please replace those desires with a desire for You, the Bible, and Your presence. I want the sinful nature to shrink and the spiritual part of me to grow, Lord.

I admit that I cannot do it without Your help, Jesus. Please change my heart. Amen

DAY 2
Choose a Relationship

An authentic, love RELATIONSHIP WITH JESUS is the answer to all of life's problems, including our food struggles. This is however not a quick fix, and therefore not a very popular solution in our society.

I do believe that God can and wants to set every woman free who struggles with food, but I also believe that He has a timetable for this to happen and that capturing your heart is the most important part of His plan. God knows when we're just in it for what we can get out of it (freedom from food) and not real relationship with Him.

If you make up your mind that God is what you want for the rest of your life, regardless of how fast you get free from your struggle, then permanent change and healing will come to all areas of your life.

In fact, I can testify that God has used this weakness (food struggle) in my life to keep me close to Him. I have became aware of idolatry, pride, control, people-pleasing, perfectionism, and other sinful patterns in my life mainly because I was seeking answers for my food addiction, and as a result fell in love with Jesus. This journey led me closer to God and taught me to keep surrendering every broken place in my heart to Him. If I start overeating again tomorrow, and fall for all sorts of temptations, I now know the only solution: Renewing my relationship with Jesus.

We are living in a time when people are looking for easy answers and ways where they can have their cake and eat it too. **If you want to run free from this food struggle, you will have to choose: Are you going to lay down every idol and give Jesus full control of your life, or are you going to keep playing around with idols and look for easier answers to your problems somewhere else?**

Please look up 2 Timothy 4:3. How does this verse apply to people who are nurturing idols in their lives?

_____

_____

 **Please read 1 John 2:17 (NIV) out loud:**

The world and its desires pass away, but the man who does the will of God lives forever.

Think about the things you desire and hold dear in the flesh. Do any of these things have any lasting value?

_____

There is an action we can take today: We can make a choice in faith.

Just like you've made a commitment to God to start taking better care of your body, I want to encourage you to choose in faith today between the desires in your flesh and the desires that God has placed in your spirit. Don't let the enemy hold you back with fear that you may fall again. In fact, you can keep making this choice daily, until it is a resounding YES in your mind for God and NO for idols.

 Please read Joshua 24:15 (NIV) out loud:

"But if serving the LORD seems undesirable to you, then choose for yourselves this day whom you will serve, whether the gods your forefathers served beyond the River, or the gods of the Amorites, in whose land you are living. But as for me and my household, we will serve the LORD."

Please answer the following questions honestly before God:
- Can you see how the enemy's noose of temptation often latches onto the hook of desires in your heart?
- Do you see a real conflict between Godly desires in your heart and those driven by the flesh?
- Are you tired of living a mediocre Christian life with not much love, joy, peace, patience, kindness, goodness, faithfulness, gentleness, and self control?
- Are you ready to start an authentic relationship with Jesus where you give Him full access to all the areas of your life regardless of what you can get out of it?
- Are you ready to let go of all the plans and quick fixes for this broken area of your life, and instead give it over to God's time table as you grow in relationship with Jesus?

We spoke previously about sorrow over the sin and the damage it causes to our relationship with Jesus, as opposed to sorrow only for the consequences of your sin (being overweight, having no clothes that fit, having bad skin and rotting teeth, losing your health, problems in your marriage, etc). I'm only bringing this up again to give you another opportunity to ask God to bring you to that place of deep sorrow for the distance the sin of idolatry has created between you and Him, and to repent from *the sin*. This time, not for what you can get out of it (freedom from food struggles), but this time because you yearn to love and know Jesus more.

We always have a choice: God gave us free will.

What will you choose today, a relationship with Jesus that can change your whole life, or an idol? Please take a minute to write a personal prayer to Jesus. This is a very personal decision, and a very important one.

_____
_____
_____
_____
_____

 I invite you to pray this prayer with me:

Lord, I repent from turning away from You, my first love, and turning to idols to satisfy the emptiness I feel inside.

Please forgive me for the years of pretending to be okay, yet sinning against You by nurturing my evil desires and neglecting the desires You've placed in my heart.

I am so sorry for not being truthful about my relationship with You all these years. Please help me from this day forward to talk to You openly about my heart's desires and to starve those evil desires and start living for You - nurturing my relationship with You.

I cannot do this without You, Lord; please help me. I accept Your love and forgiveness.

Amen

DAY 3
Live by the Spirit

Please look up Galatians 5:16 and write it in the space below

_____

_____

According to this verse, when will we NOT gratify the desires of our sinful nature?

_____

If walking by the Spirit holds the key to not gratifying the desires of the flesh, then I think you will agree that it is crucial for us to find out everything we can about the Holy Spirit, and how to start walking in step with Him.

Please read 2 Corinthians 3:17-18 (NIV) out loud:
Now the Lord is the Spirit, and where the Spirit of the Lord is, there is freedom. And we, who with unveiled faces all reflect the Lord's glory, are being transformed into his likeness with ever-increasing glory, which comes from the Lord, who is the Spirit.

Did you see that FREEDOM comes as a result of the Spirit's presence? What else happens, according to this verse, when the Holy Spirit is present in our lives?

_____

_____

You're right! If we live by the Spirit, we will not only be strengthened so we can thwart the desires of the flesh, but we will actually be changed to reflect the glory of God!

Please look up Ephesians 5:18 and write it in the space below.

_____

_____

So how do we live by the Spirit and bear fruit?
According to John 14:26, the Holy Spirit has been given to each of us who accepted Jesus as our Lord and Savior, to help us and guide us. *"But the Comforter (**Counselor, Helper, Intercessor, Advocate, Strengthener, Standby**), the Holy Spirit, Whom the Father will send in*

My name [in My place, to represent Me and act on My behalf], He will teach you all things. And He will cause you to recall (will remind you of, bring to your remembrance) everything I have told you."

There is something we should do, though, to receive the daily inflowing strength of the Holy Spirit.

 Please read John 15:5 (AMP) out loud:

I am the Vine; you are the branches. Whoever lives in Me and I in him bears much (abundant) fruit. However, apart from Me [cut off from vital union with Me] you can do nothing.

It all ties into having a close relationship with Jesus. If we make time for Him, stop our busy lives, wait in His presence and listen to the voice of the Holy Spirit, WE WILL BEAR MUCH FRUIT. If you are aware of the Holy Spirit's presence throughout your day, you can call on Him to fill you when you encounter those empty places that are really accidents waiting to happen. If we don't let the Holy Spirit fill up our emptiness by crying out to Him for counsel and help, we will keep on falling for the enemy's temptations.

Have you sometimes said "If only I had more self control, my life would be so much better"? Contrary to the word "self" in there, we cannot muster up self control in our own strength in the best of times, let alone when crisis hits and life gets hard.

 Please read Proverbs 25:28 (NIV) out loud:

"Like a city whose walls are broken down is a man who lacks self-control."

What was the purpose of a city wall during Bible times?

_____

Do you see, according to this verse, that if we don't have self control we also lack protection against the attacks of the enemy?

_____

Please look up Galatians 5:22-23 and write down the fruit of the Spirit in the space below:

_____

_____

_____

Self control is something we receive when we are FILLED WITH THE HOLY SPIRIT by abiding in the vine (relationship with Jesus) daily. If the Holy spirit empowers us to be in control of our minds, mouths, and bodies, we can also resist those desires that are not of God.

The only way to get self control is to "remain connected to the vine," dear sister. Obey God by spending time in His presence every day, and keep asking the Holy Spirit to fill your empty places.

I invite you to pray this prayer with me:

Holy Spirit, I repent from hardening my heart and not listening to Your voice calling and drawing me so often to come away to a quiet place. Thank You for being my Counselor, Helper, Intercessor, Advocate, Strengthener, and Standby. Forgive me for all the times I've ignored Your voice, or took You for granted.

Please come make me more aware of those empty places in my heart and the times when I am most vulnerable. Remind me that I can call out to You in those moments to take the veil away so that I will see the truth and be changed from glory to glory.

Thank You for the fruit of the Spirit, including self control to stand against the temptation of the enemy.

I give You full control of my life, Holy Spirit, please come fill me this very minute.
Amen

DAY 4
Protect Your Mind

 Please read Peter 1:13-15 (NIV) out loud:

Therefore, prepare your minds for action; be self-controlled; set your hope fully on the grace to be given you when Jesus Christ is revealed. As obedient children, do not conform to the evil desires you had when you lived in ignorance. But just as he who called you is holy, so be holy in all you do.

Peter instructs us to prepare our minds for action; to be self controlled and obedient. If we live by the Spirit, as discussed in Day 3, we will find the fruit of self control in our lives. We need the fruit of self control especially when it comes to our minds.

 Please read Romans 8:5 (NIV)

Those who live according to the sinful nature have their minds set on what that nature desires; but those who live in accordance with the Spirit have their minds set on what the Spirit desires.

Do you see that our minds are set on the very thing we desire? It also works the other way around - the more we set our minds on things, the stronger the desire becomes. The mind is our first line of defense against the temptation of the enemy which is why the Bible calls us to be self-controlled and prepare our minds for actions.

Take a look at this cycle that can go in a positive or negative direction depending on which thoughts we allow into our minds:

- Your thoughts control your feelings
- Your feelings control your actions
- Your actions shape your life!

Scary...isn't it? No wonder the Bible tells us to make sure we take our THOUGHTS captive. It is very difficult to stop from reacting when your emotions are already involved, but if you can catch that thought and make it obedient to the truth of God's Word before it affects your feelings, you can be victorious over the temptation.

 Please read Romans 12:2.
*Do not conform to the pattern of this world, but be transformed by the **renewing** of your **mind**. Then you will be able to test and approve what God's will is—his good, pleasing and perfect will.*

What needs to happen, according to this verse, before we can figure out God's perfect will for our lives?

_____

Let's take a look at our thought lives by answering the following questions:

 Do you still believe the enemy's lies that you are guilty and shameful?

_____

2 Corinthians 10:5 (NIV)
We demolish arguments and every pretension that sets itself up against the knowledge of God, and we take captive every thought to make it obedient to Christ.

Ask the Holy Spirit to help you spot the lies of the enemy. It is crucial for us to be reminded that we don't have to listen to the lies that the enemy and the world throws our way, we can refute it with the truth. Before our minds are renewed, we would, in fact, be wise to challenge EVERY thought.

 Do you constantly think about your own problems and worries?

_____

Philippians 4:6 (AMP)
Do not fret or have any anxiety about anything, but in every circumstance and in everything, by prayer and petition ([a]definite requests), with thanksgiving, continue to make your wants known to God.

There is only one way to counteract worries and and solve problems: PRAYER. Make a list of worries and things that bug you during the day. Refuse to think about it again, tell yourself every time it comes up in your mind: "I will pray about it later, worry accomplishes nothing." Then make a time before you go to bed at night to pray about all the issues that are on your lists, lay them at God's feet and get a peaceful night's sleep.

 Do you often dwell on conversations you had with other people?

_____

Philippians 4:8 (NIV)
Finally, brothers, whatever is true, whatever is noble, whatever is right, whatever is pure, whatever is lovely, whatever is admirable—if anything is excellent or praiseworthy—think about such things.

If you are talking to people and reading their emails all day long, your mind is not set on Christ and you can get stressed out and depressed. Limit the time you spend talking to others, rather pray for them, and then leave their problems at the feet of Jesus. He is the one who can truly help them.

 Do you often think about the perfect body, clothes, and appearance?

_____

Isaiah 26:3 (NIV)
You will keep in perfect peace him whose mind is steadfast, because he trusts in you.
Whatever we take in through our eyes get printed on our minds. What is stuck in your mind? It might be time to get your eyes off those movies, magazines, TV programs, ads, or the things you see when strolling through the mall (desiring to look and dress differently). These kind of things can keep you stuck in a thought pattern that conforms to the world. Instead renew your mind by prayer, reading the Word of God and other uplifting books, turning to media that inspires you to be all you can be in Christ, and be sure to fellowship with people who love God.

Please make sure that you have all of the above verses written on your note cards, ready for action when those weak moments of temptation hit.

I invite you to pray this prayer with me:

Holy Spirit, I put my mind under Your authority today. Please give me the self control to take every thought captive that enters my mind, and weigh it against the truth of God's Word. I no longer want the enemy and the world to abuse my mind.

Lord Jesus, please remind me to follow Your example to refute the enemy's lies with Scripture. Help me reach for the Bible and my note cards during those weak moments, even if I don't feel like it.

Please renew my mind so that I can know what Your perfect will is for my life.

Amen

DAY 5
Getting Through Weak Moments

I wanted to share this excerpt from the updated **Breaking Free Bible Study** by Beth Moore with you: "*God has reserved momentous victories and great rewards for us. But we'll never make it to our **milestones** if we can't make it through our **moments**.*"[6]

Isn't that so true? We set these milestones and we even have faith for it, but then we get to that MOMENT, that excruciating moment of temptation or weakness, and we cave, and then we lose hope…

SO HOW DO WE GET THROUGH OUR WEAK MOMENTS?

Beth goes on to explain that we sometimes don't feel that we deserve to take the exit God provides during those weak moments, and other times it comes down to this: "We just don't want to". This is very true and I've been crying out to God to change my heart and also remove the rebellious spirit from me during those times.

However, sometimes I even want to, and plan to, do the right thing, but when I get to that MOMENT… I just DON'T! Paul speaks about this struggle in his own life in Romans 7, and he concludes that it is indeed only God who can save us and help us overcome during those times. So the first and obvious answer is to learn to walk in step with the Holy Spirit moment by moment by being plugged into the vine (Jesus).

I think it's important to distinguish between two different kinds of weak moments:

1. **The weak moments that "pounce" on us**
   1 Corinthians 10:13 (NIV) says "*No temptation has **seized you** except what is common to man. And God is faithful; he will not let you be tempted beyond what you can bear. But when you are tempted, he will also provide a way out so that you can stand up under it.*"

   The very first sentence of this verse makes it clear that some temptation can catch you off guard when you least expect it. However, even though we may be "seized" by temptation at times, this verse states that it is "common to man." That means that our first thought shouldn't be "life is unfair" or "why do have I have to deal with this?" but rather an assurance that others overcome this same issue daily, through the power of the Holy Spirit, and so can we.

It goes on to say that it is NOT too hard for us to handle (with the Holy Spirit's help, of course) and that we should be on the look-out for the way of escape or "exit" sign that God provides in the midst of temptation so that we can be victorious.

Most of the time we can actually see some warning signs that a weak moment is approaching, such as feelings of uneasiness, dissatisfaction, and restlessness. Some "forced" alone time with God, especially in the evenings when we are most vulnerable, can help rid us of the stuff that piled onto us during the course of the day. We may not even know what exactly it is, but the underlying issue will most likely set us up for a weak moment.

However, there is something we can do if we suddenly find ourselves in that weak moment. **First, SPOT THE LIES of the enemy or the media. Second, RUN INTO GOD'S PRESENCE.** If I refer to "God's presence" it doesn't have to fit a certain mold; it could be as simple as finding a quiet place to cry before God, talk to Him for a few minutes, read your note cards out loud so your ears can hear the truth, or just go for a drive in your car with worship music on. Remember 2 Corinthians 3:16-18 - when we enter into God's presence, the Holy Spirit strips away the veil, and as we look into the truth of God's Word, WE ARE CHANGED!

This principle of fleeing from evil desires or temptation is very biblical. Remember how Joseph literally fled the scene when he was pursued by Potiphar's wife? Also take a look at this verse: 2 Timothy 2:22 (NIV) *Flee the evil desires of youth, and pursue righteousness, faith, love and peace, along with those who call on the Lord out of a pure heart.*

2. **Predictable weak moments**

   I asked a friend if I could quote her on this topic because she said it so well, "*I always wake up ready to take on the world and by nightfall I am a weak as a kitten."* SO TRUE!

   There are definitely certain times of day, evenings for most of us, when we are just vulnerable and weak. If we don't plan ahead for those times, we will keep falling into temptation day after day, continuing the cycle of defeat.

   I am usually super weak after a day's work, and I know that if I just end up in front of the TV, I'm in trouble. However, I've learned to be realistic about this as well. I've tried for a long time to stop watching TV or avoid the Internet all together, but this seems to only last for a little while. So I've asked God for wisdom to help me make a plan to get out and stay out of the same cycle of defeat night after night.

Recently, I've been breaking my evenings into little chunks of time. For instance, some "relax-time" with a special hot drink, a few crackers, and worship music BEFORE I start dinner for everyone else. Or maybe a long bubble bath right after dinner. Then some "God time" where I download my day before God by simply laying on my bed and getting rid of the "yuck" of the day by talking to Him, praying, crying, etc. I might pick up the Bible at this point and "eat" some of the truth of the Word. Then some "kids time" where I put my children to bed, and then some "TV and snack" time where I eat a healthy bar with a cup of tea while watching a favorite show or movie with my husband.

I have to be deliberate, though, to first of all MAKE A PLAN, and then STICK TO MY PLAN. Many nights, I have to force myself to go up the stairs after dinner to go take a bath when I just feel like flopping in front of the TV, or to go to bed early when I still want to scroll around on the Internet. I actually have to obey God while my flesh wants to be a rebellious teenager and do what it wants to do, which brings us to the next point.

Obedience is Key

According to 1 Corinthians 10:13; God is always faithful to measure the temptation that comes our way and also provide us with a way of escape. Our job: OBEY.

If we disobey God and think we're bossing ourselves, we're fooled. The Bible clearly says that we are being ruled by the enemy if we're not under God's rule (Romans 6). It's the one or the other, there's no neutral ground.

There are so many advantages to obedience.

Please look up John 15:10-11. What are some of the advantages of obedience according to these verses?

_____

_____

According to these verses we can get ourselves into a blessed upward cycle that starts with obedience:

- If you obey God because you *want to love Him*
- then you start to love and know Him more, *because you obeyed Him.*
- The more you love Him, the more you *enjoy His presence*,
- and the more you come into His presence, the *more you change.*
- The more you change, the more *your desires change:*

- you don't desire to be thin, perfect, rich, and famous anymore;
- you desire for God to be glorified in your life through the fruit of the Spirit that hangs from your tree.

See how it all started with a simple act of obedience to pick up your Bible, find a place to pray, or reach out to God when you didn't necessarily feel like doing it? Let's face it - it's difficult to get your flesh under God's control, especially if you've been doing your own thing for many years. It may be painful at first and you may cry many tears of frustration as you put down the donut to pick up the Bible, but OBEY anyway; it will be worth every tear in the end. **Psalm 126:5 "Those who sow in tears will reap with songs of joy."**

Need more evidence that we are CHANGED in God's presence?

Psalm 33:18 (AMP)
Behold, the Lord's eye is upon those who fear Him [who revere and worship Him with awe], who wait for Him and hope in His mercy and loving-kindness.

Isaiah 40:31 (AMP)
But those who wait for the Lord [who expect, look for, and hope in Him] shall change and renew their strength and power; they shall lift their wings and mount up [close to God] as eagles [mount up to the sun]; they shall run and not be weary, they shall walk and not faint or become tired.

Psalm 37:4 (NIV)
Delight yourself in the LORD and he will give you the desires of your heart.

From the above Scriptures you can see that it is so worth it to wait in the presence of God. He can restore your strength, your energy level, your endurance, and your joy! If you're in a close relationship with God you realize that His eyes are on you to reward the little things you do that nobody else even notices, let alone appreciates. He watches you like a caring mother, a very attentive husband, or a true best friend.

 Do you have a desire to delight yourself in the Lord?

_____

I know I've said this before, but let me remind you one more time: Keep asking, keep seeking God, and keep knocking. You will find Him, and that door into His presence will be opened.

I invite you to pray this prayer with me:

God I admit today that I can *not* get through my weak moments without You.

Please help me spot the lies of the enemy in that moment, and run to You, even if it feels like the last thing I want to do. Help me to be obedient and take the way of escape that You offer, in spite of my feelings in those moments. Speak to me through Your Word and Your Holy Spirit so that I will clearly see the truth, and turn my back on the temptation.

Help me to make a plan for those times when I seem to be weak everyday, Lord. I need Your wisdom to figure out how to change the cycles and patterns that I've fallen into. I recognize, though, that the best plan in the world cannot save me. I need You, Jesus. These things that have been impossible for me to overcome for years ARE TOTALLY POSSIBLE FOR YOU.

Thank You that You are always here to help me, Holy Spirit, every moment of every day.
Amen

Week 8

The Illusion of Perfection

DAY 1

Perfectionism Contributes to Eating Disorders

Perfection is an illusion and therefore searching for perfection is a waste of time. Nobody can do everything perfectly. Besides, something that *you* might perceive to be perfect, may not seem perfect to someone else at all. So perfection, like beauty, is very much in the eye of the beholder.

Doesn't God command us to be perfect? Let's investigate:

Please look up Leviticus 19:2 and write it in the space below

_____

_____

_____

Peter echoes this in 1 Peter 1:15. Please read this verse below
"But as the One Who called you is holy, you yourselves also be holy in all your conduct and manner of living."

Does this seem to you that God is calling us to be perfect?

_____

God commands us to strive for **holiness** and some translations also use the word "perfect." It refers to a pursuit of excellence in everything we do, and it's here where things get confusing because it sounds a lot like God wants us to be perfect in everything we do. But that's not true. Let's have a closer look at the difference between holiness, as the Bible commands, and perfection.

Holiness

The goal of holiness is to please God and to become more like Him. This pursuit brings forth love, joy, peace and every other fruit of the Spirit in our lives. This pursuit will end in heaven, but as we keep reaching for it here on earth it changes us in ways we never thought possible. **Also, holiness can only be achieved by the power of the Holy Spirit in us.** We can't do it ourselves. In fact we are admonished to not strive for perfection in the flesh, but to keep leaning on the Holy Spirit. Take a look at Galatians 3:3 (NLT): *How foolish can you be? After starting your Christian lives in the Spirit, why are you now trying to become perfect by your own human effort?*

Perfection

The pursuit of perfection revolves mainly around pleasing ourselves and impressing others. This pursuit brings forth obsession and anxiety in our lives. **Perfection is something we strive for in our own strength, which is limited and flawed, so the outcome is uncertain and the goal unattainable.** You can try to do everything as close to perfect as humanly possible and still be far from being holy as the Bible commands.

How does perfectionism contribute to food struggles?

Consistency breaks the yoke of food struggles, but perfection is the arch enemy of consistency. By feeding the monster of perfection, we can remain stuck in the pit of food addiction or eating disorders.

Perfectionism *keeps* us from consistency in the following areas:

Striving for the "perfect" body

People with food struggles are constantly striving to create the "perfect" body. People literally put off living until they have the perfect body. They miss out on the dreams and desires God put in their hearts and, in fact, they put off the simple joys of living such as dancing, dating, starting a new career, playing tennis, learning a craft, singing, hiking, swimming, or socializing with others. **Does all of this sound familiar to you? Maybe you have been this disconnected with your body since childhood, always putting off life until you get that perfect body. Let me pose a question to you that is bound to make you squirm with discomfort: What if it's okay to wear a size 12 forever?** Yes, even in the summer, and yes even to that reunion! I realize that some of you will be so grateful to just fit in a size 12, but trust me on this, if you don't start living your life at the weight you are right now, you may not be comfortable with your body at a smaller size either. What if you can relax and enjoy life just the way you are, right now? If you can do that, you will calm down, stop the panic, and let God help you get your body to a normal healthy weight. However, if you keep putting off life till you can wear your high school jeans again, you may waste many more years of your life, waiting.

I'm not talking about pretending to be happy with a weight that is obviously off the charts and affecting your health and your ability to live a normal life. We should all find a food plan and surrender it to the Holy Spirit to get us to a healthy weight range. I'm talking about being dissatisfied with your body because it doesn't look like the "perfect" bodies you see on TV or in a magazine, even though you might seem perfectly fine to everybody around you. You might even remember a time when you had no excess weight on your body, but you were still not happy with it, and you still kept putting off your life. Please read Week 6 of this program again if this is still a huge issue for you; your perfectionism might have lies of the enemy at the root of it.

Have you put off living until you reach the "perfect" weight or size? Please explain.

_____

_____

_____

Striving to eat "perfectly"

What if you start being consistent TODAY? What if a slip-up means nothing? What if you never eat "perfect" again? Imagine a year on a good program that lets you eat a great variety of food (or has a great variety of meal replacements) to meet all your nutritional needs and never leaves you deprived and craving junk food. Where could you have been if you started being consistent that way a year ago? What if you stop looking today for a dangerous method (purging, diet pills, and fad diets) and start looking to a program that you can follow through the ups and downs of your life? Imagine the peace in your heart, the energy in your body, and the steady weight loss...

You may have been going around in a cycle for years now of "eating perfectly" during the week and then throwing everything overboard on the weekends. You can stop this vicious cycle if you let go of any notion of "perfection" with your eating, and rather become satisfied with "good enough."

Do you give up if you cannot eat perfectly? In other words, do you start binging or overeating if you just slightly veer from your food plan?

_____

Did this prevent you from reaching a healthy weight in the past? Please explain.

_____

_____

Striving for "perfect" relationships

In order to keep relationships "perfect" and conflict-free you have to be a people pleaser. This means that you are never truthful with those around you about who you are and what you need. This destroy relationships. Also, people find it hard to relate to someone who seem to always have it all together. In most instances perfectionists hide deep-seated pain and issues by trying to please others and act perfectly. **Perfect relationships do not exist. In fact, real friendships can be messy at times, but they always allow you to be real and get something in return.** Trying to maintain perfect or conflict-free relationships can cause a lot of stress in our lives, which in turn can make us turn to food as an outlet.

 Do you strive for perfect or conflict-free relationships?

_____

Does this cause stress in your life?

_____

Striving for a "perfect" relationship with God

Consistency is the key to a healthy relationship with God. Reaching for the "perfect" relationship with God, maybe the kind we see someone else has, could be a trap of the enemy to keep us in a state of "I will never be that holy" or "only certain privileged people have close relationships with God, I'm just not one of them." If we start to make time in God's presence a daily occurrence, our appetite for His Word and our ability to hear His voice grows. We will never be free from the chains that bind us if we have spiritual ups and downs instead of a consistent flow of God's presence where we let Him into every area of our lives. **Those people who seem to have such close relationships with God learned to walk with Him daily in the minute-by-minute grind of life. Growing in your walk with God comes down to a commitment to be consistently obedient.** You cannot just dart in and out of God's presence whenever you have a need and expect something substantial from the relationship. No relationship works this way, and certainly not our most important relationship.

 Can consistency benefit you in your personal relationship with Jesus? Please explain.

Waiting for the "perfect" exercise

There is no perfect time to exercise. There is no perfect form or amount of exercise. There is no perfect place to exercise or perfect clothes to wear. There is no perfect number of days to exercise. The right time, amount, and number for you is whatever you can do consistently, nothing else.

 Have you started an exercise program by simply showing up, or are you maybe still waiting for the perfect set of circumstances?

Striving to follow this program "perfectly"

If you try to implement and do the things I recommend in this program perfectly, you will end up procrastinating and start looking for a quick fix again. So I want to let you off the hook, there is no perfect way to incorporate the principles of this program into your life. It is mainly between you and God. Most of these issues are issues of the heart that no one can see anyway. So there is no need to try and impress anyone by trying to do it perfectly. Relax, you got this far in the program, and that in itself is a great accomplishment. Remember that you can always go back over the things you don't have a handle on just yet, and ask God to help you with those. Most importantly, you're moving forward in a consistent manner, and I am so proud of you!

I invite you to pray this prayer with me:

Holy Spirit, would you please help me to live a holy life which is pleasing to you. I repent from my selfish strive for perfection to satisfy my own desires and to impress and please others.

Please make me aware of this sinful pattern of wanting to be "perfect" in my life. Help me lay it down daily as I become more aware of it. I want to be in tune to your gentle voice, Holy Spirit, nudging me to choose the path of holiness instead.

Thank you for showing me dangerous patterns in my life as I keep calling to you for freedom from my food struggle. I choose to walk the rest of my journey out in the manner that I started it; not in my own strength but through the power of the Holy Spirit (Galatians 3:3).

Amen

DAY 2

Perfection and Procrastination

Perfectionists usually have an all-or-nothing mentality. There is a definite link between perfectionism and procrastination. Perfectionists will many times procrastinate until the very last minute, because they're afraid of not doing something perfectly. This way they have an excuse to themselves for failing. They would rather not do it at all if they cannot do it perfectly.
A classic example: When starting an exercise program, the perfectionist will keep looking for the *perfect* time, place, program and price without ever finding it. This is procrastination which stems from fear of not being perfect at exercising or being humiliated when trying. Insecurities and fear of humiliation can keep the excuses going.

If you want to accomplish anything in life, you need to look at the truth that THIS MOMENT MATTERS. What you do today will shape your future, and procrastination will keep you stuck in the same place year after year.

Let's see what the Bible has to say about procrastination. Please look up the following verses and write them below:
Proverbs 13:4

_____

_____

Proverbs 20:4

_____

_____

_____

Tips to stop procrastinating

1. Stop planning and start doing
Although planning is beneficial, it can be the main downfall of a procrastinator. If you keep trying to make the perfect plan, the plan will always be the only thing you get done. You will keep procrastinating instead of actually DOING it.

2. Set realistic goals
Realistic goals would be those you can actually reach and keep doing on a consistent basis. If you set an exercise goal that you know you will never be able to keep up, you are setting yourself up for failure. Setting unrealistic goals and making unattainable promises to yourself is just another way to procrastinate.

3. Tackle issues one at a time

Break big things into bite-size pieces that you can handle. Remember the old riddle of "How do you eat an elephant? One bite at a time." Start with 5 minutes of prayer a day, just walk around the block for now, stop eating only desserts for now, or replace two of your four cups of coffee a day with water.

4. Do difficult things as early as possible

If you're having a hard time getting your six glasses or more of water in a day, then start by drinking your first glass right when you wake up and drink another one soon after that. The same goes for other things such as spending time with God or exercise. Many procrastinators say that they have to get out for that walk as soon as they wake up, or they will keep finding excuses to not do it for the rest of the day.

5. Remind yourself that perfection is an illusion

Observe what goes on in your thought life. Resist the thoughts and yearnings for perfection that come up in your mind. Remember, the enemy will present lies to you in this area, but you don't have to believe it, instead refute it with the truth. Next time you see a perfect image in a magazine, and you feel that overwhelming sadness and yearning to look like that, resist! Proclaim the truth instead "I am good enough the way I am. I have great value. I am a child of God and I strive for excellence, not perfection."

6. Remember to write in your journal

Your journal is an excellent way to keep perfectionism and procrastination at bay. On days when you feel discouraged and just want to procrastinate doing all the things you know you should do, pick up your journal. Now highlight all the amazing things God has done since you've started this course. Look at all the little things you have accomplished. Celebrate those victories! Every lie you refuted, every binge food you laid down, every act of forgiveness, every time you surrendered your heart to God, every time you put up one little boundary, and every time you said no to temptation, are huge victories. The enemy tempts us to procrastinate on days when we are emotionally fragile. He will whisper to you that you didn't accomplish anything yet and might as well quit. Precious woman of God, DO NOT BELIEVE HIM, HE IS A LIAR!

7. Sometimes you just have to DO IT

I have found that in some instances the victory lies in just doing it, regardless of my feelings. In fact on the days that I feel the least motivated to go to a support group, phone my health coach, go to a meeting, or attend a Bible study, are the days when I need it most. Trust me on this one, reaching out for support will always feel awkward, because it goes against our prideful nature, but do it anyway. Make a decision, regardless of your feelings, to take a leap of faith and trust that God will do the rest. I still have to push through procrastination many days. I do it knowing that it will probably be a humbling experience, or that I may not be able to do it perfectly or even fail at it. Writing this program was one of those things I wanted to keep procrastinating, and the only way I could finally do it was to take a leap of faith and do it while trembling with fear, not knowing what to expect. I believe this is especially true when it comes to our heart's desires. Many people never fulfill their dreams and God's purpose in and through their lives because they keep procrastinating out of fear that they won't do it perfectly or fail.

Please read the following verses:

*Luke 9:59 (NIV) He said to another man, "Follow me." But he replied, "Lord, first let me go and bury my father." Jesus said to him, "Let the dead bury their own dead, but you go and proclaim the kingdom of God." Still another said, "I will follow you, Lord; but first let me go back and say goodbye to my family." Jesus replied, "**No one who puts a hand to the plow and looks back is fit for service in the kingdom of God.**"*

Did procrastination hold you back from serving the body of Christ, or glorifying God in the past? Please explain.

_____

_____

Can you see how perfectionists miss out on half of their lives by procrastinating? In fact, they might miss the most important part, glorifying God, our ultimate purpose on this earth.

I invite you to pray this prayer with me:

Lord Jesus, I see now how procrastination could cause a lot of pent-up anxiety and stress in my life. I'm sorry that I've been procrastinating to do the things you've placed in my life or instructed me to do. I recognize that I am disobeying you, for fear of not doing things perfectly.

Please help me take the scary step to start a food plan, show up for exercising, and reach out for accountability and support, TODAY. Please remind me that when I least feel like it, I probably need it most.

I cannot do this without you, Holy Spirit. Forgive me for the times I've ignored your voice. Help me to obey you in every little thing.
Amen

DAY 3

Smell the Roses

Living in the present is one of the greatest gifts you can give yourself and teach your children.

Please read Hebrews 3:7-19. Do you see that the word TODAY keeps being repeated in these Scriptures? What are we told to do *today*?

_____

_____

People with eating disorders find it very difficult to **live in the present** and turn in obedience to God TODAY. This is mainly due to the fact that they are preoccupied with the pursuit of the perfect body, perfect weight, and sometimes even perfect relationships.

Striving for perfection is an all-consuming job:

- If you strive for perfection in appearance and relationships you may be preoccupied with the past instead of the present. You may use this present moment to berate yourself for what you've eaten and done yesterday. Guilt and shame about our past is a trap of the enemy to keep us busy with the past so that we cannot use the time that has been given to us today. You may also be checking up on relationships, making sure that you did not offend or displease anybody at yesterday's meeting, last week's Bible study, or last year's reunion.
- You may also be obsessed about the future. Your calendar might be flooded with meals to prepare, surprise parties to pull off, Bible studies at your house, and evenings where you run around and play hostess so other people can relax and mingle. You may be running around buying, baking, phoning, decorating, sending out invitations, taking care of your family, making employee of the month, being the best friend to all your friends, and keeping up your title as a truly virtuous woman at church.

Is it difficult for you to live in your present moment? Is your *today* always jam-packed with yesterday and tomorrow? Please answer the following questions to see if this is true for you.

- Are you most of the time not even aware of your present surroundings?
- Are you often occupied with anxious thoughts about your life and your relationships?
- Are you frantically trying to keep the "perfect world" you've created together?

- Are you putting off things you love or dream of doing until you can fit into a smaller size clothing?
- Are you waiting for your circumstances to change, so you can start living?

Please read this verse: Proverbs 27:1 *"Do not boast about tomorrow, for you do not know what a day may bring."*

According to this verse, do you think we have any real control over tomorrow?

_____

Take a look at Matthew 6:33-34 *"But seek first his kingdom and his righteousness, and all these things will be given to you as well. Therefore do not worry about tomorrow, for tomorrow will worry about itself. Each day has enough trouble of its own."*

What do these verses say about "tomorrow"?

_____

_____

_____

I hope you've learned from these verses that TODAY is all we really have. This moment that you are in right now is a gift from God, please don't waste it.

There is something I would love for you to do this week: STOP AND SMELL THE ROSES

Don't control anything for one day, just let it happen and get yourself in the PRESENT MOMENT. Forget about dinner, forget about tomorrow, forget especially about what happened yesterday. Focus on today. It's really happening NOW!

- Consider how it feels to not think about all the things you should have done and could have done and still have to do for tomorrow
- Consider how it feels to not have to wait until you can fit in a certain type of clothing to live
- When you wake up, spend a moment in prayer and ask God to help you see everything with new eyes, like you are seeing it for the first time that day. Keep whispering prayers to God all through the day and stay aware of the Holy Spirit's presence with you.

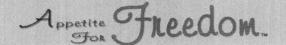

- Make it a rest day from worries and responsibilities: Try not to control anything but instead just observe and enjoy the things around you. Just let everything go for one whole day, it will be awesome!
- Don't make any plans for today. This is one of the big downfalls of a perfectionist - we have to ALWAYS have a plan. So, today, NO PLAN!
- Go outside and listen to the birds
- Just sit on the deck, take in your surroundings and do absolutely NOTHING else
- Be spontaneous: Go to a park, don't pack anything, just go and actually get on a swing or go down a slide
- Stop to notice your kids or your pets, really notice them and let the moment unfold anyway it wants (don't try to control things)
- Go to the beach (don't plan it). Just sit and watch the mighty ocean God created
- Go on a hike in the mountains and listen to God's creation around you, observe, or watch the sunrise He painted for you
- If you love swimming but haven't done so in years, just go. Feel how light your body is in the water and how free you feel

 I invite you to pray this prayer with me:

Jesus, thank you so much for giving me this day. Your Word says that "This is the day that the Lord has made, let us rejoice and be glad in it."

Please help me to set my eyes on You and as a result, on the present moment. Remind me that this moment matters, and that what I do with today will shape my future.

Please take away all fear, anxiety, and stress about yesterday or tomorrow. Fill me with thanksgiving and trust that you are in control of my life and that I can enjoy today without worrying about tomorrow.

Thank you for your love for me Jesus.

Amen

DAY 4

Make Peace with Good Enough

Remember: HOLINESS is what God requires of us, not PERFECTION!

Holiness can only be achieved by giving the Holy Spirit free reign in our lives. **When our lives are surrendered to God, He uses even our "failures" for His Kingdom. You don't have to please everyone, and it's okay if some people don't like you.** There is PRIDE in the desire that makes you want to be a perfect person in your own strength and for your own glory.

We are supposed to try and live at peace with others, but sometimes we can't do anything about another person's feelings and behavior towards us, and WE ARE NOT SUPPOSED TO.

If you struggle with perfectionism you probably know the weird feeling in the pit of your stomach when someone disapproves of you or simply doesn't like you. You might have sleepless nights and days filled with worry and anxiety over this. What is going on? You basically feel like a failure, because you didn't achieve your main goal in life: Keeping everybody happy.

Your enemy loves it when you are afraid of making mistakes and upsetting other people, because he is the one who sows the fear, it is not of God. We are going to learn more about people pleasing and setting up boundaries next week. For now, I just want you to recognize that you don't have to act perfectly in order to keep other people happy.

Is it difficult for you to forgive yourself when you've sinned, or even when you've made a simple mistake?

_____

_____

Please look up Psalm 103:12 and write it in the space below:

_____

_____

When we ask God for forgiveness, He removes our sin and we have a clean slate. We are the ones who still relive the shame and guilt. In fact we don't just dwell on the sin we've committed in our past, we are filled with shame and guilt over simple mistakes that we made, things that happen to everybody. Pride is at the root of this need to be perfect and never make any mistakes. In fact mistakes are very useful in becoming more like Jesus, it diminishes our flesh so that we can become less and Christ in us can become more.

Please write down the following key points in your journal to help you make peace with GOOD ENOUGH

Learning to make mistakes

1. Repent of Pride

Take some time today to come before God in prayer. Have you ever considered that perfectionism might have pride at its core? We sometimes think that we are so in control of our lives that we can "play God" by never making mistakes and keeping everyone happy. If this is true for you, please repent of being prideful and controlling others.

2. Make mistakes and don't try to fix it

Learn to laugh at yourself instead of shaming and scolding yourself when you make a mistake. We are sometimes our own worst enemies. Give yourself room and freedom to make mistakes. Start by telling yourself every time you make a mistake: Everybody makes mistakes, it's okay.

3. Learn to contain your own emotions

Refuse to obsess about other people's anger. Strive to live at peace with everyone as the Word says, but if they refuse to accept your apology or just don't like you, you have to learn to let it go. Ask God to help you gain control of your mind and refuse to dwell on that person's anger. If you dwell on it you are held captive by it, not the other person. However, you have to also make sure that you don't harbor any unforgiveness against the person. This could be the reason for your obsession, and in this case forgiving the person will set you free from the anxious thoughts and the hurt feelings. This might be difficult for you, so ask God to help you get to that place of forgiveness and ask others to pray with you.

4. Do not control other people's feelings

We are not supposed to control others. God has made us stewards of our own lives, not the lives of other adult people. So to try and manipulate someone's feelings and behavior by calling and constantly trying to talk to them about the unresolved conflict when they are not ready will just make matters worse. Let it go and let God deal with them if they hurt you and especially if they refuse to reconcile.

5. Silence the enemy's voice of shame and guilt

Satan will always try and attack you with guilt and shame. Don't listen to him. Remember: guilt and shame is a waste of your time, it accomplishes nothing but steals your time and ruins your life. If the Holy Spirit convicts you that you have done something wrong and need to seek reconciliation, then definitely repent and ask the other person to forgive you. However, once you have asked for forgiveness (whether they accept it or not) you don't have to feel shame or guilt. The enemy would want to keep you in a place of guilt and shame; in fact Satan tends to shame us for simple mistakes such as calling someone by the wrong name or getting in the wrong line at the Post Office.

6. Let others make mistakes without shaming them

Give other people, especially your children and spouse the freedom to make mistakes. Tell them that it's not the end of the world, and although they have to learn to take responsibility for their mistakes, they don't have to feel shame about it or berate themselves. Teach by example, don't be so hard on yourself.

I invite you to pray this prayer with me:

Lord Jesus, I'm so sorry that I let pride creep into my life in the form of perfectionism. I admit today that I've tried to keep up a perfect performance and conflict-free relationships in order to appear flawless to others. I've also tried to manipulate what others think of me and how they perceive me.

Please help me to let go of my pursuit for perfection and also let myself off the hook.

Please give me grace for my own mistakes and also the mistakes of others. Fill my heart with love for myself and others as your Word commands. Love that will cover a multitude of sin.

Thank you that you love me Lord, and that you never heap shame or guilt on me. Thank you Holy Spirit that your conviction of sin is swift to restore me to your presence, never to condemn or berate me. Amen

DAY 5

Let Down Your Hair!

Do you have a drill sergeant in your head? A voice telling you that you're never good enough, that you should have done more, and everything should always be perfect? Most perfectionists do. This could be due to a controlling parent, a legalistic background, lack of love and attention as a child, or abuse.

We learn how to talk to ourselves and treat ourselves through our parents' example. The manner in which they treated us and themselves can stay with us, and can be the voice that drives us. Even if they didn't set a strict example, we might have anticipated their expectations of perfection, which is still the driving force behind everything we do.

This is not the voice of the our Heavenly Father though. He is not a harsh or abusive parent. He is strong, just, righteous, and sovereign, but at the same time He is compassionate, kind, and merciful.

If you have the voice of a drill sergeant in your head, you can do 3 things to change that:
- **Get to know the heart and character of God, your true father, He is not a drill sergeant.**
- **Start giving yourself the kind of caring parenting you never received as a child.** You are in charge now, so be a good "parent" to yourself. Take care of your body, talk to yourself with respect, give yourself grace, and be patient with yourself.
- **Let down your hair and have some fun!**

When last did you have a good laugh?
Some perfectionists tend to take life way too serious. Studies have shown that there are so many health benefits that come from a good belly-laugh. God made our bodies and he invented laughter as medicine for a heavy soul.

 Please look up Proverbs 17:22 and write it in the space below:

_____
_____

When last did you do some fun things? You might have been so busy striving for perfection in so many areas that you have forgotten what *you* like. What makes you tick? God has made you to be a certain person, with certain qualities and interests. We've looked at our specific hearts' desires, but what do you like to do for fun? Do you love roller coasters, but haven't gone to an amusement park in forever? What about windsurfing, shopping for antiques, painting,

scrap booking, sewing, going to museums, or reading? Do you know that God created you with these interests, and He smiles when you're pursuing it and when you're just being you?

What about dancing? I just read an article a few days ago about dancing and how it releases all the right chemicals to change our whole outlook on life and aid us in our recovery from addiction. It reminded me of how I used to just put music on and dance like a crazy woman when I was younger, especially when I was really stressed. It always worked wonders and it is good exercise too!

 Please look up Psalm 30:11 and write it in the space below:

_____

_____

I believe God wants to change your mourning into dancing! I'm trusting Him for great breakthrough in the life of every lady who reads this material and opens Her heart to God. May this be the year of the Lord's favor in your life where your ashes will be turned into a crown of beauty, your mourning will be exchanged for oil of gladness, and you will receive a garment of praise instead of the spirit of despair that has enveloped you all these years! (Isaiah 61:3)

I have a challenge for you today precious woman of God. Will you step out of the boat here with me, and take the first few steps of leaving the life of a perfectionist behind? Instead, how about we take back the joy of God that belongs to us as believers and become "oaks of righteousness, plantings of the Lord, for the display of His splendor."

- I challenge you to find something to laugh out loud about this week. Rent a movie that cracks you up or see a stand-up comedian. I recommend **Bananas** for good clean stand-up comedy, you will find their DVDs at Christian bookstores or online. Also, **Anita Renfroe** is one of my favorite funny Christian ladies. Google her to find a live performance in your area and be sure to go with a bunch of girlfriends or buy her DVD. Invite some girls over for coffee and laughs.
- Try to remember what you like. Think back and try and recall long-forgotten passions. Which hobbies did you have, or better yet, which interests did you always want to pursue but never got around to?
- Get your dancing shoes on, girl! Come on, it's a challenge. Don't let the perfectionist in you wonder about dance lessons or the right music. Just do it. Put on some praise music and crank the volume up. You don't have to be young to feel young and dance your heart out. You don't have to be an extrovert or a big mouth like me, you can just be you and do it anyway you want. No one is watching except the One who invented dancing, and He's smiling. It shouldn't be perfect, it should just feel good!

 Please write down a few things you can do this week to take good care of yourself and take back the joy of the Lord that the enemy has stolen. Joy is part of the fruit of the Spirit, it belongs to you and I, we just need to give the Holy Spirit free reign in this area of our lives as well.

_____

_____

_____

_____

_____

I invite you to pray this prayer with me:

God I'm asking you to help me silence the drill sergeant that I've been listening to all these years. I know that the enemy is behind this, and I will no longer listen to His lies that nothing is ever good enough and that I should strive for perfection at all cost. Thank you that you are a merciful, compassionate Father who looks upon me with favor.

Holy Spirit, please take control of my thoughts and let the fruit of joy become evident in my life. I declare today that the joy of the Lord is my strength (Nehemiah 8:10). I will no longer let the enemy steal joy from me or keep me from enjoying the life you've given me. Thank you for the crown of beauty that you have bestowed on me, thank you for the oil of gladness, and the garment of praise. I see these things in my mind's eye today as if they were real, and I receive it in faith according to your Word.

Thank you for your love, joy, peace, patience, kindness, goodness, faithfulness, gentleness, and self-control that is starting to become more evident in my life.

Fill me with more of you, Holy Spirit.

Amen

Week 9

Healthy Relationships

DAY 1

Find Freedom in Truth

Constantly pleasing other people, or trying to save them in one way or another, can fill our lives with so much stress and anxiety that we remain in a place where we need an outlet in the form of food. At the root of people-pleasing lies a problem with establishing clear boundaries of where your responsibilities for yourself start and end and where it spills over into the lives of others. You may have been so busy with other people's responsibilities that you have forgotten all about your own personal responsibilities.

Let's take a look at what it means to have healthy boundaries in our lives.

After reading a great deal about healthy boundaries, practicing it in my own life for years, and seeing other women work at it, I narrowed it down to this very important point: **Be truthful.** This seems like a normal part of Christianity, yet so many Christians are not truthful with themselves or others about their needs and responsibilities. We need to find balance in our relationships when it comes to giving and receiving, holding close and letting go, but none of this is possible if we are not being honest with each other.

We are encouraged throughout the Bible to seek out the truth.

 Please look up John 8:32 and write it in the space below:

_____

_____

Can you see how truth is linked to freedom?

_____

Weak or non-existent boundaries in our lives essentially means that we are not being truthful with ourselves or others, and this in itself can keep us stuck in food struggles for many years.

The connection between weak boundaries and food struggles

Weak PERSONAL boundaries contribute to food struggles
The very first boundary that needs fixing is our own INTERNAL or PERSONAL BOUNDARIES. It is very important to honor our own internal boundaries. If we don't listen to our bodies' needs, we are violating our own internal boundaries. We feel sad and depressed because we are not being true to ourselves. We focus so much on the needs and happiness of others that we actually abuse our own bodies (by not getting enough sleep, rest, exercise, etc). So we make up for this by "treating" ourselves to junk food and mind-numbing activities such as watching long hours of TV.

Weak boundaries in RELATIONSHIPS can contribute to food struggles
- **Healthy relationships are all about giving and receiving.** God made us this way so that we will not become selfish, but also not burn ourselves out by only giving and never receiving. Healthy boundaries help you find the balance between "holding close and letting go." People who have been smothered with love and given free reign to do whatever they wanted as children, were never given the guidance and discipline that help them put boundaries on themselves. It affects their relationships. They might be clingy, extremely jealous, and possessive of their husbands, children and friends. The fear of being ignored or being rejected drive them daily to please others or smother them with love. This constant fear of rejection finds an outlet in food struggles.

- **Healthy boundaries help you find the balance between "my responsibility and someone else's responsibility."** Women who have been given too much responsibility at a young age or given too much emotional information about their parents' problems, also called emotional incest, could feel overly responsible for everyone. It affects their current relationships. They tend to make other people's problems their own, counsel and give advice all the time, and feel responsible for others' decisions and mistakes. They carry the whole world's sorrows and problems on their shoulders. They are most likely still taking care of their parents' problems on top of all their own responsibilities. The huge amounts of stress and anxiety also find an outlet in food struggles. Food is used to calm nerves and help them forget their huge burden, if only for a moment.

- **Healthy boundaries help you find the balance between "freedom and control."** Women who grew up in a home where they were controlled with an iron fist never forged a sense of self and stayed enmeshed with the parents' identity. It affects their current relationships. They remain in a place where others have to make decisions for them. They are afraid of conflict or to give their own opinion. They never really found out who they were and struggle with their self image. The insecurities finds an outlet: Food struggles. People sometimes use anorexia as a form of control when they feel they have no control in another area of their lives.

- **Healthy boundaries help you find the balance between "saying NO and saying YES."** People who have been abused by their parents have been robbed from their boundaries and sense of self. It affects their current relationships. They feel ashamed and afraid and tend to isolate themselves from healthy people and thus healthy relationships. They learned at an early age that they don't have any say in their own lives and that their NO doesn't mean anything, so they never honor their internal boundaries and never teach others to respect their boundaries. The few people they do let into their lives are usually broken themselves and tend to further abuse them. **All this pain and abuse need an outlet such as food struggles.** Women with binge eating disorder or compulsive overeating sometimes use weight gain to "shield" them against further abuse. Women who have been sexually abused sometimes use bulimia to "cleanse" themselves over and over from the "filth."

 Do you sense a problem with your boundaries after reading the above scenarios?

_____

_____

Do you feel that you are truthful, or do you only tell people what they want to hear?

_____

_____

Please answer the following questions to see if you might have some problems in the area of boundaries. Circle the ones that apply to you.

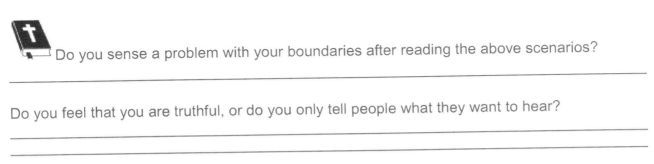

?	<ul><li>Have you ever found out what your real heart's desires are, and are you making time for it regardless of everybody else's needs and demands on you?</li><li>Do you realize that your needs are just as important as the needs of your family and other people?</li><li>Do you pride yourself in always giving your children the best attention, clothes, meals, and recreation, and do you feel guilty if you slack a little with these?</li><li>Can you take the heat and the guilt that comes when you give up the notion of "super-mom" or "super-homemaker" to go for your dreams?</li><li>Can you shut down the voices of guilt and shame, telling you that you are a bad mom and wife, when you take care of your own needs?</li><li>Do you feel like a failure when your kids have to fend for themselves for a change and the house is a mess because you're doing something you love?</li><li>Can you sleep in when you're tired, or do you feel guilty?</li><li>Can you tell your pastor in the foyer that you don't feel like smiling on this particular Sunday morning because you just had a big fall-out with your hubby in the car about tithing?</li><li>Can you ask your kids to forgive you after you've just lost it?</li><li>Can you tell your friend that you really do not feel like watching her kid again today, even if you don't have any particular excuse?</li></ul>

- Can you tell your mother that you don't agree with her and leave it at that?
- Can you say "I don't feel comfortable about giving you an answer right now, let me get back to you?"
- Can you tell the busiest super mom in church that you don't want to do the one thing she asks of you, because you frankly don't have time or energy for it?
- Can you tell someone that you're angry without profusely apologizing two minutes later?
- Can you change your mind and just go "Hey what's a mind if you can't change it" without beating yourself up about all the people you might have disappointed by changing your mind?
- Can you make mistakes and be responsible for it without being overwhelmed by a feeling of guilt, shame, and failure?
- Can you ask for what you want, without feeling guilty for wanting something?
- Can you set your own priorities and give it an important place in the family plans?
- Can you insist on being taken seriously and treated with respect, or take the necessary steps if it's not happening?
- Can you stand your ground even in the face of someone else's anger, silence, or disappointment?

Did you maybe find out, like I did, that you don't always tell people the truth? Please explain

_____

_____

The biggest revelation to me was that I mostly lied to people about me. I didn't want them to think that I was selfish or didn't care about them, so I would not tell them what I really needed or how I really felt.

David's heart cry in Psalm 51:6 became my own *"Behold, You desire truth in the inner being; make me therefore to know wisdom in my inmost heart."* (AMP)

If this is true for you then I'm sure you know by now where to start: Repentance.
Lying is a sin you know, it's not just some little character flaw, even if we didn't do it on purpose. It hurts our relationship with God and it gives Satan a foothold in our lives. On the flipside, TRUTH sets us free!

I invite you to pray this prayer with me:

Lord Jesus, I repent from the sin of deceit. I have not been truthful to myself, others and you.

You know that I didn't mean to sin against you Lord, but I thank you for showing me this area that is hurting our relationship and I ask that you will forgive me and wash me clean. Thank you for setting me on this journey and guiding me all the way to freedom. Thank you for loving me. I know you require truth in my inmost being, and I ask that you will help me to be truthful from this day on.

Bring the times that I am not really honest to my attention and help me to become someone who is truly truthful. Thank you Jesus, I accept your forgiveness. Amen

We can't get too deep into the subject of boundaries in this study. However, this could be a make or break issue in your struggle with food. If you feel that this is true for you, I want to encourage you to find a pastor or Christian counselor who can help you put strong boundaries in place in your life. Also be sure to read some of the excellent books written on the topic of boundaries by Dr. Henry Cloud and Dr. John Townsend.

DAY 2

Stop the Control

Did you ever realize that you might be trying, through your perfectionist behavior, to control other people's thoughts and feelings towards you? Control, just like perfection, is an illusion and it causes a lot of unnecessary stress and anxiety in our lives.

Your control of another person might actually be in direct opposition to what God is wanting to do in that person's life. Also, if you are controlling someone they will end up resenting you for it, and may even reject you as a result of it.

God created us to be responsible for ourselves, not other adults. Even children need to be given age-appropriate responsibilities in order to become healthy, capable adults one day.

It is not an easy thing to let go of control when it comes to our children. As moms we need to be in control of our little ones or they will not survive. For many years we control what they eat, what they wear, and what they do. Then one day we wake up and it's time to surrender a little of the control, until we finally have to completely release them. It's terrifying for most moms and can break your heart, especially if it's your first one. I still remember when my oldest son, who is now 22, started pushing for more independence. Giving him more freedom was one of the hardest things I ever had to do. **During those years a friend gave me some excellent advice. She said to remember that when separation is most difficult for me, it is probably most crucial for his future.**

Teaching your teenager boundaries is a balancing act between holding on to some control, but also allowing them some freedom. By doing this you are:
- Equipping her to face the world out there while you're still close enough to help
- Letting her find out who she is and what she likes
- Letting her develop her own relationship with God
- Keeping your door open if she wants to talk or ask for advice in the future
- Forging and preserving a new relationship with her that will go the distance

There is someone that you can and should control: YOU

Remember this verse that we read in Week 7: "Like a city whose walls are broken down is a man who lacks self-control." Proverbs 25:28

What kind of control does this verse refer to?

_____

Nowhere in the Bible do we find any indication that we should control others. However, as children of God we are admonished to bear the fruit of **self control** in our lives as we surrender more and more to the Holy Spirit. When we give our hearts to Jesus, we receive the Holy Spirit, and part of the fruit of the Spirit is self control, not the control of others (Galatians 5:22).

Unfortunately our self control with regards to our struggle with food has been worn thin by the enemy and it feels as if we don't have any control at all in this area. This is why we cannot do it alone, there is a war raging for our freedom, and we need to be reminded through the Word of God and the support of others, that we do indeed possess the fruit of the Holy Spirit in our lives, and that it includes self control.

Start today with the areas you can control.

1. **Take control of your time:** You can make time to build your love relationship with God, so that you don't need to turn to food for comfort.
2. **Take control of your thoughts:** You can take a hold of those crazy, out-of-control thoughts, recognize them as lies from the enemy, and replace them with the truth of God's Word. Our thoughts drive our emotions, which in turn affect our actions. If we can stop that thought and replace it with God's truth before it takes root, we can stop the emotion, and stop the action.
3. **Find support:** You can give up the secrecy and isolation surrounding your food struggle and reach out to someone for help and support.
4. **Stop controlling others**: Be honest with yourself about the reason you try to control or manipulate others instead of focusing on controlling yourself.

Why do we control others?

People with food struggles sometimes control others to take the focus off their own problem.

Take a minute and think if this might be true for you. Do you sometimes control and focus on the mistakes of others to take the spotlight off you and your struggle with food? Please explain

_____

_____

We are not responsible for the actions of other adults. People who feel overly responsible for others tend to control those that they "mother."

Take a minute and think if this might be true for you. Would you ask God to help you let go of the false responsibility and help you find the balance between your responsibility and someone else's?

_____
_____

People who have been smothered with love, yet never received guidance and discipline, tend to control their close family members through manipulation and guilt.

Take a minute and think if this might be true for you. Would you ask God to help you let go of this fear of rejection that comes from the enemy? Ask Him to help you find the balance between holding close and letting go.

_____
_____

Is there maybe another reason why you feel you need to control people in your life? Are you maybe being controlled by someone else? Please talk this over with God, and reach out to a counselor or pastor if you feel that control has become a huge issue in your life.

_____
_____

We were never supposed to control others or be controlled by others. It is an unnatural state and it will hurt your relationships, and keep you in bondage to food or other addictive substances.

I invite you to pray this prayer with me:

God, I realize today that I might have been so busy controlling others that I have neglected to bear the fruit of self control in my life. I see now that it is not possible to do both, and I ask you to help me let go of controlling and manipulating others in order to have the fruit of self control in my life.

Please help me restore the wall of self control around my life so that I will be protected against the attacks of the enemy. Help me to start being faithful in the small areas of my life I can control. Holy Spirit I ask you to remind me to take control of myself every time I am tempted to control someone else.

Thank you for loving me so much, and bringing the things that are harmful to my life under my attention. I love you Jesus.
Amen

DAY 3

Stop the People Pleasing

The Bible is clear that we should not be people pleasers, but rather seek to please God.

Please look up Galatians 1:10 and write it in the space below:

_____

_____

_____

Please explain in your own words what you understand from this verse with regards to people pleasing.

_____

_____

How do you handle conflict in a godly way? In other words, how can you be truthful without being hateful?
It is difficult for most women to engage in conflict. We would rather be nice than honest. We find that if we avoid conflict, our lives run pretty smooth and we like it that way and try to keep it that way. However, the "smoothness" could sometimes come at a price. Controlling our environment and relationships in this manner can rob us of internal peace and joy. This is many times the reason why people don't want to lay down the idol of food. They honestly feel that food has become the only "good" thing they have left in their lives. If you are constantly busy controlling your family and your environment, you may live a high-stress life and you might be using food to help you cope with the stress.

I recently heard a few different Bible teachers teach on the difference between a **peacemaker** and a **peacekeeper**. They derive it from the verse in Matthew 5:9: *"Blessed are the peacemakers for they will be called sons of God."*
According to the Hebrew, this word **peacemaker** refers to an active pursuit of peace, as opposed to a passive kind of peacekeeping. In order to keep the peace we need to DO SOMETHING, not just passively avoid conflict.

Being a peacemaker sometimes involves forbearance and other times calls for us to engage in confrontation. Let's take a look at what the Bible has to say about the different ways to handle conflict in a godly manner.

When do we FORBEAR?

Let's read this verse in Proverbs 25:15 (AMP): *By long forbearance and calmness of spirit a judge or ruler is persuaded, and soft speech breaks down the most bonelike resistance."*

The definition for forbearance is "tolerance and restraint in the face of provocation; patience."[7] Forbearance or patience is part of the fruit of the Spirit, and we as Christians are called to forbear and hold our tongue in many instances. I believe that most of the time, especially in close relationships, we should forbear and let love cover a multitude of sin, as the Word tells us to do. In fact, learning to forbear has humility at its core, and teaches us to become more like Jesus, and is indeed a characteristic of a peacemaker.

However, when people's actions are **dishonoring God and hurting their testimony or hurting themselves or someone else, and the only way to save the relationship is through confrontation,** then the time has come to enter into conflict in a godly manner. Keeping the peace in certain situations instead of confronting in love, is not real peace at all, it is only a temporary illusion of peace.

How do we CONFRONT?

Please read Ephesians 4:14-15. In this passage we are called to maturity, and to speak the truth. How should we speak the truth according to these verses?

_____

_____

As you can see from this verse, the Bible is clear about the fact that we should speak the truth in love. It doesn't say that we should only speak the truth when it's convenient or when it wouldn't stir up conflict.

Steps to confront in love
- **Always PRAY first:** If we are out of line and are confronting someone for the wrong reasons, such as our own selfish interests, we will not get this past God in prayer. On the other hand, if we are filled with fear, knowing that we are right to confront for the other person's sake or the sake of the relationship, then we will be strengthened and encouraged in God's presence, because God did not give us a spirit of fear.
- **Ask God to give you agape love for the person you are about to confront.** If we confront someone with the Godly love as mentioned in 1 Corinthians 13, it will be love that is not rude, selfish, or harsh in any way.
- **Seek counsel:** Counsel with elders or leaders that you know to be unbiased and whom you can trust. Never seek out counsel as a rogue to gossip, and do not turn to mutual friends or people that you are really trying to win over to your side of the argument. All of these things have pride behind it, and does not have true reconciliation at its core.
- **Try to confront in person and pick the right time:** Never confront a person in front of others, over the phone, via email, or at a time when they are stressed or obviously in a hurry.

- **Make sure that your heart is right before God:** If your motive is to get your pride restored or to make someone apologize and see things your way, you are setting yourself up for failure. There is only one motive that will cause the other person to respond favorably and that is true reconciliation. Come to the table with the restoration of the relationship in mind and you will not have to deal with your own ego and pride when things get heated. You will remain calm and look for solutions.
- **Never attack the other person's character or humiliate him/her in any way:** This is not godly behavior, and will not produce any positive results. She will just get angry or shut down and leave. Always speak in a loving and respectful tone. Anybody will be more receptive of the truth if they hear it in a non-judgmental, loving way.
- **Listen to what the other person has to say:** As a peacemaker you have to have a humble heart and be open to the possibility that you might have been wrong in your perception of things.

 Are you a peacekeeper of a peacemaker?

_____

Can you see how simply keeping the peace at all cost is only a temporary solution that can cause underlying stress and anger in you?

_____

_____

Is it difficult for you to forbear or to engage in conflict in a Godly manner? Please explain:

_____

Please ask for prayer if this is really difficult for you. Also reach out to a counselor or pastor who can help keep you accountable to start taking small steps towards becoming a peacemaker.

I invite you to pray this prayer with me:

Holy Spirit, I need your help to show me when to forbear and when to confront in my life. Please guide me and help me bridle my tongue. Let me be quick to listen, slow to speak, and slow to become angry (James 1:19).

Please give me courage to speak up during those times that I need to confront, and teach me how to speak the truth in love. I want to become truthful in my relationships and be a peacemaker, not merely someone who keeps the peace at all cost.

I desperately need you to show me how to break out of my old mold of either always keeping quiet or always fighting. Please change me to become more like you Jesus. I want to become a woman who strives for reconciliation and true peace.

Lord, help me to not get discouraged when these long-standing habits don't change overnight, but to rather celebrate every victory along the way as You change me from glory to glory.

Amen

DAY 4

Take Responsibility for YOU

Dearest woman of God, it is time to be true to yourself. Believe me, I understand why you always put others first. It's a woman thing really, we are born caretakers, God made us that way you know.

We don't mean to lie to ourselves, we just get so swept up in the role of caretaker that we lose all balance:

- We overdo it
- We forget that we're only human
- We want to be everything for everybody
- We forget to refuel
- We hate to ask for help
- We don't know how to receive tender, loving care without feeling guilty
- We betray our own opinions and preferences to please others
- We forget about the dreams we had and it stifles our potential in all areas of our lives
- Some of us were raised to exclusively become caretakers who always have to put everyone else's needs above our own. We may not even recognize that our needs matter too
- Maybe, like me, you even rebelled against this as a teenager, but once you became a mom and saw all the super moms around you, you joined the club of selfless caregivers who seemingly always smile and never complain

Please read Luke 10:27 (NIV) out loud:

He answered, *"'Love the Lord your God with all your heart and with all your soul and with all your strength and with all your mind and love your neighbor as yourself."*

Jesus teaches here that the greatest command is to love God. He also commands us to love our neighbor in a certain way - which way is that?

_____

_____

Do you see the assumption here that we should love ourselves and also love our neighbors in the same manner? The problem is that many people, especially women, have grace, love, tenderness, and compassion for everyone else, except themselves.

I know this is a very familiar passage among women, but please take some time today to read Proverbs 31. What does your picture of the Proverbs 31 woman look like?

_____

_____

Here is what I pictured when I read this passage in the past: **An amazing, selfless creature who lives only to serve her husband and children.** No wonder some of us feel guilty if we...

- take some time for ourselves
- lock the bathroom door, put music on and refuse to answer anybody
- go out for a good laugh with a few girl friends
- spend some money on ourselves for a change
- refuse to give our kids our undivided, unconditional attention 24/7

I believe with all my heart that the woman God painted for us in Proverbs 31 was such a dynamic, inspiring woman because she first took care of her spirit, mind, and body. She could love others because she first of all loved her God with all her being, and also loved herself. I believe that we can all be Proverbs 31 women if we would first make time for God, nurture ourselves, and then give to others out of our fullness, not our emptiness.

 Please answer the following questions to see if you honor your internal boundaries

	<ul><li>Can you take a NO from yourself?</li><li>Can you capture thoughts of guilt and shame and bring them under God's authority (the truth of the Bible)?</li><li>Can you stop all activity to just sit at the Father's feet ?</li><li>Can you stop eating when you're full?</li><li>Do you eat when you're hungry, sleep when you're tired, and drink when you're thirsty?</li><li>Can you stop worrying and instead lay your cares at the feet of God in prayer?</li><li>Can you calm your mind and emotions after something upsetting happened in order to do what you have to do (such as focus on your work or take care of your children)?</li><li>Can you take your thoughts captive after confronting someone about violating your boundaries, or do you keep dwelling on ways to make them happy again and to fix things?</li></ul>

Remember how we spoke about taking good care of our bodies by getting enough rest, exercising, eating well, relaxing, reading, spending time with friends, and casting our cares on God? Did you do it yet? **The sobering fact is: We either start being truthful to ourselves and others about our bodies' needs or stay in the death grip of a food struggle.**

Letting our emotions and thoughts run wild is another way of violating our internal boundaries and abusing ourselves. After a day of stress, anxiety, despair, and worry we feel drained and depressed. We might allow others to dump their problems on us, and we might even make their problems our own. We calm our anxiety by eating and turning to mind-numbing activities to drown out the stress and anxiety. **There are two things to do here: We need to set up boundaries to protect ourselves from other people's dumping, and we need to honor our personal boundaries and say NO to turning to food, but instead take our anxiety and cares to God's throne in prayer.**

Please know that you're not a failure if you can't say NO to yourself just yet. It takes time. It's like a muscle that you have to keep flexing, a little more every day, until it becomes strong. I have to DAILY flex my NO-muscle so that my spirit can grow and I can desire God above all else.

 I invite you to pray this prayer with me:

Lord thank you for giving me this body. I recognize again today that my body is not my own, it is a gift from you, and I want to honor you in my body.

Please help me to take the necessary steps to put up boundaries with the people in my life and to honor my own boundaries so that I will take better care of this great gift of life that you have given me.

Remind me, Holy Spirit, that I am not honoring you when I'm trying to be everything for everyone else and harming my own body in the process. Please help me take control of my mind by turning to you in prayer regularly. Your Word tells me to not be anxious about anything, but in every situation, by prayer and petition, with thanksgiving, make my requests known to You (Philippians 4:6).

God, please help me to say NO to my own flesh and YES to your Spirit.

Amen

DAY 5

Face your Fears

Please remember this about fear:
Satan works with fear. If he can get us to fear something, we are trapped by our own fear and we cannot move onward to freedom.

Please read 2 Timothy 1:7 (AMP) out loud:
For God did not give us a spirit of timidity (of cowardice, of craven and cringing and fawning fear), but [He has given us a spirit] of power and of love and of calm and well-balanced mind and discipline and self-control.

One of the reasons we hesitate to put up boundaries or be truthful is FEAR. We might fear any number of things such as:

- Rejection
- Loneliness if rejected
- The other person's anger and animosity
- Guilt and shame
- Losing the "perfect me" image that we upheld
- Physical or verbal abuse

IMPORTANT:	If you feel that you will be in physical danger or will suffer any form of abuse if you put up boundaries or tell someone the truth about your needs, then please refrain from doing so until you are safe.
	Please get in contact with your pastor, a counselor, a social worker, or any person in authority that can get you to a safe place. You need to be able to express your feelings and set up boundaries, but you first need to make sure that you and your children are safe.
	There are shelters and hotlines for women and children who are abused. Please search on the internet, even if you are in a different country than the USA, you will find similar hotlines and shelters in your area. <ul><li>**Abuse Recovery Ministry Services:** http://www.armsonline.org/</li><li>**Website for National Domestic Violence (USA):** http://www.thehotline.org/</li><li>**National Domestic Violence Hotline (USA):** 1 800 799 SAFE (7233) 1 800 787 3224</li></ul>

If you are NOT in physical danger or there is no real possibility of mental or physical abuse if you were to start putting up boundaries today, then the only thing that might be holding you back is FEAR.

There are many Scriptures in the Bible that refute fear. Here are a few verses to get you started. Please copy them to your note cards. Then start reading them out loud today to stand against fear in Jesus' name.

Joshua 1:9
This is my command—be strong and courageous! Do not be afraid or discouraged. For the Lord your God is with you wherever you go. (NLT)

Psalm 27:1
The LORD is my light and my salvation; Whom shall I fear? The LORD is the strength of my life; of whom shall I be afraid? (NKJV)

Psalm 56:3-4
When I am afraid, I will trust in you. In God, whose word I praise, in God I trust; I will not be afraid. What can mortal man do to me? (NIV)

Isaiah 41:13
For I am the LORD, your God, who takes hold of your right hand and says to you, Do not fear; I will help you. (NIV)

Isaiah 54:4
Do not fear, for you will not be ashamed; Neither be disgraced, for you will not be put to shame; For you will forget the shame of your youth, And will not remember the reproach of your widowhood any more. (NKJV)

Matthew 10:28
And do not fear those who kill the body but cannot kill the soul. But rather fear Him who is able to destroy both soul and body in hell. (NKJV)

Romans 8:15
The Spirit you received does not make you slaves, so that you live in fear again; rather, the Spirit you received brought about your adoption to sonship. And by him we cry, "Abba, Father" (NIV)

Hebrews 13:5-6
For He Himself has said, "I will never leave you nor forsake you." So we may boldly say: "The LORD is my helper; I will not fear. What can man do to me?" (NKJV)

1 Peter 3:13-14
Who is going to harm you if you are eager to do good? But even if you should suffer for what is right, you are blessed. "Do not fear what they fear; do not be frightened." (NIV)

1 John 4:18
There is no fear in love. But perfect love drives out fear, because fear has to do with punishment. The one who fears is not made perfect in love. (NIV)

Even if there is no real physical danger involved, there is always a chance that you will be rejected, that someone will get angry, or that you will experience guilt and shame for putting up boundaries. During these times you want to stay close to God and people who can support you such as family, friends, a spouse, a pastor, or a counselor. First practice setting boundaries with someone you can trust, for example, start saying no to your family members and warn them beforehand that it is difficult for you, but you are learning to set healthy boundaries for yourself. Stand your ground once you set a boundary, and call your support people for prayer and encouragement if you start to feel guilt and shame.

Please know that I don't say any of these things lightly. I am aware that there are ladies out there who will have to fight for their FREEDOM. But I also know that weak or non-existent boundaries will keep your eating disorder in place year after year. If you want to be free you have to become someone who tells the truth. If you are a victim of abuse you especially need to tell someone the truth.
Please opt for the TRUTH, it might be the hardest thing you ever do, but it can be the beginning of a new life of freedom for you.

 I invite you to pray this prayer with me:

Lord Jesus I don't want to be fearful of speaking the truth anymore. Please remove all traces of fear from my heart. I believe today that the truth of your Word will set me free (John 8:32). Please help me to read and learn more of your Word so that I can love you more and live free from all fear.

Lord, I cry out with King David today: "You desire truth in the inner being; make me therefore to know wisdom in my inmost heart." Show me if there is a harmful way in my heart where I still lie to myself and others. I don't want to be a people-pleaser anymore Lord, but I want to please you above all else.

Thank you that you love me and that you are drawing me closer to your heart every day so that I will live a life of abundance, not a life in bondage.

I love you, Jesus
Amen

Week 10
Forgiveness and Healing

DAY 1
Looking Back to Move Forward

Why do we have to dig through things in our past that are best left alone?

There exist at least two very good reasons why we have to take this journey into the past:

- According to various eating disorder experts, also the ones who specialize in biblical counseling, our relationships with our parents and close family members could have played a major role in our food struggles. **However, we should never look back with the purpose of finding someone to blame, this is not helpful and certainly not biblical.** We are simply looking back in order to forgive and make amends where appropriate.

- Also, it is often said that eating disorders are just the symptoms of much deeper issues or "roots". Some of these issues such as bitterness, unforgiveness, shame, guilt, and pride originated in past experiences and relationships. So in order to remove the underlying root or sin we have to dig a little deeper. **As we forgive those who hurt us, we can move forward and not repeat the same mistakes in our present families**

Don't play the blame game:

As previously stated, we are not trying to find someone to blame for our sin. We are looking to mend broken relationships, put up clear boundaries, and extend forgiveness, so that we can break free from the chains of bitterness and anger that might be keeping us stuck in this pit of food struggles.

It is important to note right here at the beginning of this week that God commands us to honor our parents. **He didn't say we should only honor them if they deserve it,** because He knew that parents are human and they will make mistakes and most likely hurt their children at times. This command is not only for the parent, but also for the spiritual and emotional well being of the child.

 Please look up Exodus 20:12 (NIV) and write it in the space below:

_____

_____

According to Ephesians 6:1-3 (NIV) this is the first commandment with a promise. Please read this verse below:

Children, obey your parents in the Lord, for this is right. "Honor your father and mother"—which is the first commandment with a promise— "that it may go well with you and that you may enjoy long life on the earth."

What is the promise if we obey this command?

_____

Let's look at a few different scenarios where we are instructed to honor our parents:

1. When we are still under their authority, we should obey our parents
Colossians 3:20 (NIV)
Children, obey your parents in everything, for this pleases the Lord.

Proverbs 1:8-9 (NIV)
*Listen, my son, to your father's instruction and do not forsake your mother's teaching.
They will be a garland to grace your head and a chain to adorn your neck.*

2. Another way of honoring them is to not despise them or mock them, thus be respectful even if you don't feel that they deserve it.
Proverbs 30:17 (NIV)
The eye that mocks a father, that scorns obedience to a mother, will be pecked out by the ravens of the valley, will be eaten by the vultures.

We are kidding ourselves to think that we can treat our parents anyway we want and not reap the consequences. Not honoring our parents can greatly influence the course of our lives, according to the following verse:
Proverbs 20:20 (NIV)
If a man curses his father or mother, his lamp will be snuffed out in pitch darkness.

3. If we are able to help care for our elderly parents and we refuse, God will hold us accountable. We have an obligation, according to the Word, to return some of the love that they have given to us as children. 1 Timothy 5 speaks about caring for your parents and not let them be a burden to the church if you are able to take care of them.

Note: Sometimes it is difficult to love an elderly parent, or a parent who didn't treat us like they should have when we were children. Even in this instance God calls us to love everybody (even our enemies) with a godly agape love. You can ask God to give you a godly love for your parents, even if you don't "feel" love towards them..

IMPORTANT	You need clear boundaries with a parent who abused you or is still abusing you in any way. God never expects us to stay in a situation where we are abused. On the contrary, I believe that God will personally judge and deal with people who have harmed children according to this verse
	Matthew 18:6 (NIV)
	But if anyone causes one of these little ones who believe in me to sin, it would be better for him to have a large millstone hung around his neck and to be drowned in the depths of the sea.

How do we look back?
Looking back involves the following simple steps:

- Open up your heart to God in prayer
- Resist the fear that comes from the enemy
- God never convicts us to harm or destroy us, He always convicts us to bring healing and reconciliation.
- Even if you cry and go through difficult emotions, God will hold you safely in His hand. Remember that He is the potter and we are the clay and He has promised to never leave us nor forsake us. In Isaiah 9:6 God is called Wonderful Counselor, Prince of Peace, Mighty God, and Everlasting Father. Please remember that your pain is not too big for God
- Ask God to help you forgive those who hurt you and caused you to believe lies about yourself
- Look for verses in the Bible, or ask a pastor or mature Christian to help you find verses, that refute the lies you have believed about certain areas of your life and read those verses daily

 Start by answering these questions in your journal. Don't rush it. You might not be sure about some of the answers right now, so take the rest of this week, or as long as you need to think and pray about it

> **?**
>
> **Ask the Holy Spirit to help you discover truth about the pain in your past, and the lies that kept that pain alive. When you feel Him stir something in your heart, please don't ignore it, try and find some time alone to talk it through with your Heavenly Father**
>
> 1. List some things about your parents which you are grateful for. Thank God for those things (list your mom and dad separately if you want). For those who have grown up without parents or don't have many positive memories, list at least one thing you are grateful for from your childhood.
> 2. Now list the things between you and your parents that you regret or that you wish could be different. Talk to God about these and be honest with Him about where you're at in the process of forgiveness and letting it go.
> 3. Think about your relationship with your parents when you were a child. Did you get any negative messages about their attitude towards food and their bodies?
> 4. Describe your relationship with your parents today
> 5. Did your parents only accept the "good" parts of your personality and not the "bad" or weaker parts?
> 6. Did this cause you to try and be the perfect daughter?
> 7. Do you feel angry with your parents, and have you ever been able to tell them how you feel without getting into a huge argument?
> 8. Do you think that you've honored your parents?
> 9. Are you holding grudges against your parents?

10. Do you suffer from a broken heart due to the actions of either one of your parents?
11. Did you feel that either one of your parents abandoned you when you were a kid? How did this impact your life?
12. Was either one of your parents chronically ill or had an addiction that kept them away from you?
13. Could you ever be honest with your parents about your true emotions without them falling apart or getting really angry?
14. Do you fear conflict as a result of this?
15. Did either one of your parents try to control you, and do you feel that your food struggle gives you some control over your own life?
16. Have you been able to separate from your parents as a teenager? In other words, do you know who you are apart from your parents' input and approval?
17. Do you still find it difficult to say no to either one of your parents? Do you feel guilty if you do?
18. Do you try to please your parents, sometimes even at the cost of your own family?
19. Did either one of your parents judge others based on their appearance, and do you maybe also struggle with prejudice in this area?
20. Do you depend on your parents to help you make decisions?
21. Do you depend on your parents to hear from God, or do you have your own intimate relationship with Jesus?

I invite you to pray this prayer with me:

God, please help me this week as I take the necessary steps to look back at my past in order to forgive and find healing.
I don't want to revisit old ruins again and again Lord, but instead I want you to do a deep surgical work in my heart to remove any splinter of unforgiveness, bitterness, or anger that I might have left in there.
Holy Spirit please be my guide. I can not do this on my own. Remove the layers of pride and denial so that I can see the lies that are still holding me captive. Help me to refute every one of those lies with the truth of the Bible.

God, thank you for loving me so much that you've sent your Son to die for me, set me free, and bring healing to my broken heart. I trust you with the hurts from my past. I know that only you can bring permanent restoration to my life.
Amen

DAY 2
Moms, Daughters, and Food

Most women find it hard to look back at their relationships with their moms. The first time I talked to ladies in a group about their moms, their response caught me off guard. They reacted in anger towards me for even mentioning their moms. I was baffled. When we started talking more about it and looked into the reason some of them responded so strongly, we found that many of us had this in common: Being women ourselves, we feel a deep loyalty to our moms. Even though we may have been hurt or negatively influenced by them, it is not easy for us to dig in this almost sacred ground.

I pushed the ladies in that group to talk more about the connection they felt with their mothers. One lady mentioned that she felt as if she was a part of her mother, and that looking critically at her mother would be to put herself under a microscope as well.
I think this is very true for most of us. Not only do we share genetic makeup with our moms, but they were our first female role models and laid the foundation in our formative years of what it means to be a woman and how to treat our own bodies. We also end up walking the same path as we grow older as far as dealing with various women's issues such as PMS, pregnancy, childbirth, marriage, raising kids, being a single mom, or facing challenges in the corporate world. Somewhere along the path of life we start to understand many of our mother's pressures and rationalize many of her faults.

A friend who lost her mom to cancer told me that it was incredibly hard for her to have to look back. She said it felt as if she was dishonoring her mother's legacy, and yet she knew in her heart that her mom would have wanted her to find healing. It is not selfish at all to let Jesus heal this broken area of our lives, because if we heal we also bring healing to the generations before and after us. Every woman who stops and takes care of herself and finds healing also gives this gift to her mom and her daughters.

The biggest challenge in all of this is that in judging our mothers we are essentially judging ourselves. Thinking about the pain they caused us, would be to think about the pain we are causing. Asking them to change would require us to change, and forgiving them would give us the opportunity to forgive ourselves as well. So to look back at our relationships with our mothers is truly bitter sweet. So much good can come of it, but it will be difficult before it gets better. Before it can truly heal us, it will hurt to look back, and yet, healing can not come any other way.
One final word on this: Your animosity toward this subject may be an indicator that you need to dig a little. I found that women who don't have hidden pain in this area don't mind thinking and talking about it at all. It usually hurts or scares us, because there is something there.

Mom's example

Let's take a look at moms and food:
Children learn primarily by what we model and not so much by what we say. Hence the expressions: "teach by example" or "practice what you preach". That which your mom modeled through her eating habits, physical activity, dieting behaviors, and body image influenced you greatly. The shocking part is that these influences start at a very early age. Just as a little girl likes to put on Mommy's shoes and jewelry, she "tries on" Mom's way of eating, taking care of herself, and talking about herself.

There are two sides to this coin: The child who sees her mom over-eat and watch TV frequently is at risk, but the one who sees her mom obsess about calories and skipping meals, is also in grave danger of developing an eating disorder. **We sometimes make the mistake, I know I did, of thinking that our children don't see, because they don't say anything. Yet one day you might find them act just like you, because they did see, and they internalized this as the correct way to behave towards food and their bodies.**

Because girls are usually more sensitive than boys, they are especially at risk when they hear their moms talk about their own bodies in derogatory terms. They can easily project their mother's words on their own bodies: *"If she think she's fat and ugly then I must be fat and ugly too."* Girls also tend to pick up on nonverbal cues, such as: Not taking care of our bodies and ignoring its needs for healthy food, exercise, rest, and restoration in God's presence. If they see you work from dawn till dusk, never resting, never praying, and hardly eating, they will find it extremely hard to take care of their own bodies.

Pleasing Mom

All girls live to please their moms. We have an overwhelming yearning for them to see us, and to approve of how we look and act. A lady in one of my groups told us how she struggled to let go of her mother's approval. Her mom had physically abused her into her teenage years, and she was still verbally abusing her as an adult, yet, she couldn't stay away from her mother or be assertive about what she needed.

This ties in with the most basic need that every child has: To be loved and taken care of by his or her mother. She is the first person we encounter, the first one we depend on for survival, and the first one we look to for love and affirmation. If this is withheld from a child, it causes deep seated emotional problems. Like my friend, a child who has been deprived of basic necessities, might keep going back to the one who was responsible for the pain, always looking and hoping to find something. So how could she stop this unhealthy attachment? She has to let go of the picture she created in her mind of the perfect mother and face reality. She has to work through the pain and the process of grieving her lost childhood, and ask God to help her forgive and let go of unrealistic expectations. I know I make it sound so simple but it never is. **If you find yourself in a situation such as this, I want to urge you to get the help of a Christian counselor and attend classes that can teach you to put up clear boundaries.**

FIRST: Let go of the "perfect mother"
Many of us walk around with a perfect ideal of a mother in our heads. To be free from the pain surrounding that ideal we have to face reality: There is no such thing as a perfect mother. Mothers are just human: They make mistakes, they hurt themselves and their children, they control, they abandon, they sin, and they can even love too much.
The bottom line: They usually do the best they can with the circumstances they have. As long as we keep wanting our mother to be a "real mother" or be a "decent grandma", we are still imposing our ideas of the "perfect mother" on her. It is too much to handle for any human being. You can not be the perfect daughter and she can not be the perfect mom. Just let it go! This doesn't mean you have to let her hurt you. You can decide what you can handle and how much. Let her live her life, but don't let her control yours. If your mom never accepted the "not so good" parts of your personality, but always pushed you to perfection, you might expect the same of her. It's time to let each other off the hook. Life is too short to try to be perfect. It takes an enormous amount of energy, time, and money to chase after perfection, just to realize in the end that it was only a phantom. By accepting this reality, we also let ourselves off the hook. We can relax and stop trying to be perfect at mothering. We can never do everything right. We will hurt our children without meaning to or even knowing that we did. But by letting them know that the perfect mother does not exist, we free them from the burden of unmet expectations.

SECOND: Let go of the "perfect daughter"
The perfect daughter is an unattainable image that Satan uses to keep us in bondage. If we keep hanging on to the illusion of being a perfect daughter, and becoming the one that has our mother's unwavering approval, we will never get rid of our food struggles. All this stress of trying to be someone other than yourself needs an outlet, and food or starvation provides exactly that.

Here are some steps for you to say goodbye to the perfect mother and daughter image that you might have been hanging onto over the years. Please copy these points to your journal so they can really resonate with you.

- Let go of the expectations you've put on your mom
- Let go of the high standards you've placed on yourself to be the perfect mother
- Accept the fact that you and your mom are both human
- Let go of the fantasy about a perfect mom-and-daughter relationship
- Relax and enjoy the relationship you have with your mom, even though it's not perfect
- Accept the fact that she's made some mistakes with you, and some of that could have played a part in your eating disorder
- Accept the fact that she might make some more mistakes
- Face the fact that you might have made similar mistakes with your kids and that its not the end of the world either
- Be honest with yourself and your children about your own humanity and ask their forgiveness when you hurt them
- Stop trying to be the perfect daughter, it is unattainable and exhausting
- Stop feeling responsible for your mom, she is an adult, let her make her own decisions and bear her own consequences
- Tell your mom what your needs are and how much you can do for her

- Forgiveness is the key that keeps families together, start asking God to help you forgive your mom for hurting you

Before we end our discussion on moms I want to specifically encourage those ladies whose moms were absent or abusive. If you've never experienced the tender care of a mother, and you feel that it left a gaping hole in you, then I have good news: **God can give you that nurturing love you've never had. Did you know that God has all the qualities that we need from both our mother and father?** Take a look at these verses where God's love is also compared to the loving nurture of a mother:

Isaiah 49:15 (NIV)
Can a mother forget the baby at her breast and have no compassion on the child she has borne? Though she may forget, I will not forget you!
Isaiah 66:13 (NIV)
As a mother comforts her child, so will I comfort you
Matthew 23:37 (NIV)
O Jerusalem, Jerusalem, you who kill the prophets and stone those sent to you, how often I have longed to gather your children together, as a hen gathers her chicks under her wings, but you were not willing

Please remember to reach out for help and support if you feel overwhelmed or deeply impacted by this week's material.

I invite you to pray this prayer with me:

Lord Jesus, thank you for opening my eyes to denial surrounding the relationship with my mom. Please help me to deal with habits and behaviors surrounding my eating that I might have picked up from my mom and continued in my own family.

I know that it's time to let go of my need to be the perfect daughter. Please help me to also let my mom off the hook, by letting go of any expectations I might have had surrounding her.

Thank you Jesus that you came to heal my broken heart, also in the area surrounding my relationship with my mom. I surrender those broken places to you today and ask you to heal me and help me extend forgiveness to my mom.

Thank you that according to your Word you will never forget me even though my mom might have forgotten me. Thank you that you are always ready to comfort me, as a mother comforts her child.
Amen

DAY 3
Dads and Little Girls

There is a big correlation between a girl's self image and her relationship with her dad. Our dads are the first male figures in our lives and the way they behave towards us play a huge role in how we see ourselves.

A dad's comments can have a profound impact on his daughter, and his deeds, whether good or bad can shape the way she sees herself. Now if you've had a loving dad who affirmed you, complimented you, and instructed you in the Word of God, then you are one of the rare ones out there who probably do not struggle with a low self image.
The reality is that most women did not have this positive experience. We live in a society where dads are emotionally distant or absent all together. In a staggering number of instances dads are also physically, mentally, or sexually abusive. All of this wreak havoc on the heart of a little girl.
It can cause her to believe the lie that she has no value, that she is not worthy of love and respect, and that no decent man would ever want her. Research has shown that negative comments from male family members such as dads or brothers can cause a girl to start dieting at a very young age, even if it was just meant as "teasing".

Why some Dads Leave, Neglect or Abuse

I believe that Satan especially target the men in our society because they are the appointed heads of their homes, and they represent God the Father to their families here on earth. They are supposed to love, protect, and care for their families. The enemy is always trying to get dads to abdicate their God given position, so that he can wreak havoc in the lives of the women and children involved. He uses things such as work pressure, luring pleasures, temptation, divorce, suicide, depression, violence, addiction, incarceration, and abuse to remove husbands and fathers from the scene.

These absent fathers leave behind emotionally shattered women and vulnerable and confused kids. Children usually believe that they are to blame for their dads' absence and most of the time their moms are not able to refute these lies, because of their own brokenness and preoccupation with fighting for survival.

The enemy will use vulnerable times of pain to plant lies in the heart of a little girl:

Let's refute some of those lies with the truth of God's Word. Would you please make the appropriate note cards for your specific situation.

When Dad was Absent

THE LIE:
I'm to blame for my Dad's absence. There must be something wrong with me: The only way I can have value is if I change my APPEARANCE and PERFORMANCE

THE TRUTH:
Your dad failed you! He failed to love and protect you, and he failed to tell you the truth that you have value as a person, as a woman, just the way you are right now

1 Samuel 16:7b (AMP):
For the Lord sees not as man sees; for man looks on the outward appearance, but the Lord looks on the heart.

Psalms 139: 13-16 (AMP)
For You did form my inward parts; You did knit me together in my mother's womb. I will confess and praise You for You are fearful and wonderful and for the awful wonder of my birth! Wonderful are Your works, and that my inner self knows right well.
My frame was not hidden from You when I was being formed in secret [and] intricately and curiously wrought [as if embroidered with various colors] in the depths of the earth [a region of darkness and mystery].
Your eyes saw my unformed substance, and in Your book all the days [of my life] were written before ever they took shape, when as yet there was none of them.

When Dad Left

A girl whose dad left, for whatever reason, might feel deep rejection and abandonment. Fear of rejection can easily become the driving force of her life. She will work feverishly to avoid rejection by trying to please everyone around her, especially the men in her life.

THE LIE:
I have to do anything to keep my man happy or he will leave me

THE TRUTH:
I am not supposed to keep other people happy. This is a waste of time, because they will not stay happy, and I can not serve both God and men.

Galatians 1:10 (AMP)
Now am I trying to win the favor of men, or of God? Do I seek to please men? If I were still seeking popularity with men, I should not be a bond servant of Christ (the Messiah).

When Dad was Emotionally Distant

A girl whose dad was emotionally distant may have many unanswered questions. "Was I not pretty enough? Was it something I did? Was he ashamed of me? Why could he never give me a hug? Why would he never talk to me or look at me? Why could he never take me with him?"

It is really tragic because a father's emotional distant behavior has to do with his own inadequacies, and background, NOT with the behavior of his children. However, many children take this as a sign that they are not good enough or important enough to be noticed. A little girl might believe the lie that she is not worthy of a man's affection, and as a result start chasing after the attention and affirmation of men. She might become flirtatious and promiscuous and even trade sex for a speck of love, acceptance, or attention.

Some girls might try to get their dad's attention by working very hard in school and their careers, or excelling in sports. In the same way they might try to do everything perfectly to gain dad's respect or approval. All of this is an accident waiting to happen. These "perfect" girls can not maintain the high stress and their bodies will eventually start to rebel against the harsh treatment. Binging can easily become an outlet for the pent up pain, or starvation can be used to gain some control of a runaway life.

THE LIE:
I need to do whatever it takes to obtain the attention and approval of men

THE TRUTH:
God loves me just as I am. He is my Father and He has unconditional acceptance and love for me. He can offer me more than the best earthly father could ever give me.

Psalm 86:15
But you, Lord, are a compassionate and gracious God, slow to anger, abounding in love and faithfulness.

Romans 8:38-39
For I am convinced that neither death nor life, neither angels nor demons, neither the present nor the future, nor any powers, neither height nor depth, nor anything else in all creation, will be able to separate us from the love of God that is in Christ Jesus our Lord.

When Dad was Abusive

This is one of the most devastating things that can happen to the heart of a little girl. The one who was supposed to protect her and give her confidence and strength, robbed her of it all. So much damage occurs in the life of a girl who has been hurt in this horrific way.
Her view of men might be so distorted that she turns to a lesbian lifestyle. She might believe the lie of the enemy that no man will ever be able to understand her or meet her emotional and

physical needs. Others who have been sexual abused may go the opposite way and become promiscuous, always trying to get the attention of men, unable to say no.

We have already touched on this topic in Week 6. Please go have another look at the notecard you made to refute the enemy's lies with the truth of the Bible in this area.

Many women who have been abused by their fathers blame themselves, and still try to please their dads after everything they have gone through. These girls sometimes use perfectionism to keep external things in order; trying to hide the chaos they feel inside.

I strongly urge you to seek counsel if you have been abused. Abuse leaves us shattered, but God can pick up our broken pieces and create beauty from it. He works through His Word, the Holy Spirit, and the body of Christ (the church). Please reach out for support, counseling, and prayer.

Finding Hope and Healing

The only way to fill the emptiness your dad left in your life, is to accept the love of your everlasting Father. God is the perfect Father, however, if we were abused, rejected, or hurt it might be difficult for us to accept or even understand this. I believe this is why God gave us the Bible. In His Word we discover the character of our true Father. We also learn that He created us, that He knows us like no one else does, and that He will never leave us nor forsake us.

Please make time to read the Bible. Purchase a Bible study, or better yet, join a women's Bible study at your church. This way you will get to know the Father heart of God, while also having the support and encouragement of other women.

Another way to get to know God's heart is to simply talk to Him. God created us to have communion with Him. It might feel weird at first, but just imagine the most compassionate, loving Father, waiting for you to talk to Him, every moment of every day. You have His undivided attention and nothing you could say could ever make Him love you less. He will not get angry or interrupt you. He will not get bored or be rude to you. He will not humiliate or discourage you. He really listens and speaks through His Word with more wisdom than any earthly father could ever possess. The depth of your sorrow, your pain, or your addiction will not overwhelm Him or scare Him off. He will not turn away from your raw emotion or feel uncomfortable with your sensitive feminine side. He made you, He knows how you work, He knows what you need, and He knows your future.

I challenge you again to wait in His presence. There you will find rest for your soul, wisdom for your problems, unspeakable joy, and you will be changed for good. There is nothing that changes us like a word directly from God. People can try and tell you something for years, but when you hear it from God, you finally get it.

Please move away from the faulty thinking that God is just like your earthly dad. God is not a man, He doesn't have faults or issues.

📖 Please look up the following verses about God the Father and write it in the space provided:

Numbers 23:19

_____
_____
_____

2 Corinthians 1:3

_____
_____
_____

 Please read the following verse out loud: Romans 8:15 (NIV)

For you did not receive a spirit that makes you a slave again to fear, but you received the Spirit of son ship. And by him we cry, 'Abba, Father'

This word _Abba_, which is used to describe the father heart of God, translates as Daddy, a tender word used by little children. This word evokes the feelings of intimacy and security. God does not only want to be a father figure to you, but a Daddy who will pick you up on His lap, dry off your tears, and listen to the heart's desire of His little girl.

You, my dearest friend, are God's little girl.

I invite you to pray this prayer with me:

God, please help me understand and accept that You are my Abba Father, even if I never had the example of what that means.

Thank You that You are compassionate and gracious, slow to anger, abounding in love and faithfulness. Teach me through Your Word and the Holy Spirit how to trust You more and grow in relationship with You as my everlasting Father. I need Your wisdom, Your guidance, Your strength, and Your love. I believe that all these things that have been missing from my life can be found in You.

Teach me to wait in Your presence, climb up on Your lap, and share my heart openly with You. Help me to make my time with You top priority. I know that in Your presence there is fullness of joy (Psalm 16:11), there is healing for my broken heart (Isaiah 61), and there is permanent change (2 Corinthians 3:18).

Thank you for being my Abba, my Daddy. Amen

DAY 4
The Path of Forgiveness

Extending Forgiveness

Do not think for one minute that people who committed atrocities will go scot-free. God will personally avenge our broken hearts. Take a look at these verses:

Romans 12:19 (NIV)
Do not take revenge, my dear friends, but leave room for God's wrath, for it is written: "It is mine to avenge; I will repay," says the Lord.

Matthew 18:7 (NIV)
"Woe to the world because of the things that cause people to sin! Such things must come, but woe to the man through whom they come!"

Forgiveness is not for our perpetrators, it is for us. We need to forgive for the following reasons:

- If we don't forgive we grieve the Holy Spirit, whom we desperately need to guide and lead us, every day of our lives (Ephesians 4:30-32)
- If we don't forgive others, we drive a wedge between us and God. The Bible says that God doesn't forgive us if we don't forgive others (Matthew 6:14-15)
- According to the Bible we give Satan a foothold, or a standing place, in our lives if we don't forgive (2 Corinthians 2:10-11)

Please look up 2 Corinthians 2:10-11 and write it in the space below

_____

_____

_____

_____

Please add the following note card to your collection, and read it daily if you still struggle to forgive your perpetrator

Holy Spirit, I repent of any sin in my life that might GRIEVE you. Please open my eyes especially to UNFORGIVENESS so that I can repent and keep God's forgiveness flowing in my own life.

Ephesians 4:30-32 (AMP)
And do not grieve the Holy Spirit of God, with whom you were sealed for the day of redemption. Get rid of all bitterness, rage and anger, brawling and slander, along with every form of malice. Be kind and compassionate to one another, forgiving each other, just as in Christ God forgave you

Matthew 6:14-15 (NIV)
For if you forgive men when they sin against you, your heavenly Father will also forgive you. But if you do not forgive men their sins, your Father will not forgive your sins

Believe me, the last thing I want to do is pretend that to forgive is easy. I realize that for some people this is an extremely difficult thing to do because of the deep wounds that have been inflicted.

Let me urge you again though that to hold onto that hurt and anger, is to keep yourself bound to the person who hurt you, forever. If you forgive, you are not doing you perpetrator a favor, you are cutting yourself loose so that you can live again.

Forgiveness is a supernatural step in faith that starts with our willingness. **I believe that it is impossible for us to forgive in our own flesh, but the Holy Spirit who lives in us can empower us to forgive, so that we can be free from this stronghold in our lives, forever.**

Please take a moment to talk to God about this person that you can not yet forgive. Write your own personal prayer and ask the Holy Spirit to help you forgive.

_____

_____

_____

_____

_____

Finding Forgiveness

We came before God in repentance many times during the past weeks. Please let the Holy Spirit search your heart again for areas where anger, bitterness, and unforgiveness toward your parents or perpetrators caused you to sin.

- Maybe you feel that you have already made the same mistakes with your children that your parents made with you.
- Maybe you feel that you have given your children issues with food through your own example
- Maybe you feel like a total failure as a mother
- Maybe you feel that you didn't honor your parents or didn't act in an honorable way towards them. This might be especially difficult if they passed away, and you can not ask their forgiveness or change things now.

There is something you can do about it: You can repent from your sin before God, accept His forgiveness, and also forgive yourself. You can not help anyone, especially not yourself, by staying in this pit of guilt that the enemy built for you. Once we've repented of the things we have done wrong God promises to remove our sin as far away from Him as the east is from the west (Psalms 103:12).

You have set your feet on a journey to turn your back on idols and put God first in your life. By letting God change you, you are also paving a different path for your children: You are teaching by example. If the enemy comes to you with guilt and shame, and he will always try, then stand against his lies with the truth of God's Word. You are no longer guilty, you don't have to feel ashamed anymore. Remember Romans 8:1 (NIV): *Therefore, there is now no condemnation for those who are in Christ Jesus.*

I invite you to pray this prayer with me:

Lord Jesus, please help me forgive the people who have sinned against me. I cannot do this in my own strength, but I believe that it is possible through the power of the Holy Spirit who lives in me. I want to be free from the cords of unforgiveness that bound me to my perpetrators, please help me to release them to Your judgement, Lord.

God, I ask You to also forgive me for the sin I have committed as a result of their sin. Forgive me for the anger and bitterness I have harbored and for picking up idols to help me cope with it all. I repent from my sin today, and choose to set my feet on a new path, free from guilt and shame.

Thank You that You are giving me a second chance to forgive, change, and positively affect my children and the generations who will come after me. I am so amazed at Your love for me, God. Thank You for forgiving me.

Amen

DAY 5
A Brighter Future

You can make a difference: You can change the future for your children. I've once heard it said that it takes only ONE person to change the course of a whole family line. Will you be that person who changes the destiny of the generations after you?

Let's talk for a minute about changing eating habits in your immediate family:
- There is a very thin line between encouraging your kids to eat healthy, and making their weight a big issue. You do not want to jump in and rock the boat too much, especially if you're dealing with teenagers who already have unhealthy eating patterns
- According to experts in this field, the best thing you can do for your kids, to prevent or help with food issues, is to LEAD BY EXAMPLE

We do ourselves a huge favor if we start to take care of our own bodies. However this is also the greatest gift we can give our children. They learn by observing and copying what we do.

We have talked a lot about our habits, and if you follow a healthy food plan, exercise regularly, drink enough water, and make time to rest, you will most definitely pass these habits on to your children. Please don't give up if this doesn't happen overnight; they are waiting to see if you are for real. If you stick to your guns they will come around eventually.

There is another issue that we need to teach our children: THE TRUTH about God and about them. They need to know that we as parents are only human, and that where we lack because of our vulnerabilities, they will always have God as their ULTIMATE PARENT.

Again, the only way to teach this to your children is to believe the truth about your God and about you, and live it yourself.

The Truth about God: He is Enough

 Please look up Psalm 27:10 and write it in the space below:

_____

_____

- **There is no one like our God:** "Remember the former things, those of long ago; I am God, and there is no other; I am God, and there is none like me." (Isaiah 46:9)

- **God is a righteous judge:** God does not ask anything of us that we can not do through the power of the Holy Spirit who lives in us. God is a loving God, but He is also a righteous judge. We bear the consequences if we keep disobeying God (Gal 6:7-8)

- **God is waiting for you:** Like the father of the prodigal son, He is looking and waiting for you to return to His loving embrace, even though you failed miserably (Luke 15:11-32)

- **God knows everything about you:** He counted the hairs on your head (Luke 12:7)

- **God is ever present:** His eyes are on you and He's attentive to your cry (Psalm 34:15). He never sleeps nor slumbers (Psalm 121:4)

- **God fights for you:** He says that He will fight for you and avenge you (Romans 12:19). Jesus has already slain your worst enemy on the cross of Calvary.

- **God has compassion on you:** He wants to shelter you under His wing (Psalm 36:7). He cares about your emotions. You can cry on your Father's shoulder and He will comfort you and lead you through dark times. He will keep you safe in His hands while you grieve and heal (Isaiah 43:2)

The Truth About the Daughter of the King

Please look up these truths about you in the Bible. This is your real identity. Please write it in your journal or put it up somewhere we you can see it daily.

1. I am fearfully and wonderfully made (Psalm 139:14)

2. I am regarded with numerous precious thoughts (Ps 40:5, Ps 139:17)

3. I am loved (John 3:16 ,17:23)

4. I am more than a conqueror (Rom 8:37)

5. I am bought with a price (1 Cor 6:20)

6. I am a new creation (2 Cor 5:17)

7. I am chosen (John 15:16, 1 Peter 2:9)

8. I am royalty (1 Pet 2:9)

9. I am holy (1 Pet 2:9)

10. I am a child of God (1 Peter 2:10)

11. I can do all things through Christ who gives me strength (Phil 4:13)

What we don't seem to get is that the King of kings, the Creator of all things, the Everlasting Father DOESN'T MAKE ANY MISTAKES! He didn't make a few beautiful people, a few athletic ones, a few smart ones, and the rest were just duds that he thought "Oh well, just toss them in with the bunch". God knew exactly what He was doing when He created you and me, He knew exactly what our purpose was.

You, precious woman of God, are so valuable! Right now, just the way you are. If you and I can grasp God's love for us, we can be changed forever, and give our children a brighter future as we lead by example.

 I invite you to pray this prayer with me:

Lord Jesus, please help me to accept the fullness of Your love for me. You are enough for me, even if I've never experienced the love and acceptance of my parents. I believe that You are the ultimate parent to me and to my children.

Help me to daily refute the lies of the enemy with the truth of Your Word. I believe that You've created me with a very special purpose to glorify You. Thank You for making me aware of the fact that I have great value, not because of my appearance or performance, but because I am Your daughter.

Please help me live out this truth in a visible way by making You my top priority and taking good care of the body You've given me. Help me to do this in a consistent manner for years to come so that my example will change the course of history for my family.

God, I am so grateful that I have You as my Father, and that I no longer have to live in bondage to my past. Thank You that You sent Your son Jesus so that I can have a brighter future.

Amen

Week 11
Completing the Race

DAY 1

Keep Up Your Guard

One of the greatest lessons we can learn through our struggle with food is to think soberly about ourselves: **We should know that we can not stand alone against the enemy. In fact, taking him on alone will get us in trouble. That said, we are not helpless either, we are daughters of the King and with the Holy Spirit on our side we are more than conquerors.**

Please look up 1 Corinthians 10:12 and write it in the space below:

_____

_____

_____

Have you let your guard down in the past, after times of great victory? Please explain

_____

_____

_____

_____

As soon as God starts to work in us, some of the layers of pride and denial start to come off, we gain some control over our eating, life seems easier, and then we sometimes let our guards down. A flashing red light is when we become consumed again with ourselves and our appearance. The moment your motive for getting control of your eating is no longer to glorify God, but rather to impress others, you are playing with fire and setting yourself up for a fall. Sometimes we learn this lesson after the first fall, and sometimes it doesn't dawn on us until we fell a dozen times or more.

In the past, when I let down my guard, I would slowly but surely start to spiral downward, until I found myself back in the pit of food addiction. I describe the sequence of events below to serve as a warning to you. I trust that it will help you identify the signs early enough to pull yourself out of that nosedive:

- After some weight loss on a solid food program, I would think to myself: "This is great, at this rate I can be a totally different woman by summer. I think I will start cutting out starches all together, just to help this on a bit." **Do you see how I start to make some changes to my plan that I've initially surrendered to God?**

- After altering the plan I would stop calculating the food I ate, and also stop writing in my journal. I would think to myself "I have calculated this so many times, I know exactly how much to eat. It's a waste of time, I'll do it again tomorrow" or "I don't have to keep journaling, it's becoming a legalistic thing"

- Before I knew it a week would go by where I didn't write down what I ate, didn't write in my journal, and didn't exercise regularly. I would usually use busyness as an excuse for my slacking.

- Usually one week wouldn't make much of a difference in my weight, and I would pretty much still stay the course without too much indulgence. So at this point, instead of repenting of pride and getting back on track, I would have my aha-moment: "I must be totally there. I must finally be over my bizarre eating spree". I would wonder how on earth I could have let myself be ruled by such vulgar behavior. Maybe I never really suffered from eating disorders, maybe I should have just straightened myself out a long time ago. **Can you see how I start to believe the lies of the enemy and pride and denial creep back into my life?**

- After another week I would start to buy some of my binge food here and there. Next, I would start preparing dishes I know I have no business preparing. I would invite people over, and make plans to go dine out. All the while I would stay busy, busy, busy. I would avoid God's presence and pretend that I don't even own a Bible.

- Next I will start to make some full-fledged "binge runs" and eat some binge food in secret. I would appear happy, too happy, talking fast and loud and being silly and crazy at times, alternated by times of total depression. Everybody would comment on my funny mood and laugh, and I would laugh too, but at this point I would have already started crying on the inside, and anxiety would have lodged itself in the pit of my stomach.

- After weeks and months of this I would stand in front of my closet one morning with nothing to wear. By now I would feel bloated and tired every day, I would watch TV into the early morning hours and just fall into bed afterward. I would wake up with heartburn and a headache from a sugar and fat hang over every morning. Yet, unable to stop the cycle I would reach for coffee and doughnuts for breakfast, mixed with tears of despair.

- I would finally look up from my pit of denial and admit that I could not stop eating, that I've ignored my body and avoided God for months again, that I've isolated myself from people again, and that it all started when I let pride back in and thought I would just help God a little. I would cry out to God again, and He would stretch out His hand and help me up where I laid in the miry clay...

Do you see that every time I thought I was standing just fine on my own and that I didn't REALLY need God, I would fall? Through trial and error I've learned that this girl on her own is actually very vulnerable, but when she runs to her Father and climbs up on His lap, she can look life straight in the eye and stop being afraid.

I've learned and I am still learning that without Him I can do nothing, but with my God all things are possible. So for the rest of my days, may I get it through my thick head, there is only one place that I am truly safe: Tucked in under His wing.

 Please look up 1 Corinthians 16:13 and write it in the space below:

_____

_____

_____

You have come far, my dearest sister in Christ, but don't dare to think that you will be okay on your own. Please hear me on this one: You never want to be on your own again, it's not good, and it's not safe. Stay close to the One who loves you more than anyone, JESUS

I invite you to pray this prayer with me:

Lord Jesus, thank You for being strong for me when I am weak. Please remind me as I start to grow stronger in You, and the fruit of self control becomes evident in my life, that it's ALL YOU!

I am totally dependent on You, Holy Spirit. I surrender all of my life to Your guidance once again. Please help me every moment of every day to resist temptation and stand strong, especially in the area of food. Make me aware of pride and denial that are still hiding in the corners of my life, or that I might have picked back up again.

God, please remind me to put You first every day so that You can have full control of my life. Increase my faith to believe that the things that still seem impossible to me are totally possible with You.

Thank You for setting my feet on this journey of healing and freedom with You, God. Please help me to keep up my guard and remember that the most important thing I can do in all of this is to stay close to You, tucked in under Your wing.
Amen

DAY 2

How to Get Up When You Fall

Let me warn you that while we're still walking out our journey to freedom, and being transformed by the renewing of our minds, we may still fall. In fact, the people around us who seem so successful and have it so together have learned only ONE thing that we didn't: **How to get up quickly when they fall!**

Don't get too discouraged by this though: We most definitely start to fall less, and I'm convinced that we can reach a place where we are so fully surrendered to Jesus in every area of our lives that we no longer fall.

However, if you've just started this journey, or you're still in the process of letting the Holy Spirit renew your mind, then you will most likely still fall from time to time. In fact, in spite of great victories and years without sugar you might find yourself in front of the freezer, eating ice cream straight from the tub, when life throws you a curveball.

Now, as I've mentioned before, I do believe in miraculous healing. I believe that God can and will heal you from food addiction in an instant if He so chooses. However, if His will for you is to walk out your journey to freedom to bring you closer to Him, and create growth in your life, then I want to advise you to not live in denial, but rather arm yourself for the journey. To say **"I will never, ever, ever fall for that again"** is just setting yourself up for failure, self condemnation, guilt, and shame. In fact, striving for the "perfect" track record can become a form of bondage in itself that can keep you stuck and prevent you from moving forward to victory in Jesus.

So now to the question: How do you get up when you fall?
What is the first thing that comes to mind after you have fallen and your eating is spiraling out of control? I'm not talking about the pre-fall stage where you're still toying with a bite of this here and a morsel of that there, because at that point you might still feel that you have things under control. No, I'm talking about the flat-on-your-face-stage where you know you've once again lost all control, you binged for one week straight, all you can think of is your next meal, and you've easily gained five to ten pounds. When you hit that place, you know you're on your knees, you don't wonder anymore.

I usually experience the following emotions and thoughts after a fall: First guilt, then shame, followed by its evil twin condemnation. Next I start looking around for someone or something to

blame. In the end despair and hopelessness sweeps over me as the enemy whispers in my ear "You will never overcome this, you might as well give up."

I know all too well how intense these emotions of hopelessness can be and therefore I want to encourage you to not listen to the enemy in that place of despair. If you give up, and keep laying down, the enemy joins you there in your pit of despair. He comes and whisper all kinds of lies in your ears, and the more he talks the deeper you sink into the pit, until you can hear nothing but lies, and can not see the light of day anymore. That place where you have fallen can change into a pit of captivity that can be your home for the next few months or even years.

Here is the truth: VICTORY IS NOT FAR AWAY, BUT YOU HAVE TO ACT QUICKLY!
If we humble ourselves before God we can quickly recover from a stumble or even a fall. The enemy only wins if we believe his lies and STAY DOWN.

WHAT NOT TO DO:

1. **Don't look for a diet.** Resist the urge to go on the internet and read up for hours on the latest diets out there. You will end up eating stacks of food while trying to find a "quick-fix" that DOES NOT EXIST.
2. **Don't go over every little detail trying to figure out how it happened.** It probably happened gradually and you can not change the past. Rather spend your energy on getting up and moving forward.
3. **Don't blame your husband, your kids, your friends, a food program, or God for your fall.** The blame game will just ruin your relationships and keep you laying down longer. Rather take responsibility and repent.

WHAT TO DO: Always Get Back to Basics

1. **Come back to God FIRST.**
   REPENT of the sin you let back into your life. Then ask God to help you get up and on track again. Commit to spend time with Him first of all. It's really useless to first try and get your eating or your exercise routine back in place before repairing your relationship with God.
2. **Kick denial and pride out of your life!**
   Ask God to help you stop the denial and show you any traces of pride so you can repent from it. Also ask God again to give you true sorrow for your sin if you're not ready to lay down your idol. True sorrow about the sin that nailed Jesus to the cross will lead you back to true repentance and repair the relationship between you and God.
3. **Tell family and friends who have supported you in the past the truth about your fall, and ask them to pray with you as you're getting back up.**
   Ask them to especially pray for you during the next 21 days as you again surrender to God and resist the enemy (James 4:7), while ridding your body of addictive substances

4. **Bring your pain before God and let Him search your heart.**
   God wants to restore you and heal you if you've gone through a trial or a difficult time. Open your heart to Him again and start writing in your journal. Write down your deep heart's desires again, and surrender these to God.

5. **Start building up your body again.**
   Get away from the diet mentality where you promise yourself every morning that you will start tomorrow (you've probably been doing that again for a while without any success). Rather start adding some water, fresh fruit, and vegetables to everything else you're eating RIGHT NOW. Show up for exercise today. It doesn't have to be perfect, you just need to show up.

6. **Get your healthy food plan up and running again.**
   Keep to your menus and shopping lists, or start a program that has it all in place for you. Don't listen to the enemy's lies that you will now be deprived and you should start binging before the diet. Remember, a healthy program is not a diet.

7. **Get a handle on your thought life again.**
   Start to read your note cards every morning when you wake up so you can hear the truth of God with your own ears. Keep these around the house, especially the kitchen, and keep reading the truth throughout the day.

8. **Use your weapons of warfare (Ephesians 6:10-18).**
   Give praise to God during the day and put on the full armor of God to stand against the enemy. Put some worship music on when you feel tempted and start praising Him. Remember that prayer and time in the Word are also weapons at your disposal to overthrow strongholds (2 Cor 10:4-5). Expect temptation and be prepared to resist. Run to your room again during those first days and just cry your heart out before God when you just want to give in. You will even experience grief again because you formed a new attachment to the food. Just go through these emotions, but let God into it, let the Holy Spirit counsel you and let Jesus heal your heart.

9. **Forgive yourself and others who contributed to this fall.**
   Move away from the pit of despair and keep moving forward on this journey. The faster you get up and forgive yourself and others, the easier all of this will be.

10. **Don't see this as failure, but see it as schooling, lessons learned to be wiser for the rest of the journey.** There might be more times of falling, don't be afraid of it though, instead make up your mind that you are completing the race, no matter what.

Let me remind you once again of this verse in Proverbs 24:16 *"for though a righteous man falls seven times, he rises again, but the wicked are brought down by calamity"*

Righteous men and women may fall, but their victory lies in GETTING UP!

 Please look up Psalm 40:2-3 and write it in the space below:

_____
_____
_____
_____

Did you see that your story of being pulled out from the pit will not only bring joy to your life, but it will also spill over as a testimony to others and affect their lives? _____

Can you think of people in your life who may be touched when they see that, even though you fall, you keep calling out to God to pick you up and help you move forward?

_____
_____

I invite you to pray this prayer with me:

Lord Jesus, I'm so sorry that I have turned to the idol of food, starvation, and purging again. Please forgive me. I do *not* want to be mastered by food or any other behavior. I repent from my sin and surrender all of my life again to You this day.

Please help me to get up from where I've fallen. I believe Your Word that I am more than a conqueror through Christ, and that I don't have to be defined by this slip-up. I take every lie of the enemy captive and refute it with the truth of Your Word. You, God, are my strength and You will lift me up from this miry clay and set my feet on the Rock, Jesus.

I commit to come back to Your Word and Your presence TODAY.
Amen

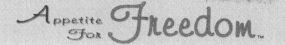

DAY 3

Never Quit!

This journey to freedom can be long for some of us, and we might feel tempted along the way to throw in the towel and quit. You need FAITH to keep going.

At some point during my struggle with food I started taking a hold of God for my deliverance. I started believing with my whole heart that God could set me free from this eating disorder: I knew from His Word that He is able and willing to do so and I took the promise as my own. I also learned from Hebrews 1:6 that without faith it is impossible to please God. I wanted faith and I started asking God to give me more faith and forgive my unbelief.

 **Please read Hebrews 11:1 out loud:**
Now faith is the assurance (the confirmation, the title deed) of the things [we] hope for, being the proof of things **[we] do not see** and the conviction of their reality [faith perceiving as real fact what is not revealed to the senses] (AMP)

Did you grow in faith during the last 12 Weeks? Do you believe that God can and wants to set you free from your food struggle, even though you might not actually see it happening this very minute?

_____

Submit to God's time table
I want to remind you again though that faith is not a way to manipulate God. We can not tell God when and where we want things done and if it doesn't happen that way, we lose our faith and trust in God. We have to remember that He is sovereign and that He does things for a reason and with our best interest at heart. So His timing in all of this is also for our sake. We can't see the future. In fact, we can see a very small piece of the big picture. So we would be wise to believe that God will set us free, and also to believe that we can trust Him with the timetable.

Please look up Isaiah 55:8-9 and write it in the space below:

_____
_____
_____
_____

Have you submited to God's timetable for your healing and freedom yet?

_____

According to the above verses God's ways and thoughts are higher than ours. Have you considered that He knows your future, and that He knows what is needed to equip you for it? Have you considered that a quick miracle might not be God's best for you? Please explain

_____
_____

Let me ask you this: Have you considered that God might even allow some of the times you fell along this journey to bring you to a place of healing and freedom?

_____

I get this question a lot: Was it God or the enemy who caused me to fall?
We've learned in Week 7 that we are tempted by the enemy, the world, and our own flesh. The enemy will tempt you in the areas where you still have weakness, and use these slip ups to discourage you. The Word says that in the last days he will try to wear out the saints. Satan knows that by tripping us up, and by sending waves of busyness and temptation our way, he might get us to fall and even stay down. However, I also believe God allows it to happen sometimes as part of our journey to freedom. He knows that we will destroy our own lives if we keep those desires alive. So He gives us an opportunity to hurt a little, so that we will recognize that we still have sin in our lives and repent, before it hurts a lot. **God will never allow sin to remain in our lives, because that sin nailed Jesus to the cross, and it can cost us eternal life.**

Please read Romans 2:6-8 (NLT) below
He will judge everyone according to what they have done. **He will give eternal life to those who keep on doing good,** seeking after the glory and honor and immortality that God offers. But he will pour out his anger and wrath on those who live for themselves, who refuse to obey the truth and instead live lives of wickedness. (Emphasis mine)

To whom, according to this verse, will God offer eternal life?

_____
_____

The topic of "not giving up" can be found throughout Scripture. We are admonished that in order to be overcomers, reap a harvest, and obtain eternal life we should NEVER QUIT reaching for righteousness!

Please read Revelation 3:12 (AMP) below to inspire you to become an overcomer:
He who overcomes (is victorious), I will make him a pillar in the sanctuary of My God; he shall never be put out of it or go out of it, and I will write on him the name of My God and the name of the city of My God, the new Jerusalem, which descends from My God out of heaven, and My own new name.

Now read Revelation 12:10-11 and answer the following questions:
Who is the accuser of the saints?

_____

How do we overcome according to this verse?

_____

_____

Did you see that we overcome by the blood of Jesus, and by the WORD OF OUR TESTIMONY!

Start telling the world around you what God has **already** done for you.
- Did He help you to forgive?
- Did the Word came alive to you?
- Did He reveal Himself in a way to you that you have never seen or felt before?

Precious woman of God, I know you have something to share, don't keep it to yourself and don't let the enemy rob you from your testimony by telling you that you're not totally free yet. Remember: Satan is a liar. In this passage we see that he is also the accuser of the saints, the one who keeps loading shame and guilt on us. However, you don't have to believe the lies anymore. Keep telling others about God's goodness.

Here are some important questions for you to consider:
What if you decided to quit this time and you stop one "getting-up" short of the victory?
What if you decide today to get up one more time, and this is _your time_?
- _The time_ when you break through the last barrier
- _The time_ when you fully surrender and let God rip the sin of idolatry out of your heart
- _The time_ that you will tell others about for the rest of your life...

I invite you to pray this prayer with me:

Lord Jesus, I don't want to stop one "getting-up" short of victory. I know that according to Your Word You have good plans for me, plans to prosper me and not to harm me, plans to give me hope and a future (Jeremiah 29:11).
Help me to fully submit to Your timetable, and to trust that You are working everything for good in my life. I don't want to lean on my own understanding in these matters, Lord, because I can so easily get discouraged while I only see a small piece of the puzzle. Help me to trust You with all my heart, and know that You work out my life for me in the most glorious way.
I know that freedom and healing is on the agenda for my life, according to Your Word. However, it means nothing if this journey doesn't rid me of my sin and doesn't teach me how to surrender my whole life to You.

I desire more of You, Lord. Please help me to keep searching after You with all my heart. Amen

DAY 4

Two Crucial Points

If there are only two things you take away from our 12 weeks together then I hope it will be the two very important issues of SURRENDER AND CONSISTENCY.

Surrender

We spoke a lot about surrender: All the knowledge in the world isn't worth much if you don't surrender to God by actually doing what He tells you to do. **True surrender produces true obedience.** Just hearing the Word and going through programs like this doesn't mean anything if we don't OBEY and put it into action.

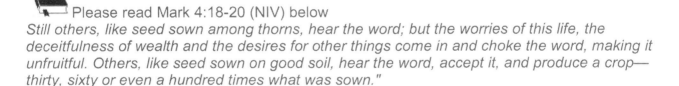 Please read Mark 4:18-20 (NIV) below

Still others, like seed sown among thorns, hear the word; but the worries of this life, the deceitfulness of wealth and the desires for other things come in and choke the word, making it unfruitful. Others, like seed sown on good soil, hear the word, accept it, and produce a crop—thirty, sixty or even a hundred times what was sown."

According to these verses, what happened to the seed sown among thorns?

_____
_____

Did you see actual fruit in your life from the Word of God sown in your heart during these past weeks? Please explain

_____
_____
_____
_____

Consistency

Consistently working at something produces great results. Nothing in life that is truly worth having comes without consistency. Seriously, think about it: A happy marriage, a well behaved child, a successful business, a degree, a sports trophy, a promotion, a beautiful garden, a healthy body, a strong relationship with God, a life free from addiction, they're all fruit of consistency.

Give yourself a year, starting today, to be consistent and surrender to God. You can not see the true impact of all the habits you've picked up in our 12 weeks together, over a short period of time. Rather commit to go one year without diets or dangerous methods, but rather

use a food plan that can build up your body and rid you consistently of excess weight. You can do it! The enemy will ALWAYS try and tell you that one more day wouldn't make a difference. This is one of the biggest lies the enemy uses in our lives. It is all of those days that supposedly didn't matter (count together) that got you to this place. **Don't fall for it any longer. Write this down everywhere in your house as a reminder: THIS MOMENT MATTERS!**

Please read Hebrews 12:11 below:

"No discipline seems to be joyful for the present, but painful, nevertheless, afterwards it yields the peaceable fruit of righteousness to those who have been trained by it."

According to this verse, what can we expect **at first** when we crucify our flesh and submit it to God?

_____

What can we expect if we keep doing it **consistently**?

_____

_____

How are you doing?

Let's look for a minute at where you're at after our 12 weeks together:

Have you had great victory during the 12 Weeks? Please explain

_____
_____
_____
_____
_____
_____
_____

If you have made great strides and feel that you are totally healed from this food struggle then I rejoice with you! All the glory to God, He is the *only One* who can truly set us free. I felt this joy of deliverance when God set me free from bulimia. I had to work at it, make no mistake, but when it was over I just knew it was over, and I haven't looked back for many years. It was a clean break with purging and I can not thank the Lord enough for that.

I want to encourage you to share your testimony. God wants to use you to help others in this struggle. Pray about it. You might want to start up a group like this at your church, allowing God to use your victory for His glory.

Appetite For *Freedom*

218

Did you not quite receive the breakthrough that you were hoping for? Please explain

_____
_____
_____
_____
_____

Let me encourage you with this verse
Philippians 1:6 (NIV)
"Being confident of this, that he who began a good work in you will carry it on to completion until the day of Christ Jesus."

My heart truly aches for you, my dearest friend, who may not feel quite so blessed, but rather discouraged to be at the end of this study, yet you're still not free. I believe that God has kept some of this pain and disappointment in my life, in the form of compulsive overeating, so that I can still relate to you and encourage you while I am writing this. I have come a long way with my food struggle, but I can not say that I am 100% free from overeating. I can say that I don't fall often and that I get up quickly these days, but it is not quite the same as with bulimia where I had a clean break and never looked back to binging and purging (for more than 10 years now)

So please let me say this to you: It's okay. We all have different times of healing, because we have different layers that need to come off. On top of that: not all those layers just peel off like onion layers, some need to be literally chiseled off by the Master Sculptor. Are you already asking yourself: "What did I miss?" Please trust me on this: If you went through the whole course and applied the principles to your life (not perfectly, just to the best of your ability) then you did great and God changed exactly the things in you that needed changing in these 12 Weeks.

However, if you think that this can not possibly be *it*, then you are right, it isn't! This is just the beginning of your journey. I got you started but I believe that the Holy Spirit will take you beyond human knowledge and understanding. I truly believe that when we're at our wits end, we finally surrender it all to God. I am excited to know what God is going to do in you. He is willing and able to set you free as you keep surrendering to Him.

Please go through the material again if you need to. You may want to join another group, or just go through it by yourself. God's timing plays a role in all of this for sure and I am convinced that He led you to this program and that He began a great work in you, even if you can not quite see it.

Keep the faith girl, and please don't give up! You are actually being changed a little bit every day, into "a planting of the Lord, for the display of His splendor" (Isaiah 61:2)

© Copyright 2012. Surrendered Hearts Ministries: www.SurrenderedHearts.com

✝ Would you again today commit to do the two most important things: SURRENDER TO GOD and do it CONSISTENTLY. Remember, you may not be in control of your eating just yet, but you are in control of your time. Surrendering your time to God is a step of obedience. Please write your own prayer of commitment to God in the space below

_____

_____

_____

_____

_____

 I invite you to pray this prayer with me:

Thank You Jesus that You will complete the good work You've started in me and bring freedom and healing to my world.

Please give me more faith so that I will keep fighting the good fight consistently, even though I can't always do it perfectly. Help me to keep getting up and moving forward as many times as it takes.

Please remind me that even though this discipline is painful right now, it will bear fruit of righteousness and joy in my life. I resist the lies of the enemy that I should quit. I choose to believe Your Word that I will reap a harvest of freedom and healing if I do not give up. I will discipline my body daily to be quiet in your presence, choose healthy food, and get moving, and I know that I will reap what I sow.

I surrender my life again to You today, and commit to doing it consistently.

Amen

Day 5

Still Running the Race:
Heleen's Story

I've given you ladies a brief overview of my testimony in the introduction video of this program, so I thought it would be fitting to end with my full testimony of God's ongoing work in my life. I pray that this will encourage you to not give up if you're still falling, and especially inspire you to start working for God, regardless of where you're at in your journey.

10 Years Free from Bulimia!

July 2011 has been 10 years that God has set me free from the binging and purging cycle of bulimia. It took a journey and a lot of healing, but there was a definite time when I knew something happened and that I would never be the same again. There's a song that Darlene Zschech of Hillsong sings "I will never be the same again…" I heard this song years ago when God brought freedom to this area of my life, and I have been singing it every since. I especially hold on to the verse "There are higher heights, there are deeper seas, whatever You need to do, Lord do in me; the Glory of God fills my life and I will never be the same again"

Patience with the growth process

I am not very patient and the hardest thing that I had to do was to wait for God's timing for my healing. I wanted it yesterday and I wanted it all done at once. It didn't work that way. I have seen and heard of people who had it happen like that, but they are by far in the minority. So I had to learn to trust God with the His particular "plan of healing" for me.

I know He was trying to teach me patience, but He was really also testing my heart and testing my motives. I told you ladies before that my relationship with God consisted for a long time of me asking Him to make me skinny. It wasn't a sincere relationship, but rather me bargaining with God. The biggest mistake I made was to think that He didn't know. As if He's not God Almighty who can see in the heart of every human. I am ashamed when I think of that, but I have asked God to forgive me and help me love Him in a way that is worthy of Him. A pure and genuine way that has all to do with Him and nothing to do with what I can get out of Him for my own gain.

But in spite of all of this I still get impatient, because I don't feel that I can say "I will never fall again" and I so want to say that. In these instances I argue with God that surely I have suffered enough and have enough patience by now. Can He not just speak a word now and let it be done? But then there are times when I just come before Him, so in awe of His beauty, so in love with Him that I just blurt it out: "Oh Lord I don't care if I will never be totally free from this, I don't care if you never give me anything again, just let me love You like this for the rest of my life"

And indeed it is this attitude that kept me going. It is in this "making peace" with the fact that I probably will have to deal with falling and getting up (obviously in a lesser fashion) for the rest of my life, that I felt some peace come over me. By not reaching for the perfect track record anymore, I have actually given things over to God's time table. I am doing what I can to keep things going, but if I slip, I don't beat myself up anymore. I don't go into a three year relapse anymore and I don't think: I will never be free from this. Because, really I am free. Every day that I give this struggle over to the Holy Spirit I am free. Every time I start to think about food a lot and start to buy things I haven't bought in a long time, I know to check my spiritual thermometer.

So come to think of it: If God is using this to keep me close to Him, isn't it then a blessing in disguise?

I still have times when I look at people's houses that are just spotless and so beautifully decorated and I think about picking up my slack and getting things shipshape (really perfect in my mind) again. But just for a minute, because then I remember the anxiety, the binging, and the stress that goes with it and I let it go.

I definitely have moments where I just want a certain someone to like me more and I let go of my boundaries and overextend myself. But just for a moment, then I sigh, pick up the phone and let them know that I made a mistake, I would after all not be able to do whatever they were requesting. I put the phone down, shake off the guilt and thank God for freedom.

None of this is easy, there's a price to pay: No more compliments about your squeaky clean house, no more admiration from young mothers about your awesome ability to juggle so many things at once, no more bragging with your long list of things to do, no more special mention at the year-end function of the women's ministry of your devoted service and enormous supply of energy.

However, the reward is priceless: Freedom, freedom, freedom and a special place in the arms of the One you now know as counselor, friend, savior, husband, helper, and everlasting father. Also real friendships with men without any ulterior motives and with women without their insecurities standing on end.

Hard times with food during the last 10 years
I know you probably hoped that I never fall anymore, and that I could tell you that for the past 10 years I have never binged or looked at a fad diet. What I can tell you is: seldom. These times of falling seems to happen when there is some area in my life that God wants to work on and I

refuse to let Him. During times like these I inevitably turn back to my old lover: food. So if I can just get a clue, that will be helpful right?

Let me tell you about two specific incidents these past 10 years when I picked up my crutch of overeating again. I'm so grateful that I never opened the back door of huge binges and purging again, but I have to admit that I would start to 'graze' again during those times, and then start looking for a fad diet to help me with the weight gain.

Birth of my baby girl (2006):

By God's grace my eating disorders didn't flare up during my pregnancy with my sweet little gift from God five years ago. However, afterward panic struck me because of the weight I had to lose. I wrote all about this in my 40 day journal on the members area of my online program. The bottom line: I was looking for a quick fix because I hated the extra weight and I was scared that I would always look that way. After some kicking and screaming, I finally followed the same steps I've written down for you throughout this program. Basic biblical principles of repenting from all unbelief, pride, and denial and letting the Holy Spirit search my heart and heal the things that still needed healing. After trying a few fad diets I finally turned to a decent program – Weight Watchers, and slowly shook off the weight and regained my peace with God's help and the support of friends and Weight Watchers groups.

Season of change (2010 – 2011):

My close circle of friends and also those of you who have been faithfully following my blog will know that this past year (2010-2011) has been a tough one on our family. My husband lost his job, couldn't find another, and as a result we started up a bunch of Internet businesses. We have been doing website design just for fun before and had a few e-commerce businesses that didn't bring in a lot of money in the past, but now this became our main source of income. You imagine the chaos of having your business smack in the middle of your home while trying to homeschool your kids and still support others; it was a nightmare at best! Our financial situation kept looking bleaker and the stress accumulated as the year went by.

With all this busyness you can just imagine that I started spending less time with God, and less time in the Word. I've warned you ladies many times that if we don't get washed by the water of the Word and lay our cares at Jesus' feet in prayer that we start to "stink" because of the filth and worries of this world. This is exactly what happened to me this last year, and I turned to an old familiar outlet – food. I'm so grateful to God that I never turned back to serious binging and purging, however I started eating all day long to get rid of the stress, only, it didn't help of course.

My husband and I each picked up about 40 pounds over the course of a year, and the shame and guilt I felt became my daily companion. FINALLY I turned again to the biblical principles of this program. I repent once more of **the pride** (that I could fix our situation by working super

hard), **the denial** (that I'm in control of my eating when I clearly have not been for a year) and **the unbelief** (that God couldn't not possibly save me AGAIN)

I also started crying out to God for a program to help both me and my husband lose the weight we had gained. Weight Watchers wasn't working this time around. I tried doing it online but couldn't attend a group meeting and because of no accountability I just dropped the ball every day. Our new schedule also left me with absolutely no time for regular shopping and menu planning, so after 12 hours behind the computer and going hours without food I kept just "giving up" and eating junk food. Tony was actually the one who found us something that could help in the midst of our crazy busy lives. He told me that friends of ours at a neighboring church were doing a program and losing weight. I didn't want to hear of it because it consisted of meal replacements! It sounded like a fad diet to me if ever I've heard of one. I kept arguing with him about the price of the food and how I can just make similar healthy meals for us (as if I've not tried doing that many times before). Long story short, I reluctantly submitted to my husband, the guy who in my mind "knew absolutely nothing about food stuff". This tool ended up being used by God in a mighty way in our lives. We lost all of our weight and kept it off. More importantly, it turned out to provide exactly what we needed in this busy time of our lives, and the support made all the difference for me. It caused me to lay down my pride and admit that I actually needed accountability in this area of my life on a regular basis. I'm so grateful to God for yet another tool that I can suggest to you ladies.

As for the future: I know that as long as I do the things that I taught you in this program consistently, stay far away from perfection, and stay as close as humanly possible to God, I will be just fine.

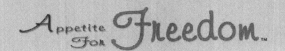

A Special Note for You

My dearest friend, I can not believe that we are at the end, and yet, it's only the beginning of a new life of freedom for you.

Whether you're all the way there, or still on your journey, I believe that you can never be the same once you've truly looked into the face of Jesus and started your own intimate love relationship with Him.

I am so honored and incredibly grateful that you let me into your world these past 12 weeks. Thank you!

Please remain in the Word of God daily, join hands with other women who love Jesus, pray more than you talk, and don't forget to let the Holy Spirit into all the moments of your life.

In God's amazing love,
Heleen

 Let's pray one last prayer together:

Lord Jesus, thank You that You have called each one of us by name, and that You know us like no one else on this earth. We are so grateful that You also know exactly what it will take to bring each of us to place of healing and freedom in You. Your Word says that we can call to You, and You will answer us, and show us great and unsearchable things we never knew. We therefore call upon You to show us Your glory, and change us forever!

Jesus, You hold the answers to the tough questions in our lives, so we know for sure that freedom from food struggles is wrapped up in a close relationship with You. Please use whatever it takes to keep drawing us closer to You, all the days of our lives. We cannot live without You, and we don't want to either. Teach each one of us how to hide under Your wing, how to be quiet in Your presence, and how to rely 100% on You for everything in our lives.

How easily we forget that it's all about You, Lord. Please remind us that life is not about us, or even about our freedom, but that we are here to glorify You. Use even our struggle with food to change us, humble us, and make us more like You, Jesus.

Please come search our hearts and see if there is still a harmful way in us. Remove all traces of pride, denial, idolatry or any other sin. Draw us into Your presence daily, so that the veil will be stripped away, and as we look into Your Word, we are changed from glory to glory.

We love You, Jesus. There is none like You. Thank You for loving us!
Amen

Endnotes

1. Beth Moore, *Breaking Free* (Lifeway Press 2009) 193

2. Max Lucado, *It's not about me* (Integrity Publishers 2004) 18

3. Heleen Woest, *God will I ever be free?* www.SurrenderedHearts.com

4. Andrew Murray, *Absolute Surrender* (Vancouver Eremitical Press 2009) 54

5. Beth Moore, *So Long Insecurity (*Tyndale House Publishers, Inc*)*

6. Beth Moore, *Breaking Free* (Lifeway Press 2009) 76

7. www.thefreedictionary.com

Available Resources in This Series

LEADER KIT - Contains one copy of this member book, one leader guide, and a DVD set (12 teaching sessions). Available at www.SurrenderedHearts.com

DVD SET – Includes 12 sessions (30 minutes each) of live teachings at All Things New, a ministry of City Bible Church in Portland Oregon.
Available at www.SurrenderedHearts.com

LEADER GUIDE - Suggestions for small group leaders.
Available at www.SurrenderedHearts.com

AUDIO CDS - The audio portions of Heleen's teaching. Useful for review or when a participant misses a session. Available at www.SurrenderedHearts.com

DOWNLOADS - Video and audio available at www.SurrenderedHearts.com

ONLINE PROGRAM - Women Struggling with Food: 12 Week Online Program and Member Forum. Available at www.SurrenderedHearts.com

Additional Resources

The greatest resource I can recommend for your journey to freedom and healing is THE BIBLE. However, these Bible studies and books could also bless you as you continue to draw closer to God and surrender your food struggle to Him daily.

Bible Studies:

Breaking Free: Making Liberty in Christ a Reality in Life by Beth Moore

Living Beyond Yourself: Exploring the Fruit of the Spirit by Beth Moore

First Place 4 Health Bible Study Series by First Place 4 Health

Jonah by Priscilla Shirer

Books about relationship with Jesus:

Absolute Surrender by Andrew Murray,

Captivating by John and Stasi Eldredge

The Purpose Driven Life by Rick Warren

Finding favor with the King by Tommy Tenney

The Sacred Romance by Brent Curtis and John Eldredge

The Dream Giver by Bruce Wilkinson

Crazy Love: Overwhelmed by a relentless God by Francis Chan

Just like Jesus by Max Lucado

Walking with God by John Eldredge

Books about Spiritual warfare:

Victory over the darkness by Neil Anderson

When Godly people do ungodly things by Beth Moore

Waking the Dead by John Eldredge

Battlefield of the mind by Joyce Meyers

Books about prayer:

Living Free: Learning to pray God's Word by Beth Moore

The power of a praying women by Stormie Omartian

The power of simple prayer by Joyce Meyers

The Prayer of Jabez by Bruce Wilkinson

Books that deal with the issues surrounding food struggles and addiction:

Get out of that pit by Beth Moore

Boundaries by Henry Cloud and John Townsend

Hope, Help and Healing for Eating Disorders by Gregory L Jantz

Mercy for Eating Disorders by Nancy Alcorn

Approval Addiction by Joyce Meyers

Inside Out by Larry Crab

The power of forgiveness by Joyce Meyers

Conflict free living by Joyce Meyers

Food and Love by Gary Smalley

Books that deal with the issues surrounding food struggles and addiction:

Love to eat Hate to eat by Elyse Fitzpatrick

How People Grow by Henry Cloud and John Townsend

Made to Crave by Lysa Terkeurst

Addictions: A banquet in the Grave by Edward T Welch

The Christian Counselors Manual by Jay E Adams

When People are Big and God is Small by Edward T Welch

Books about healthy living:

Set Free to Live Free by Sandra Dalton Smith MD

The Maker's Diet by Jordan S. Rubin

Body for Life for Women by Peeke Pamela

Master you Metabolism by Jillian Michaels

Winning by Losing by Jillian Michaels

Dr A's Habits of Health by Wayne Scott Andersen

For a list of online resources please visit www. SurrenderedHearts.com

Made in the USA
Charleston, SC
10 November 2012